The Declaration's
Forgotten Liberties

For Youth

Charles A. Castleberry

The Declaration's Forgotten Liberties For Youth (Forgotten Liberties, Book 2)

Copyright © 2025 by Charles A. Castleberry

All rights reserved. No part of this publication may be reproduced, distributed, or transmitted in any form or by any means, including photocopying, recording, or other electronic or mechanical methods, without the prior written permission of the author, except in the case of brief quotations embodied in critical reviews and certain other noncommercial uses permitted by copyright law. Please do not participate in or encourage piracy of copyrighted materials in violation of the author's rights.

No part of this book may be used for the training of artificial systems, including systems based on artificial intelligence (AI), without the copyright owner's prior permission. This prohibition shall be in force even on platforms and systems that claim to have such rights based on an implied contract for hosting the book.

Cover Image Citation:
Ferris, Jean Leon Gerome, Artist. *Writing The Declaration of Independence, / J.L.G. Ferris.* ca. 1932. Cleveland, Ohio: The Foundation Press, Inc., July 28. Photograph.

Library of Congress Control Number: 2025905446

Paperback ISBN: 978-1-966283-51-5
Hardcover ISBN : 978-1-966283-52-2

1. Main category—History › United States › Colonial Period
2. Other category—History › United States › Revolution & Founding
3. Other category—History › United States › General

Published by American Real Publishing
Binghamton, NY
americanrealpublishing.com

Introduction

The Declaration of Independence: More Than Just Words

The Declaration of Independence is one of the most important documents in American history—but how much do we really know about it? Over the years, myths, mistakes, and even stretched stories have made it hard to see the real story of America's fight for freedom.

Have you ever wondered:

- **Why was Thomas Jefferson chosen to write the Declaration?**
- **Did he come up with the ideas himself—or borrow them from others?**
- **If the Declaration says, "all men are created equal," why did Jefferson own slaves?**
- **What were the real reasons the colonies wanted to break away from Britain?**
- **What happened to the part of the Declaration that condemned slavery—and why was it removed?**
- **Did Jefferson and Adams really spend two weeks in a Philadelphia tavern writing the Declaration together?**
  No—that story is a later invention. Jefferson wrote the draft alone at the Graff House, drawing on years of his earlier work. Adams and Franklin suggested only a few edits before it went to Congress. The "tavern collaboration" is a myth that grew out of confusion between their shared service on the drafting committee and Adams's later recollections of debate.

The answers to these questions are important—they help us understand the America we inherited.

A Bold New Idea

The Declaration wasn't just about breaking away from Britain. It shared a bold idea: governments should serve the people—not the other way around.

But winning freedom wasn't easy. It took a long war, a new Constitution, and generations of people working to make those words real. Even today, the fight for freedom and fairness continues—not just in America, but around the world.

This book goes beyond the famous words of the Declaration. It reveals forgotten stories that helped shape our nation, such as::

- How Jefferson changed the word subjects to citizens—a small change with a big impact.
- Why British trade laws hurt everyday colonists—not just because of a tax on tea.
- The truth about the Three-Fifths Clause—and why it's not what most people think.
- How early leaders, even Jefferson and Mason, worked to end the slave trade and stop slavery from spreading.

Why the Grievances Still Matter

A lot of people think of the Declaration as just a list of complaints against the King. But these grievances weren't only complaints—they were lessons. The Founders knew that if future generations didn't learn from these mistakes, they could happen again.

That's why these grievances still matter today. They shaped our Constitution, influenced our laws, and continue to affect our rights and freedoms. Each one tells a story—some surprising, some inspiring!

A Call to Think for Yourself

History isn't just about memorizing dates and names. It's about asking questions and finding answers. The Founders believed in thinking for yourself, debating ideas, and standing up for what's right.

As you read, ask yourself:

> Would I have had the courage to sign my name on the Declaration, knowing it could cost me everything?

The Power of Words

The American Revolution wasn't just fought with soldiers and cannons—it was also fought with ideas and words. Thomas Jefferson's words inspired people to act and helped give birth to a new nation.

Even today, words can change the world. They can start movements, bring people together, and inspire justice. Never forget the power of your voice—and the courage it takes to use it.

The Story of Slavery in America

Many students learn about slavery, but not always how it connected to the Revolution. Slavery was part of a global system that lasted more than 300 years.

This book includes easy-to-understand charts that show:

- Which countries were most involved in the Transatlantic Slave Trade.
- How the Three-Fifths Clause and the 20-Year Clause really worked.
- How decisions made during America's founding shaped the fight against slavery.

By learning the whole story, we can see both the mistakes of the past and the progress toward freedom.

Why This Story Still Matters

The Declaration of Independence was the first big step in securing the freedoms we enjoy today. But the fight for liberty didn't end in 1776.

Even after independence, slavery continued in America. The struggle for equality took generations—and still continues. Today, millions of people around the world are trapped in forced labor and human trafficking—modern forms of slavery.

By understanding how past generations stood up to injustice, we can find courage to do the same. The words in the Declaration—that all people are created equal and deserve life, liberty, and the pursuit of happiness—still matter today.

What Inspired This Book
Key moments that inspired this book

This book began with two unforgettable discoveries.

The first was when I found a book filled with the writings of America's Founders. One entry stood out—Thomas Jefferson's Summary View of the Rights of British America, written in 1774. Jefferson wrote it for Virginia's delegates to the First Continental Congress, but they thought it was too bold.

As I read it, I began to notice ideas that later appeared in *The Declaration of Independence*. My research showed that almost every principle and Grievance in the Declaration had its roots in this earlier work. Later, those same principles became protected by law in the U.S. Constitution.

The second moment came when I saw the Rough Draft of *The Declaration of Independence* in person. A major collector of early American documents, Glenn Beck, brought a rare copy to St. George, Utah, as part of a large historical exhibit at the St. George Tabernacle.

For three days, I was honored to this document to thousands of people and saw their amazement as they listened to its powerful words.

What surprised most visitors was learning about the Slavery Clause—a passage in the Rough Draft that condemned slavery but was later removed by the Second Continental Congress just before it was printed. Hardly any visitor had ever heard of it, and were saddened to learn why it was removed the final Declaration. Jefferson later wrote that Congress "mangled it" when they took it out of *The Declaration of Independence*. America's history may have been very different if it had remained.

As I shared these discoveries in many cities, people often asked me to turn them into a book. Now, after years of more research, here it is —ready to celebrate 250 years of Independence!!

More Secrets Await in the Afterword
By the time you finish this book, you'll have discovered the Declaration's hidden truths and forgotten stories. But there's more! In the Afterword, you'll meet unsung heroes—men and women who stood up for liberty long before 1776.

In *The Declaration's Forgotten Liberties* you'll read about:

- The 1688 Germantown Petition Against Slavery, America's first written protest against slavery.
- The boy who fell off the Mayflower—but survived to help shape the New World.
- The "Quaker Comet," a dwarf abolitionist as brave as a lion.
- A Black mathematician who helped design Washington, D.C., and debated Thomas Jefferson.
- The fearless Daughter of Liberty known as the Mother of the Boston Tea Party.
- Black Civil War heroes and hidden truths about the Emancipation Proclamation.

Their stories—and many more—are waiting for you!

From Subjects to Citizens

History doesn't disappear just because it happened long ago. It disappears when it gets turned into simple stories that leave out important parts. When that happens, history stops asking us to think.

Over time, America's founding has often been told as a neat and heroic story. But the real story is more interesting than that. Some hard questions are skipped. Some details are left out. Big events are shortened into catchy phrases. What many people learn are familiar *MythTakes*—stories repeated so often that they begin to sound true.

The Declaration of Independence is not a fairy tale. It is a serious document with real costs. It was written by one man, but it spoke for many. Thomas Jefferson knew his words could change everything. He wasn't perfect, but he thought deeply about freedom and fairness—and he helped put into words ideas that many Americans already believed.

So what does *From Subjects to Citizens* mean?

Before independence, Americans were subjects. That meant they had to obey a king they didn't choose and laws they didn't help make. After the *Declaration of Independence*, Americans claimed something new. They said people should help choose their leaders, have a voice in their government, and share responsibility for their country. That is what it means to be a citizen—and why it mattered so much.

The Declaration didn't just change who ruled America. It changed what Americans believed about themselves.

Table of Contents

INTRODUCTION	4
TABLE OF CONTENTS	8
PROLOGUE: THE JOURNEY BEGINS	10
AMERICA'S CHARTERS OF FREEDOM	18
THE GOLDEN APPLE IN A SILVER FRAME	22
OPENING LINE OF THE DECLARATION OF INDEPENDENCE	24
WHEN, IN THE COURSE OF HUMAN EVENTS	26
WE HOLD THESE TRUTHS	28
DID GEORGE MASON INSPIRE JEFFERSON'S PREAMBLE?	30
WHEN A LONG TRAIN OF ABUSES	34
LET FACTS BE SUBMITTED TO A CANDID WORLD	42
PRESENTING THE GRIEVANCES	44
1. He Refuses to Assent to Necessary Laws	46
2. He Forbids Passing Laws of Pressing Importance	48
3. He Suppresses Representation	50
4. He Burdens Legislatures with Fatiguing Measures	52
5. He Dissolves Parliaments & Opposes Rights	54
6. He Endangers Us by Neglecting Elections	56
7. He Controls the Settlement of Lands & Naturalization	58
8. He Blocks Local Administration of Justice	62
9. He Has Made Our Judges Dependent on His Will	64
10. He Erected New Offices & Sent Swarms of Officers	66
11. He Keeps Armies Among Us in Times of Peace	68
12. His Military is Superior to Our Civil Authority	70
13. He Subjects Us to Foreign Jurisdiction	72
14. For Quartering Large Bodies of Troops Among Us	74
15. He Protects Foreign Soldiers by Mock Trials	76
16. For Cutting Off Global Trade	78
17. Taxation Without Representation	82
18. Deprived of Trial by Juries	84
19. Transporting Us Beyond Seas for Trial	86
20. Enlarging the Borders of a Neighboring Province	88
21. Taking Away Charters and Valuable Laws	92
22. Suspends Legislatures & Assumes Power	96
23. Abdicating Governance and Protection	98
24. He Plundered, Ravaged, Burnt & Destroyed	100
25. Foreign Mercenaries Terrorize Our People	102
26. Taken Captive to Bear Arms Against Fellow Citizens	104
27. Inciting Insurrections & Unleashing Merciless Forces	106
THE SLAVERY CLAUSE	108

THE KING IS DISQUALIFIED BY HIS TYRANNY	114
ENEMIES IN WAR, IN PEACE FRIENDS	116
THEY PLEDGED THEIR LIVES	118
SIGNING THE DECLARATION	120
THE PRICE THEY PAID	122
COMPARING THE GRIEVANCES	123
WORKING COMPOSITION DRAFT	130
JEFFERSON'S EPIPHANY	131
BEFORE THE DECLARATION	132
JOURNEY TO PHILADELPHIA	134
REFINING THE LANGUAGE OF LIBERTY	135
CLASSICAL EAR AND ARCHITECTURAL PROSE	139
NOTES ON THE STATE OF VIRGINIA	140
A WOLF BY THE EARS	142
AFTERWORD	144
THE "DUTY BOYS" OF 1619	145
THE ORIGINS OF SLAVERY IN AMERICA	146
SLAVE SHIP BROOKES	147
TRANSATLANTIC SLAVE TRADE	150
HORRORS OF SLAVERY IN AFRICA	151
THE THREE-FIFTHS COMPROMISE	156
THE THREE-FIFTHS AND 20-YEAR COMPROMISES	158
AMERICAN SLAVE MERCHANTS	162
THE DISTORTED LEGACY OF JEREMIAH DIXON	163
THE FIRST SLAVERY PROTEST	164
A HOUSE DIVIDED AGAINST ITSELF CANNOT STAND	166
BLOOD AND TREASURE: THE CIVIL WAR	168
FORGOTTEN HEROES	170
COLONEL GEORGE MIDDLETON	172
JOHN HOWLAND	174
BENJAMIN LAY	176
SARAH BRADLEE FULTON	178
MERCY OTIS WARREN	180
BENJAMIN BANNEKER	182
FRANCES ELLEN WATKINS HARPER	186
POLLY COOPER, ONEIDA ANGEL OF VALLEY FORGE	189
THE FIGHT GOES ON	190
A FINAL REFLECTION	192
BIBLIOGRAPHY	194
END NOTES	196

Prologue: The Journey Begins

A Journey Into Forgotten Liberties

Welcome to an incredible journey into the founding of our nation.

The Declaration's Forgotten Liberties is more than a story about the past. It helps us understand how America was built—and why ideas like freedom, fairness, and unity still matter today.

The Declaration of Independence was written 250 years ago, and today we still celebrate—and live by—its words. What did it really mean? How did it change the world? And what can we still learn from it today?

A Surprising Family Discovery

My journey into history began with a discovery—one that connected my own family to the fight for justice in early America.

I grew up on the West Coast, far from where the American Revolution took place. But years later, after moving to Pennsylvania, I learned about relatives who had lived there long before America became a country.

One of my ancestors was Heinrich Kesselberg, later known as Henry Castleberry. He came from Germany to Pennsylvania in the 1680s. His future wife, Catherine, made the journey too.

Their story connects to something remarkable—one of the first protests against slavery in America. Family tradition tells that Catherine was at that first protest.

The First Protest Against Slavery

In 1688, four men living in Germantown, Pennsylvania, wrote the first protest against slavery in the American colonies. One of them was Abraham op den Graeff, a weaver and farmer. His family later married into mine. Abraham lived near Evansburg, Pennsylvania, and is buried nearby in the Skippack Mennonite Cemetery.

Over time, four Castleberry stone homes were built on that land. Two still stand today. One of them was later used as General George Washington's headquarters during the Revolutionary War.

Abraham and many early German immigrants were Quakers and Mennonites—people who believed in peace and in treating all people equally. At a time when slavery was common, they chose to speak out. Their words became known as the 1688 Germantown Petition Against Slavery.

Leaving Europe Behind

Life in Europe was very difficult for many people. At the same time Africans were being taken from their homes and enslaved, millions of people in Europe were also suffering. Wars spread across the land again and again, leaving death and destruction behind. Armies and rulers took food, livestock, and supplies, leaving families with very little. In many places, far more civilians died than soldiers.

Families had to make hard choices. Many left everything behind, seeking a new life across the ocean. They were not only escaping war—they were also escaping unfair rulers and punishment for their religious beliefs as well.

A book called *Martyrs Mirror*, first published in 1660, tells the stories of thousands of people who suffered because of their faith. These stories help us understand why so many were willing to risk everything to sail into the unknown. They were searching for a place where they could live in peace—and be free.

Finding Home

The people who left Europe had faced terrible hardships—wars, religious persecution, and constant danger. They were desperate to find a place where they could live in freedom and safety.

That place was Pennsylvania. William Penn, the colony's founder, invited German Quakers and Mennonites to settle in his land, promising them religious freedom and a fresh start. In 1683, a group of them left their homes in the Rhine and Rühr River Valleys and boarded a ship called the *Concord*, bound for America.

One of the largest family groups on the ship was the Op den Graeff brothers, cousins of William Penn. They traveled with their families, including their elderly mother, hoping to build a better life. The Concord became known as the *"German Mayflower"* because of its important role in bringing German refugees to America.

For these early immigrants, America was a place of hope—a chance to live in peace without fear. But when they arrived in Pennsylvania, they found something quite shocking: Slavery was everywhere.

Restoring the Old Home

The photos on the next pages show a special place—the Casselberry farm in Evansburg, Pennsylvania, first purchased in 1722. Over 200 years ago, four Castleberry (Casselberry) homes were built on this land.

In 2016, my wife, Vanet, and I purchased one of them—the abandoned Anne E. Casselberry House. We spent the next five years restoring it to its former beauty. This home is part of the Evansburg National Historic District, which helps preserve the history of William Penn's vision for Pennsylvania. Here's what the photos show:

1. **Anne E. Casselberry House:** The original section was built in the mid-1700s, with an addition in 1798. The sturdy stone walls are nearly two-feet thick. We remained true to colonial colors and schemes as we restore this home.

2. **1820s Addition:** This is the "new" addition. This part of the house has a modern kitchen, a "winder staircase," and a bedroom and bath upstairs. A fun feature of this kitchen is the Dutch door.

3. **Colonial Kitchen:** This home has two kitchens! We kept the colonial kitchen just as it was in the 1700s. Visitors love it!

4. **Updated Second Kitchen:** This kitchen is in the 1820s addition. It has a Dutch door that leads to a porch which was added some time later.

5. **Dining Room:** This room, plus the entry hall, staircase, and an upstairs bedroom, were built between 1795 and 1800. The fireplace woodwork and cabinets are original.

6. **The Casselberry Barn:** A German stone bank barn built in 1831. The name John Casselberry and the date August 1831 are carved into the stone.

7. **Derrick Casselberry House:** Washington's Headquarters! On September 20, 1777, George Washington stayed here during the Revolutionary War. The first section was built in 1734. This photo is from a century ago. Today, most of the white stucco has been removed and it is in need of restoration.

8. **President Washington's Visit:** Washington honored fallen soldiers at St. James Episcopal Church. This reenactment includes historical actors and Father Mike Sowards, who shared historical documents with me. Local stories say Washington spent the night at Anne E. Casselberry House.

9. **Tomb of Unknown Soldiers (Revolutionary War):** This burial mound holds over 150 unknown soldiers. The Daughters of the American Revolution placed a plaque to honor them. The first church on this site was built in 1700, replaced by a stone church in 1721. Today's "new chapel" was built in 1845.[1]

1. Anne E. Casselberry House with two front doors—mid 1700s phase on the left, 1790s addition on the right

2. 1820s addition on back left before restoration

3. Mid 1700s colonial kitchen in the front left of the house

4. Updated 2nd kitchen in the 1820s addition

5. Dining room and fireplace, circa 1795 with original woodwork

6. Casselberry German Bank Barn, circa 1831

7. Adjacent Derrick Casselberry House, first phase circa 1734

8. Re-enactment of President Washington visiting fallen comrades

9. Tomb of Unknown Soldiers, Revolutionary War, placed by the Daughters of the American Revolution

A Visit from President Washington

On September 20, 1777, during the Revolutionary War, George Washington stayed at the Derrick Casselberry House, which sits near the home we restored.

He was there to honor fallen soldiers, including those buried in the nearby Tomb of Unknown Soldiers. More than 150 Revolutionary War soldiers are buried in that sacred place.

Local stories say that after visiting the cemetery, Washington may have spent the night at the Anne E. Casselberry House.

A Web of Family History

The more I researched my family history, the more surprises I found!

One of my ancestors, John Howland, was a passenger on the Mayflower. He signed the Mayflower Compact, which helped shape the government of Plymouth Colony. He even worked as a clerk and scribe for the governor—so it's very possible he wrote the Mayflower Compact himself!

Another ancestor, John Rolfe, played a major role in Jamestown's history. In 1609, he was shipwrecked on the island of Bermuda before finally arriving in Jamestown. He later introduced sweet tobacco seeds to the colony—creating the American tobacco industry.

John Rolfe married Pocahontas, and together they had a son. They traveled to England, but tragically, Pocahontas died just before their planned return to Jamestown.

These discoveries weren't always easy to process. The tobacco industry later became tied to slavery, something I struggled with as I learned more. But history is full of both triumphs and tragedies—and we must study both to understand our past.

Jefferson's Vision and The Declaration of Independence

As I continued my research, I found more and more connections between early American documents. One of the biggest discoveries was how Thomas Jefferson prepared for writing the Declaration long before 1776.

Two years earlier, in 1774, he wrote *A Summary View of the Rights of British America*, outlining ideas that would later appear in the Declaration. He wrote that for the Virginia delegates to the First Continental Congress.

Then, in May 1776, while Virginians were writing their state constitution while Jefferson was in Philadelphia. He included a list of grievances against King George III in his proposed Virginia Constitution. Within days, he used that list (much was word-for-word) while drafting *The Declaration of Independence*.

Most are familiar with the opening words of the Declaration, but did you know that 65% of the Declaration is a list of grievances—a "full train of abuses" (a phrase borrowed from John Locke) against the King?

Understanding these grievances helps us see why the American Revolution happened and why the Founders believed freedom was worth fighting for.

As Long as the Sun Shall Shine
Lessons from the Iroquois Confederacy

On May 27, 1776, a group of twenty-one Iroquois leaders from four different tribes arrived in Philadelphia to meet with the Continental Congress. They stayed for over a month, lodging on the second floor of the Pennsylvania Statehouse—the same building where the Founders were preparing to declare independence.

On June 11, 1776, an Onondaga **chief** addressed the delegates, calling them "Brothers," and shared a message of unity and friendship. They expressed hope that the bond between the Iroquois and the American colonists would last "as long as the sun shall shine and the waters run." [2]

John Hancock, president of the Congress, was given a special honor—an Iroquois name: Karanduawn, meaning "The Great Tree."

The very day the Iroquois addressed Congress, June 11, 1776, Thomas Jefferson began writing *The Declaration of Independence*—inspiring words that would soon give birth to a nation.[3]

How the Iroquois Inspired America

For many centuries, the Haudenosaunee (Iroquois) Confederacy has united different tribes under a system of shared leadership, peace, and cooperation. This idea fascinated the Founding Fathers, who were trying to unite the thirteen colonies.

In 1744, an Iroquois leader named Chief Canassatego of the Onondaga Nation met with colonial leaders. He warned them that unless they learned to work together, they would remain weak.

To prove his point, he picked up a single arrow and snapped it in half. Then, he bundled multiple arrows together and tried again. This time, they would not break.[4] His message was clear: Divided, the colonies would fall. Together, they would be strong.

Later, this powerful symbol inspired the Founding Fathers as they created a government for the United States. Even today, the Great Seal of the United States carries this message—the eagle holds a bundle of arrows in one talon, not as a symbol of war, but of the strength that comes from unity.[5]

The Great Law of Peace

The Haudenosaunee Confederacy (People of the Longhouse) was created long before the United States even existed. Their laws were passed down through oral tradition and recorded on wampum belts.

The **Great Law of Peace** includes many important ideas, including:

- **Leaders should serve the people, not rule over them.** Chiefs (called sachems) were chosen by the people and could be **removed** if they failed to lead with wisdom and fairness.
- **Decisions should be made by consensus.** Instead of one person making all the choices, leaders discussed issues and worked together to find solutions that benefited everyone.
- **Peace is stronger than war.** The Haudenosaunee believed in resolving conflicts through discussion instead of fighting. This is why they buried their weapons of war beneath the Great Tree of Peace.
- **Future generations matter.** Leaders were expected to think seven generations ahead—making decisions not just for themselves, but for their children, grandchildren, and beyond.
- **Unity makes a nation strong.** Just like a bundle of arrows is harder to break than a single arrow, the Iroquois knew that when people stand together, they are much stronger.[6]

THE IROQUOIS NATION'S GREAT LAW OF PEACE
The World's Oldest Constitution

SENECA NATION — CAYUGA NATION — ONONDAGA NATION — ONEIDA NATION — MOHAWK NATION

Wampum belts—intricately woven, beaded memory belts—recorded treaties, laws, and agreements. One of these belts tells the story of the Great Tree of Peace, a sacred white pine where former enemies buried their weapons of war beneath its roots and agreed to live together in harmony.[7]

America 250

As we celebrate 250 years of *The Declaration of Independence*, history still has important lessons to teach us. How can we bury our "weapons of war"—hate and envy—and become more united as a people?

The fight for freedom and equality is not over. But by learning from the past, we can protect those liberties for the future—**as long as the sun shall shine.**

America's Charters of Freedom

The Charters of Freedom are three of the most important papers in American history. They helped build the United States and protect the rights and freedoms that Americans have today.

You can see these documents in a special room called the "Rotunda for the Charters of Freedom" at the National Archives in Washington, D.C.

The Charters of Freedom include:
- *The Declaration of Independence* – The document that declared America's freedom from British rule.
- **Constitution of the United States** – A set of rules that created our government and explains how it works.
- **Bill of Rights** – The first ten amendments to the Constitution that protect our rights.

Thomas Jefferson said these documents should always help guide our country. He called them:

*"The creed of our political faith;
the text of civic instruction."*

Jefferson warned that if America ever strayed from these principles, we should quickly return to them:

> **"These principles form the bright constellation which has gone before us and guided our steps through an age of revolution and reformation… and should we wander from them in moments of error or of alarm, let us hasten to retrace our steps, and to regain the road which alone leads to peace, liberty, and safety."**
>
> —Thomas Jefferson, First Inaugural Address, March 4, 1801[8]

Why This Book Matters

This book will help you see why these documents were written and how they changed our country. We'll take a close look at *The Declaration of Independence*, breaking it down to understand its meaning, and how the Constitution and Bill of Rights protect the liberties it declares.

The Three Charters of Freedom

These documents were created during a time of great struggle and change. The people who wrote them wanted to build a fair government and protect individual rights.

1. The Declaration of Independence (1776)

Written mostly by Thomas Jefferson, this paper was America's way of saying, "We are free from Great Britain!" But it was more than just a breakup letter to King George III—it laid out big ideas about freedom, equality, and human rights. The Declaration states that:

- **All people are created equal.**
- **Everyone has rights that can't be taken away, like life, liberty, and the pursuit of happiness.**
- **Governments must protect these rights, and if they don't, people have the right to change or replace them.**

These ideas came from great thinkers like John Locke, who believed rulers should only have power if the people agree. *The Declaration of Independence* took these ideas and put them into action!

2. The Constitution (1787)

After America won its independence, the new nation needed a plan for how to run itself. The first plan, called the Articles of Confederation, wasn't strong enough. In 1787, leaders gathered to write the Constitution, which created:

- **A government with three branches:** Executive, Legislative, and Judicial divide power so no one person or group controls everything.
- **A system of checks and balances:** To make sure the government followed the rules.
- **A federal system:** Where power is shared between the national government and the states.

The Constitution is still the highest law in America today. It begins with the words "We the People," showing that the government's power comes from its citizens.

3. The Bill of Rights (1791)

When the Constitution was first written, many Americans were worried it gave too much power to the government and didn't do enough to protect people's rights. A leader named George Mason fought hard to include a list of rights during the Constitutional Convention but was overruled—leading him to refuse to sign the final document. Other states, especially Massachusetts and Virginia, refused to support the Constitution unless a Bill of Rights was added.

The pressure was too great to ignore. James Madison, who had strongly opposed adding a Bill of Rights at the convention, promised to introduce amendments during the first Congress to secure ratification. It was only because of relentless demands from the states that Congress finally drafted and passed the Bill of Rights, which was ratified in 1791. The first ten amendments protect our fundamental liberties, including:

- **Freedom of speech, religion, and the press**
- **The right to protest and gather peacefully**
- **Protection from unfair searches and arrests**
- **The right to a fair trial**

Living Documents: Why the Charters of Freedom Still Matter

The Charters of Freedom aren't just old papers sitting in a museum—they still shape our lives today. When we talk about fair laws, voting rights, free speech, or justice, we are talking about ideas that started with *The Declaration of Independence*, the Constitution, and the Bill of Rights. These documents connect the past, present, and future—reminding us that freedom isn't something we receive once and forget about. It has to be protected, defended, and passed down to future generations.

Without fair rules, chaos could take over. The Constitution sets up a system that keeps power balanced and protects everyone's voice. The Constitution provides the framework that ensures fairness, balance, and representation for all. It is the foundation our government must follow to function properly.[9]

The Constitution: A Plan That Adapts

One smart idea the Founders had was to make the Constitution something that could be changed when needed. The Founding Fathers knew they weren't perfect, and they knew the country would face new challenges in the future. That's why they included a way to amend (change) the Constitution when needed. For example:

- The 13th Amendment ended slavery.
- The 19th Amendment gave women the right to vote.
- The 26th Amendment lowered the voting age to 18.

Because of the system they created, America can grow and improve while still staying true to its original values.

The Power of the Bill of Rights

The Bill of Rights is a promise that protects our freedom. It protects every American by guaranteeing rights that the government cannot infringe upon.

- It guarantees the right to free speech, allowing you to voice your opinions, even if they challenge authority.
- It ensures the freedom to practice your religion or live without religious constraints.
- It safeguards you from unjust treatment by the government or law enforcement.

The Bill of Rights makes sure that everyone is treated equally and fairly under the law—no matter their background or beliefs.

The Bill of Rights ensures that laws apply equally to everyone—no matter who they are. These rights are so important that people fought and died to defend them. Every time you hear about a court case, a protest, or a news story about people standing up for their rights, you're seeing the Bill of Rights in action. It affects your daily life in ways you might not even realize—from what you post online to how you express your opinions at school or in public.

It's because of the Bill of Rights that newspapers can report on the government without fear, why people can gather to demand change, and why no one can be arrested without a reason. It even protects your right to defend yourself if you're accused of a crime, making sure trials are fair and just.

But rights are only as strong as the people willing to defend them. If we take them for granted, we risk losing them. The Bill of Rights is more than just words and lofty ideals—it's a promise that **freedom will always have a protector—the Constitution**. And that promise only holds if every generation understands and values it.[10]

Your Role in Protecting Freedom

The Charters of Freedom weren't written just for the people in 1776, 1787, or 1791—they were written for YOU and for future generations. Every American has a responsibility to understand these founding documents, protect their freedoms, and keep them strong.

You don't have to be a president, a judge, or a politician to make a difference. You can:

- **Learn about your rights** so you understand how they protect you.
- **Speak up** if something seems unfair or unjust.
- **Respect other people's rights**, even if you don't agree with them.
- **Stay informed** about how the government works and vote when you're old enough.

These simple actions help keep the ideas of *The Declaration of Independence*, the Constitution, and the Bill of Rights alive and strong.

Moving Forward

As we move forward in this book, we will take a deeper look at *The Declaration of Independence*. We'll uncover the meaning behind its powerful words, the struggles that led to its creation, and how its message still echoes through history.

> **Think About It:** How can you protect freedom—not just for yourself, but for those who will follow?

The Golden Apple in a Silver Frame

President Abraham Lincoln once said *The Declaration of Independence* was like a **"golden apple in a silver frame."**

He meant that the Declaration was the bright and shining center, and the Constitution and the Union were the frame that protected and supported it. [11]

The Golden Apple: The Declaration of Independence

The Declaration is like a golden apple because it holds America's most precious ideas.

It says that all people are created equal and have rights that no one can take away—like life, liberty, and the pursuit of happiness.

These ideas are the heart of our freedom and the reason our nation was born.

The Silver Frame: The Constitution and Union

The Constitution and the Union are like the silver frame that holds the golden apple in place. The frame keeps it safe and lets everyone see its beauty.

The Constitution gives rules to help protect the rights in the Declaration. It makes sure power is shared, leaders follow the law, and people stay free.

The Union brings all the states together, helping the whole country stand as one. [12]

Modern Interpretation

Today, Lincoln's words remind us that the Declaration shows the goals of America, and the Constitution gives the plan to reach them. The Declaration shares our beliefs about freedom and equality.

The Constitution helps make those beliefs real by setting up laws and leaders who must follow them. Both are needed—ideas alone aren't enough, and power without principles can become unfair.

This message shows how America's founding documents work together. The Declaration gives the heart of our freedom. The Constitution gives it **a strong body** to live and grow.

From Hope to Reality: Building a Framework for Liberty

When *The Declaration of Independence* was signed in 1776, its promises were still hopes, not yet real.

The Founders had said that everyone has the right to life, liberty, and the pursuit of happiness, but they still had to fight for those rights.

The war for independence was the first step toward making freedom more than words on paper. The Declaration showed the dream; the fight showed the courage to begin making it real.

The First Step Was to Win the War

The Revolutionary War was long and difficult. It tested the courage and unity of the new American people.

Unless America won the war, they could not claim the liberties they cherished. Winning the war proved that freedom was worth the cost—but victory was only the beginning.

Now the young nation had to build a government strong enough to protect those freedoms for everyone.

Weakly United Under the Articles of Confederation:

After the war, the first government plan was called the Articles of Confederation. It tried to bring the states together, but it didn't give the national government enough power.

It couldn't make laws work fairly between the states or collect taxes to support the army.

Without stronger rules, the new country was too weak to protect its people and their rights.

A Government that Endures

To fix these problems, the leaders met again and wrote the Constitution. This became the "silver frame" that protected the "golden apple" of the Declaration.

The Constitution set up a fair system with three branches of government and clear limits on power.

It made the Union stronger and helped America's promises of liberty last for generations.

Together, the Declaration and the Constitution created a nation built on freedom, guided by laws, and strong enough to endure.[13]

Opening Line of The Declaration of Independence
"The unanimous Declaration of the thirteen united States of America."

The Power of a Single Word: "united"

At first, this line may look simple—but one word tells a big story. The word "united" starts with a lowercase "u." That's because, in 1776, the thirteen colonies were not yet one big country. They were thirteen separate states with their own governments, laws, and leaders.

When Jefferson wrote "united States," it meant that the states had chosen to work together for independence, not that they were already one single nation. The capitalized word "States" looked stronger than "united," showing that each state still held its own power and wanted to protect its freedom from being controlled by a king—or any central government.

Thirteen Separate Colonies, One Common Goal

The colonies joined together for one important purpose: freedom from British rule. Even after winning independence, the states wanted to make sure no government would ever grow too powerful again. That's why they first created the Articles of Confederation, which protected each state's independence.

Later, when the Constitution was written, the Founders agreed the country needed a stronger government to stay united—but they also added protections to make sure the federal government could never take away the rights of the states or the people.

Power Sharing Between States and the Federal Government

James Madison, one of America's Founders, explained that the federal government's powers should be "few and specific"—limited mostly to things like defending the nation, handling foreign affairs, and managing trade between states. Most powers, he said, should stay with the individual states.

Before the Constitution, each colony had its own laws, money, and leaders. The Articles of Confederation kept them independent but made it hard for the nation to act as one. *The Declaration of Independence* had called for unity, but not at the cost of freedom for each state.

This careful balance between state and federal authority became one of America's most important principles. It prevents too much power from resting in one place and keeps the nation strong through cooperation rather than control.

The Challenge of Staying United

Even after the war for independence, America's unity was fragile. The states had grown used to running their own affairs, and the first plan for government—the Articles of Confederation—didn't give enough power to hold the nation together.

- This caused problems across the new country:
- Some states made their own money.
- Trade arguments broke out between borders.
- The government couldn't collect taxes to pay soldiers or debts.
- There were no strong rules for trading with other nations.

Without a stronger system, the young nation was in danger of falling apart.

The Constitution Strengthened the Union And Protected the States

To solve these problems, America's leaders met again to create a new plan: the Constitution. It gave the national government more power to unite the country while still protecting the rights of each state.

The Constitution balanced power between the national and state governments. This balance is one reason the United States has remained strong and free. When our nation stays united—while still respecting state independence—freedom works best.

Constitutional Safeguards

- **The Tenth Amendment** says that any powers not given to the national government belong to the states or the people. This keeps the government from taking power it was never meant to have.
- **The Founders' plan** created a system where national powers were limited, and most day-to-day authority stayed with the states.
- **The federal government** cannot create new rights—it can only protect rights people already have by nature or birth.
- **The Thirteenth Amendment** ended slavery and confirmed that freedom must exist in every state, making equality the shared law of the entire nation.

When, In the Course of Human Events

"When, in the course of human events, it becomes necessary for one people to dissolve the political bands which have connected them with another, and to assume, among the powers of the earth, the separate and equal station to which the laws of nature and of nature's God entitle them, a decent respect to the opinions of mankind requires that they should declare the causes which impel them to the separation."

Historical Background

The American colonists thought of themselves as British citizens, but they had no real voice in how they were governed. British laws and taxes were forced on them without their consent, and they had no representatives in Parliament to speak for them.

Over time, this felt deeply unfair. The colonists were treated as second-class citizens, denied the same rights as people in Britain. Each new law and tax made things worse, leaving them frustrated and powerless. When they tried peaceful petitions and protests, British soldiers were sent to keep order and enforce unpopular rules.

Eventually, the colonists realized they had to make a choice: stay silent under unfair control or stand up for their rights. They knew the world would ask why they were breaking away, so they wrote a clear explanation to show they weren't acting out of anger, but out of duty.

That is why *The Declaration of Independence* begins with such a strong statement—sometimes people must separate from a government that no longer protects their rights, but they must give good and honest reasons.

How Did This Shape America?

This bold opening made it clear that America's Revolution was not just a fight against a king—it was a fight for a new idea of government. The Founders believed that leaders should only have power if the people agree to it. This is called "consent of the governed."

By declaring independence, the Founders showed the world that people have the right to choose their own government. Their example inspired later revolutions for freedom in France, Haiti, Latin America, and other parts of the world.[14]

A Decent Respect to the Opinions of Mankind

Jefferson wrote that the colonies should show "a decent respect to the opinions of mankind." He meant that America needed to explain its reasons clearly and fairly. The world was watching, and the colonists wanted others to see that they weren't just rebelling—they were standing up for what was right. They wanted freedom, but also the world's respect.

Summary

The Declaration of Independence declared that people have a right to govern themselves. But freedom isn't automatic—it must be protected by laws that make sure people's rights are respected. The Constitution later provided that framework, keeping power in the people's hands.

Modern Interpretation

The idea that government should serve the people is still vital today. When people feel their government is unfair, they have the right to speak up, vote, and work to make things better—just like the colonists did in 1776.

Every debate over laws, justice, or elections connects back to these same founding ideas. From peaceful protests to Supreme Court rulings, Americans still rely on the principles of the Declaration to protect freedom and fairness.

Constitutional Safeguards

- **The government serves the people:** The Constitution begins with "We the People," showing that power comes from citizens, not rulers.
- **The government can't take total control:** The three branches of government—Legislative, Executive, and Judicial—share power so no one group dominates.
- **Rights are protected:** he Bill of Rights guarantees freedoms like speech, religion, and fair trials.
- **The people can change laws:** Amendments and elections let citizens fix unfair rules and improve their government.
- **Laws must be fair and applied equally:** The Fourteenth Amendment ensures equal protection under the law.
- **Leaders must follow the rules:** The Constitution is the highest law of the land, keeping even government officials accountable.

The Ninth Amendment also protects rights not specifically listed—just as the Declaration said all people have natural rights that can't be taken away.

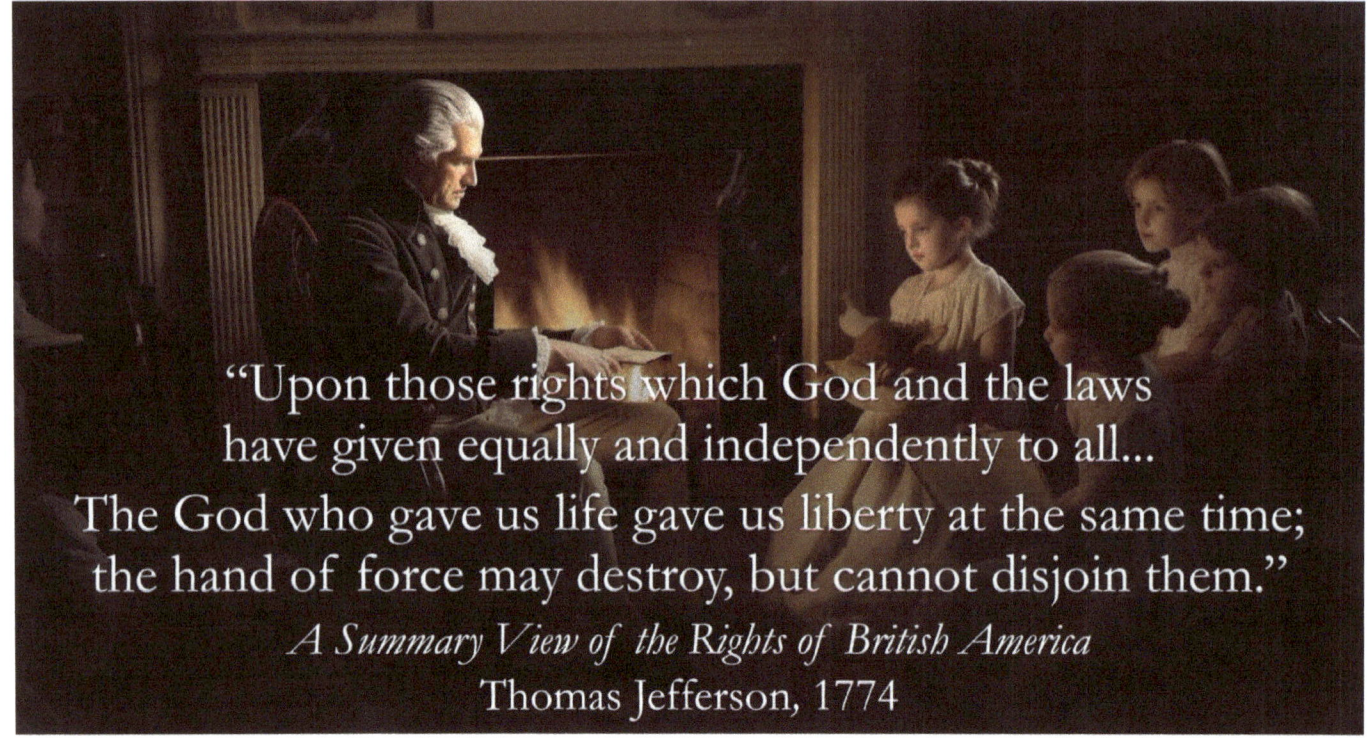

"Upon those rights which God and the laws
have given equally and independently to all...
The God who gave us life gave us liberty at the same time;
the hand of force may destroy, but cannot disjoin them."
A Summary View of the Rights of British America
Thomas Jefferson, 1774

We Hold These Truths

"We hold these truths to be self-evident, that all men are created equal, that they are endowed by their Creator with certain unalienable Rights, that among these are Life, Liberty and the pursuit of Happiness.—That to secure these rights, Governments are instituted among Men, deriving their just powers from the consent of the governed,—That whenever any Form of Government becomes destructive of these ends, it is the Right of the People to alter or to abolish it, and to institute new Government, laying its foundation on such principles and organizing its powers in such form, as to them shall seem most likely to affect their Safety and Happiness."

From Jefferson's 1774 *Summary View of the Rights of British America*

The God who gave us life gave us liberty at the same time; the hand of force may destroy, but cannot disjoin them… Kings are the servants, not the proprietors, of the people.

Franklin changed Jefferson's phrase **"sacred and undeniable"** to **"self-evident,"** shifting the Declaration from theology to reason—turning belief into proof. Yet what was said to be self-evident—that all men are created equal—was not self-evident in practice. Enslaved Africans and Native peoples stood outside the circle of equality Jefferson described. Even so, those words lit a fuse that generations would carry forward, forcing America to measure its conduct, even today, against its own immortal claim.

Historical Background

The Founders had been raised on Enlightenment ideas that emphasized reason and truth. John Locke and other thinkers taught that people could discover truth through reason—not just accept what they were told.

Jefferson took these ideas and applied them in his writings, including *The Declaration of Independence*.

Many of these ideas came from something called **natural law**—*the belief that every person is born with rights given by God*, not by kings or governments.

These ideas include:

- **Natural Rights:** Every person is born with rights like Life and Liberty that cannot be taken away
- **Consent of the Governed:** Government only has power because the people allow it
- **Right to Revolution:** If a government abuses its power, the people have a right to change or replace it
- **Reason and Moral Law:** Truth can be learned by thinking, observing, and learning—not just by tradition
- **Life, Liberty, and the Pursuit of Happiness:** Government exists to protect freedom, allowing people live happy and meaningful lives

They show that liberty comes from truth and reason—not from rulers or governments. These rights come from God.

Modern Interpretation

Each generation must decide what freedom means—and how to protect it. If liberty is ignored, it can slowly disappear.

The Declaration reminds us that our rights do not come from leaders or from popular opinion. They come from a higher law—one that applies to all people.

The Declaration is not just a document from the past. It is a call to stay aware, to think for ourselves, and to stand up for what is right.

Summary

The Declaration of Independence brought together both belief and reason. Jefferson built on ideas from thinkers like John Locke, who taught that people are born with natural rights.

Locke wrote that people should seek true and lasting happiness through thoughtful choices.

Jefferson turned these ideas into action. He argued that governments exist to protect these rights. When they fail, the people have both the right—and the duty—to change them.

Constitutional Safeguards

Through the Declaration, Jefferson gave these ideas a clear voice. Later, representatives met to create a Constitution—establishing a government strong enough to protect liberty, but limited enough to preserve it.

- **Article I:** Creates a Congress chosen by the people, so laws reflect their will.
- **Article II:** Establishes a president who must protect and defend the Constitution.
- **Bill of Rights:** Guarantees freedoms like speech, religion, and fair trials, while limiting government power.

Together, these protections help ensure that liberty is preserved and protected by law.

Did George Mason Inspire Jefferson's Preamble?

For more than a hundred years, historians and teachers have said that Thomas Jefferson got ideas for *The Declaration of Independence* from George Mason's Virginia Declaration of Rights. Both men wrote about life, liberty, and the right to change unfair governments. But the evidence tells a different story—one that shows Jefferson may have written his ideas first.

Mason's declaration was adopted on June 12, 1776. But Jefferson began writing the Declaration the day before, on June 11. Two years earlier, in 1774, he had published his *Summary View of the Rights of British America*, which included the same ideas. That means Mason's version followed Jefferson's—not the other way around.

What if we've been looking at this backward? What if Mason was actually influenced by Jefferson's earlier work?

Jefferson's Ideas Were Already in Print

Thomas Jefferson did not need to borrow from Mason—because he had already written these concepts himself. Two years before drafting the Declaration, Jefferson wrote his *Summary View of the Rights of British America*, written in July 1774, a bold and revolutionary argument against British rule. This document, published and widely circulated, contains strikingly similar language to both Mason's Virginia Declaration of Rights and Jefferson's own *Declaration of Independence*.

Jefferson did not claim his ideas were original—he was stating principles that were well known to the colonists, drawn from mutual experiences and great thinkers like John Locke.

Comparing the Texts

Below are three excerpts from *The Declaration of Independence*, Jefferson's *Summary View of the Rights of British America*, and Mason's Virginia Declaration of Rights. When viewed side by side, the similarities between Jefferson's *Summary View of the Rights of British America* and *The Declaration of Independence* are undeniable—while Mason's language, though similar, appears less like a source and more like a parallel reflection.

1. Natural Rights & the Creator's Gift of Liberty

Declaration of Independence (Jefferson, June 1776):

"We hold these truths to be self-evident, that all men are created equal, that they are endowed by their Creator with certain unalienable Rights, that among these are **Life, Liberty** and the pursuit of Happiness."

Summary View of the Rights of British America (Jefferson, July 1774):

"Upon those rights which **God and the laws have given equally** and independently to all… **The God who gave us life gave us liberty** at the same time; the hand of force may destroy, but cannot disjoin them."

Jefferson taught that freedom was a gift from God, not a favor from kings. Mason wrote that people are naturally free, but his version sounded more like English law than Jefferson's belief in divine rights.

Virginia Declaration of Rights, (Mason, May–June 1776):

"**That all men are by nature equally free and independent** and have certain inherent rights…namely, **the enjoyment of life and liberty, with the means of acquiring and possessing property, and pursuing** and obtaining happiness and safety."

Mason's text does not mention a Creator or divine authority—his wording is closer to English legal traditions than Jefferson's moral and philosophical stance.

2. The Purpose of Government & the Consent of the Governed

Declaration of Independence (Jefferson, June 1776):

"That to secure these rights, Governments are instituted among Men, deriving their just powers from the consent of the governed."

Summary View of the Rights of British America (Jefferson, July 1774):

"They know, and will therefore say, that kings are the servants, not the proprietors of the people… And this his majesty will think we have reason to expect when he reflects that he is no more than the chief officer of the people, appointed by the laws."

(Jefferson's earlier writing already establishes the idea that government is a servant of the people, subject to their will.)

Virginia Declaration of Rights, (Mason, May–June 1776):

"That all power is vested in, and consequently derived from, the people; that magistrates are their trustees and servants and at all times amenable to them."

(Mason echoes Jefferson's point, but the key idea—that rulers should serve the people—is already fully developed in *Summary View*, two years prior.)

3. The Right to Overthrow an Unjust Government

Declaration of Independence (Jefferson, June 1776):

> "That whenever any Form of Government becomes destructive of these ends, it is the Right of the People to alter or to abolish it, and to institute new Government."

Summary View of the Rights of British America (Jefferson, July 1774):

> "When the representative body have lost the confidence of their constituents… their continuing in office becomes dangerous to the state, and calls for an exercise of the power of dissolution."

Jefferson directly calls for the dissolution of an untrustworthy government—a sentiment later reflected in the Declaration.

Virginia Declaration of Rights, (Mason, May–June 1776):

> "When any government shall be found inadequate or contrary to these purposes, a majority of the community has an indubitable, inalienable, and indefeasible right to reform, alter, or abolish it."

There's no proof Jefferson copied Mason. Jefferson had already written the same ideas in 1774—two years before Mason's Declaration of Rights.

Many historians think Jefferson read Mason's work while drafting the Declaration, but that's just a guess. Jefferson never mentioned Mason as an influence. His earlier writings and the thinkers of the Enlightenment explain his ideas more clearly than any single source.

Historical Background

The Declaration of Independence was not created in isolation, nor was it copied from a single source. Thomas Jefferson had already been writing about these principles long before June 1776. His *Summary View of the Rights of British America* shows that he, like many of his peers, was deeply engaged in the debates about natural rights, self-governance, and the role of government long before Mason's Virginia Declaration of Rights was even written.

Many historians point to comparisons between the Declaration and Mason's work as proof that Jefferson borrowed from Mason. One history book even follows this pattern—lining up three sections of text from both documents to make the case. However, in the very next paragraph, it admits that Mason was familiar with Jefferson's *Summary View* but fails to compare Mason's text to Jefferson's earlier writings. It then claims that, while Jefferson's writing was superior, he certainly introduced no new ideas but merely reworded Mason's text.

A better approach is to compare original source documents and let the evidence speak for itself, rather than writing to prove a theory. The reality is that Jefferson had already put these ideas to paper two years before Mason's draft existed. *The Declaration of Independence* remains one of the greatest political documents in history—not because it borrowed from Mason, but because it captured and perfected ideas that had been evolving for decades. Jefferson did not copy Mason—he expressed the will of a people who were already determined to be free.

Summary

There's no proof Jefferson copied Mason. Jefferson had already written the same ideas in 1774—two years before Mason's Declaration of Rights.

Many historians think Jefferson read Mason's work while drafting the Declaration, but that's just a guess. Jefferson never mentioned Mason as an influence. His earlier writings and the thinkers of the Enlightenment explain his ideas more clearly than any single source.

However, none of this diminishes George Mason's importance in shaping America's founding principles. James Madison is credited as the Father of the Constitution. But **it was Mason who insisted on a declaration of rights at the Convention. Mason rose 136 times to speak, advocating for the inclusion of protections for individual liberties. When the final draft lacked a Bill of Rights, he refused to sign the Constitution**. Madison initially opposed adding one, but when Massachusetts and other states made ratification conditional upon future amendments, he finally agreed to push for a in the first Congress. Seven of the ten amendments in the Bill of Rights came directly from Mason's work, cementing his legacy as the true Father of the Constitution.

By examining Jefferson and Mason's contributions side by side, we can appreciate the unique roles both men played—Jefferson as the voice of the Declaration and Mason as the champion of individual rights that would later shape the Constitution's Bill of Rights.

More Food For Thought

As we compare the writings of Mason and Jefferson, more similarities come to light. Thomas Jefferson's 1776 draft of a Virginia Constitution was more than just a list of grievances or an alternative to the version being written in Williamsburg. It foreshadowed elements of both the U.S. Constitution and the Bill of Rights. It arrived in Williamsburg too late to be considered, but its depth and structure reflected Jefferson's vision for a government designed to protect liberty and prevent tyranny.

Jefferson's draft established a clear separation of powers among the executive, legislative, and judicial branches—principles later enshrined in the U.S. Constitution. He proposed a bicameral legislature to check tyranny, with both houses elected by the people.

Among his boldest provisions were term limits (to prevent a new aristocracy among the political class). Even more striking, his draft contained a list of fundamental rights, anticipating later constitutional protections:

- **Equal inheritance laws** – He proposed Gavelkind, ensuring equal land distribution, but uniquely included women in inheritance rights.
- **A ban on slavery for future arrivals** – "No person hereafter coming into this county shall be held within the same in slavery under any pretext whatever."
- **Religious freedom** – "All persons shall have full and free liberty of religious opinion; nor shall any be compelled to frequent or maintain any religious institution."
- **Right to bear arms** – "No freeman shall be debarred the use of arms [within his own lands]."
- **Opposition to standing armies** – "There shall be no standing army but in time of actual war."
- **Press freedom** – "Printing presses shall be free, except so far as by commission of private injury cause may be given of private action."

When a Long Train of Abuses

"Prudence, indeed, will dictate, that governments long established, should not be changed for light and transient causes; and accordingly, all experience hath shown, that mankind are more disposed to suffer, while evils are sufferable, than to right themselves by abolishing the forms to which they are accustomed. But when a long train of abuses and usurpations, pursuing invariably the same object, evinces a design to reduce them under absolute despotism, it is their right, it is their duty, to throw off such government, and to provide new guards for their future security. Such has been the patient sufferance of these Colonies; and such is now the necessity which constrains them to alter their former systems of government."

NOTE: Freedom is not lost all at once—it fades little by little when people put up with wrong things too long. The colonists tried many times to fix the problems peacefully, but nothing changed. After years of waiting, they realized they could not wait any longer. Below is a paraphrase of what he wrote in 1774.

Thomas Jefferson's 1774 Summary View of the Rights of British America (Paraphrased)

When leaders lose the trust of the people, begin to give away their rights, or take powers they were never given, they become dangerous. When that happens, the people have the right to remove them and choose new leaders.

Breaking down the phrases

"Prudence, indeed, will dictate, that governments long established, should not be changed for light and transient causes"

> Jefferson begins with the word *prudence*, meaning careful and wise judgment. He explains that people shouldn't throw out things they already know for small or passing reasons. Patience and stability are good, but if taken too far, they can let wrongs grow out of hand.

"…and accordingly, all experience hath shown, that mankind are more disposed to suffer, while evils are sufferable, than to right themselves by abolishing the forms to which they are accustomed."

> Jefferson notes that people often put up with unfair treatment because it feels safer than taking risks. Many would rather stay with what's familiar, even when it's unfair, than face the dangers that may come with demanding change.

"But when a long train of abuses and usurpations, pursuing invariably the same object, evinces a design to reduce them under absolute despotism, it is their right, it is their duty, to throw off such government, and to provide new guards for their future security."

> Here Jefferson makes his key point. When a government's abuse becomes a pattern, it's no longer a mistake—it's a plan to take away freedom. In that case, people not only can change their government, they must. Their duty is to build something new that protects liberty.

"Such has been the patient sufferance of these Colonies; and such is now the necessity which constrains them to alter their former systems of government."

> After years of patient suffering, the colonists had reached their limit. They had tried every peaceful way to correct the wrongs, but nothing changed. Jefferson says the time for waiting is over—the time for action has come.

This part of the Preamble carefully explains why revolt was not only their right but it was their duty. Jefferson's text moves from general principles to the specific case of the colonies, linking the two to build a compelling case why it was finally necessary to change their government.

> ### This Means
> Jefferson wanted the world to see that the colonies didn't rush into rebellion. They endured years of mistreatment before deciding that only liberty could bring lasting security.

Overview

This section of the Declaration's Preamble explains when people are justified in changing or replacing a government. Jefferson argues that claiming rights and overthrowing tyranny must never be done for trivial reasons. But when a government constantly violates people's rights, it loses its claim to power. At that point, it becomes the people's duty to create a new system that defends their safety and liberty.

This reasoning became the foundation of America's independence—and continues to inspire free nations everywhere that rise when justice is denied.

Historical Background

The ideas in this part of the Declaration came from Enlightenment thinkers—people like John Locke—who taught that government is a social contract between leaders and the people. In that agreement, rulers are supposed to protect people's rights, not take them away.

These ideas helped the colonies explain to the world why their fight for independence was fair and reasonable. They wanted other nations to see that they were not rebelling out of anger, but acting from long experience and moral duty.

The Enlightenment Thinker, John Locke, used the phrase, "a long train of abuses" in his 1690 *Second Treatise on Government*, Section 225.

> But if a long train of abuses, prevarications, and artifices, all tending the same way, make the design visible to the people, and they cannot but feel what they lie under, and see whither they are going, it is not to be wondered that they should then rouse themselves, and endeavour to put the rule into such hands which may secure to them the ends for which government was at first erected.[15]

Jefferson had already written about these ideas before 1776 in his Summary View of the Rights of British America. It was considered too bold by some, but it clearly showed his belief that leaders serve the people—and that when leaders betray that trust, people must act.

The American Revolution was not the first time people had resisted tyranny. English history included earlier struggles for liberty, such as the English Civil War and the Glorious Revolution. Jefferson and the Founders saw their own cause as part of that same story—people standing up for the rule of law and natural rights.

The Colonial Charters

Each colony in America had been founded under a charter—a kind of contract from the King of England. The charters granted land and outlined how the colony would be governed. Over time, these documents became symbols of freedom and self-rule. Colonists believed their charters gave them rights that even the King could not take away.

When Britain began changing or ignoring these charters, many colonists felt betrayed. The charters had guaranteed their liberty and property, but Parliament treated them as temporary permissions instead of lasting promises. This conflict planted the seeds of independence.

Early Troubles and Restrictions

As trade grew, Britain started passing laws that limited colonial manufacturing and shipping. These laws—like the Navigation Acts and the Molasses Act—were meant to keep money flowing to England. But to the colonists, they felt like chains.

Each new restriction made life harder for farmers, merchants, and shipbuilders. Taxes and trade barriers fueled resentment and created a growing sense that the colonies were being used, not represented.

Diverging Views on Charters

By the 1760s, the gap between Britain and the colonies had become clear. Britain saw the charters as privileges that could be changed or taken away. The colonists saw them as sacred agreements that guaranteed their rights. This disagreement deepened mistrust and laid the groundwork for open conflict.

Rising Tensions and Committees of Correspondence

As British pressure grew, colonial leaders began to organize. They formed Committees of Correspondence—early networks of communication between colonies. These committees helped share information, coordinate protests, and keep unity alive. The first was started in Virginia in 1773 and soon spread throughout the colonies.

List of British Acts and Colonial Responses

Britain kept passing new laws and taxes to control the colonies and raise money. Each one made the situation worse. Colonists responded with boycotts, petitions, and protests. The "long train of abuses" Jefferson described was not just about taxes on tea—it was about years of being ignored, punished, and ruled without consent.:

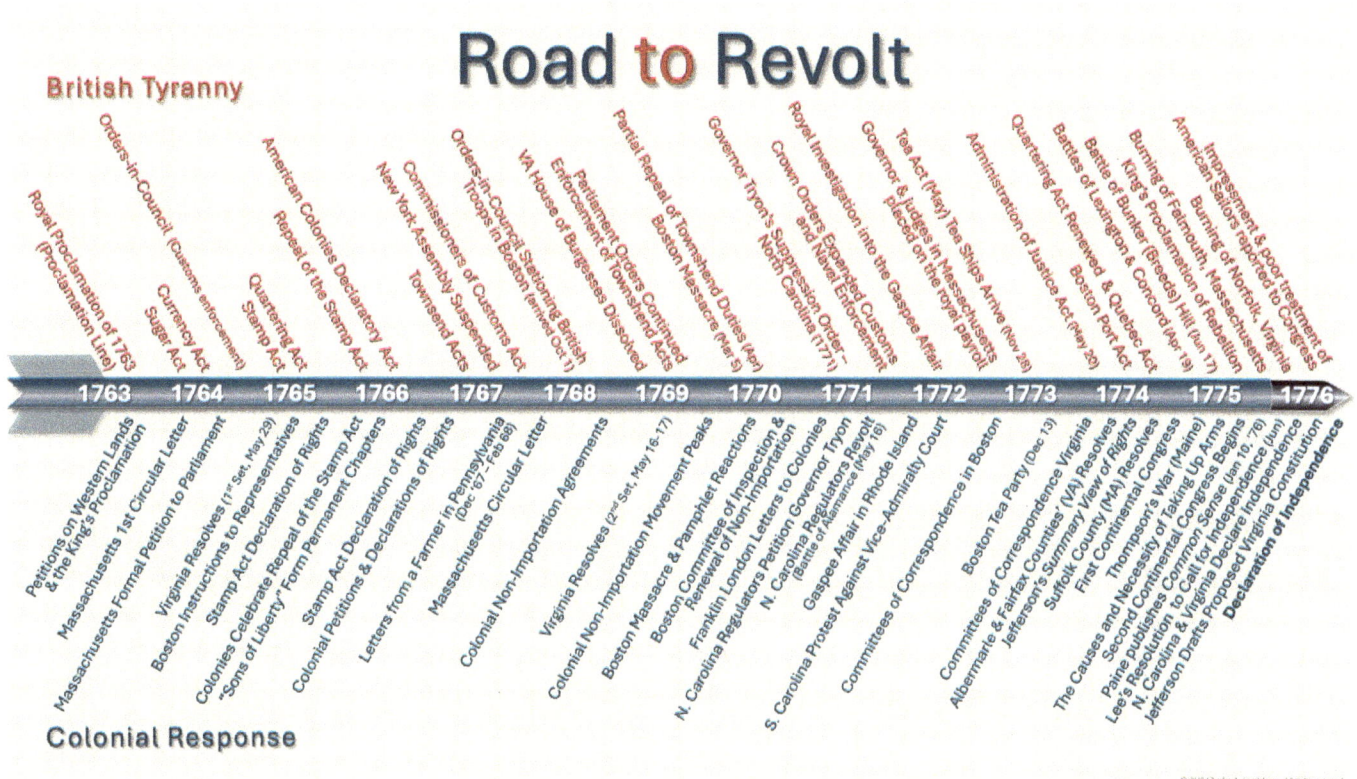

Each act of British tyranny provoked a colonial response—and the clash of wills led to the birth of a nation.

The Spread of Resistance

Resistance spread quickly across the colonies—from the crowded streets of Boston to the fields of Virginia and the harbors of South Carolina. Wherever British power tried to tighten its grip, Americans pushed back.

Events like the Boston Tea Party became symbols of courage and unity. The colonists' protests showed the world that they were no longer afraid of standing up to an empire.

The Road to Revolt: British Acts and Colonial Responses

The British government passed law after law trying to control the American colonies and raise money. Each new act made life harder and fueled growing resentment. These weren't just taxes on tea—they were signs that the colonists were losing control over their own lives.

Navigation Acts (1651)
- **Purpose:** These laws required colonial goods to be shipped only on British vessels so England could profit from trade.
- **Significance:** The Acts limited who the colonies could trade with. They helped Britain grow rich but left colonists feeling trapped and used for profit.[16]

Molasses Act (1733)
- **Purpose:** This act taxed molasses, rum, and sugar from non-British islands.
- **Significance:** Colonial merchants often ignored the tax and smuggled goods instead. It became one of the first sparks of defiance against unfair trade rules.[17]

Currency Act (1751)
- **Purpose:** This act stopped colonies from printing their own paper money.
- **Significance:** Without local money, farmers and shopkeepers struggled to pay debts. Britain's rule over the colonies' economy grew even tighter.[18]

Albany Congress (1754)
- **Purpose:** Representatives from several colonies met to discuss common defense and unity.
- **Significance:** Although their plan for cooperation wasn't adopted, it set the stage for later teamwork that would lead to the Continental Congress and, eventually, independence.[19]

Proclamation Line of 1763 (Royal Proclamation)
- **Purpose:** After the French and Indian War, the King forbade settlement west of the Appalachian Mountains to avoid conflict with Native tribes.
- **Significance:** Frontier settlers were furious—they had fought in the war and expected to claim that land. Britain's restriction convinced many that London didn't respect colonial sacrifices.[20]

Sugar Act (1764)
- **Purpose:** Lowered the tax on imported sugar but increased enforcement of trade laws.
- **Significance:** Colonists viewed it as another way for Britain to take money without consent. Even a cheaper tax felt unfair when imposed by a distant Parliament.[21]

Currency Act (1764)
- **Purpose:** Extended the earlier ban on colonial paper money.
- **Significance:** It deepened financial hardship and made trade even harder. Many saw it as another example of Britain ignoring local needs.[22]

Stamp Act (1765)
- **Purpose:** Required colonists to pay taxes on printed items—newspapers, legal papers, even playing cards.
- **Significance:** For the first time, the tax touched nearly everyone. Colonists protested loudly, arguing "No taxation without representation!" until the act was repealed.[23]

Quartering Act (1765)
- **Purpose:** Forced colonists to house and supply British soldiers stationed in America.
- **Significance:** Families resented having troops in their homes. To many, it felt like living under occupation rather than protection.[24]

Declaratory Act (1766)
- **Purpose:** Declared that Parliament had the right to make laws for the colonies "in all cases whatsoever."
- **Significance:** Even after repealing the Stamp Act, Britain reminded colonists that their obedience was expected—deepening distrust and anger.

Townshend Revenue Act (1767)
- **Purpose:** Placed new taxes on glass, paper, paint, and tea.
- **Significance:** Colonists responded with boycotts, smuggling, and protests. Tensions grew as British troops arrived to enforce the laws—paving the way for open conflict.[25]

> ### This Means
>
> Every new law or boundary change made colonists feel less like free participants in their own government and more like people being **stomped on by a tyrannical power.**
>
> The seeds of independence were planted not in a single protest—but through 120 years of frustration from trade restrictions, lost rights, and ignored petitions.
>
> By the late 1760s, nearly every part of colonial life was ruled by British law.
>
> Through bitter experience, the colonists learned that liberty and obedience could not live side by side under tyranny.

For ov 120 years, Britain had passed laws to shape, tax, and restrain the colonies. Each act added weight to the growing burden of control. By the 1770s, tension had reached a breaking point.

The next few years would ignite open conflict—when petitions turned to protest, and protest to revolution.

Boston Massacre (March 5, 1770)
- **Event:** A confrontation between British soldiers and a mob of colonists in Boston led to the soldiers firing into the crowd, killing five colonists.
- **Significance:** The Boston Massacre further inflamed anti-British sentiment in the colonies and was used as propaganda by colonial leaders to rally support for resistance efforts.[26]

Tea Act (1773)
- **Purpose:** This Act granted the British East India Company a monopoly on tea sales in the American colonies and allowed the company to sell surplus tea directly to colonial merchants.
- **Significance:** The Tea Act was seen as another attempt by the British government to assert its authority and maintain the principle of parliamentary taxation. It led to the Boston Tea Party and further heightened tensions between Britain and the colonies.[27]

Boston Tea Party (1773)
- **Event:** Colonists disguised as Mohawk Indians boarded British ships in Boston Harbor and dumped chests of tea into the water in protest against the Tea Act.
- **Significance:** The Boston Tea Party was a dramatic act of colonial defiance against British taxation policies and monopoly control over colonial trade. It led to harsh reprisals by the British government and the passage of the Intolerable Acts.[28]

Intolerable or Coercive Acts (1774)
- **Purpose:** These Acts were a series of punitive measures passed by the British Parliament in response to the Boston Tea Party. They aimed to punish Massachusetts and assert British authority in the colonies.
- **Significance:** The Intolerable Acts included the Boston Port Act, the Massachusetts Government Act, the Administration of Justice Act, and the Quartering Act, among others. They further escalated tensions between Britain and the colonies, significantly galvanizing colonial opposition and unity.[29]

The Boston Port Act (March 31, 1774)
- **Purpose:** Closed the port of Boston until damages from the Boston Tea Party were paid for.
- **Attitude in the Colonies:** This was seen as an egregious attack on the rights of the colonists and a blatant act of retaliation by the British government.[30]

The Massachusetts Government Act (May 20, 1774)
- **Purpose:** Altered the Massachusetts charter of government, granting the British-appointed governor significant power and restricting town meetings.
- **Attitude in the Colonies:** Viewed as an assault on colonial self-government and an attempt to undermine representative institutions.[31]

The Administration of Justice Act (May 20, 1774)
- **Purpose:** Allowed British officials accused of crimes in the colonies to be tried in Great Britain or another colony, where it was believed they would receive a more sympathetic trial.
- **Attitude in the Colonies:** This was seen as a violation of the principle of trial by jury and an affront to colonial legal rights.[32]

The Quartering Act (June 2, 1774)
- **Purpose:** Expanded the scope of the Quartering Act of 1765, allowing British troops to be quartered in private homes, including unoccupied buildings and barns, if necessary.
- **Attitude in the Colonies:** It was perceived as an infringement on colonial property rights and personal liberties, further fueling resentment towards the British military presence.

The Quebec Act (June 22, 1774)
- **Purpose:** Expanded Quebec's boundaries and granted religious freedoms to French Catholics while extending Quebec's jurisdiction into the Ohio Valley.
- **Attitude in the Colonies:** Seen as a direct threat to colonial land claims and religious freedoms, exacerbating fears of British tyranny and Catholic dominance.[33]

Modern Interpretation

The long train of abuses that inspired this part of the Declaration are important to understand. They remind us that people have the right to resist when a government becomes unfair or abusive. Jefferson's point wasn't to offer an excuse for rebellion, but to explain why and when it becomes necessary.

Jefferson explained that change must come from reason and principle—not anger or revenge. These words help every generation judge whether leaders are protecting liberty or destroying it.

Summary

The founders didn't rush into independence. They waited, reasoned, and pleaded for change before deciding that freedom was the only path left. This section shows that overthrowing a government should never be done lightly.

But when leaders ignore the people's rights and repeat the same abuses, the people not only have the right to act—they have the duty to act. Jefferson's words still inspire free nations to stand against tyranny and defend human liberty.

Constitutional Safeguards

The U.S. Constitution weaves the Enlightenment principles underpinning the Declaration's Preamble into the governance framework. The Constitution establishes a government empowered and constrained by the rule of law. The system of checks and balances among the three branches of government ensures that no single entity can become tyrannical, reflecting the Declaration's caution against despotism.

- **Article IV, Section 4** guarantees every state a republican form of government, ensuring that power always comes from the people.
- **Article V** provides a peaceful way to amend the Constitution, allowing change without the need for revolt.
- **The Bill of Rights** protects individual freedoms and limits government power, preserving the people's inalienable rights.

Together, these safeguards fulfill Jefferson's call **"to provide new guards for their future security."**

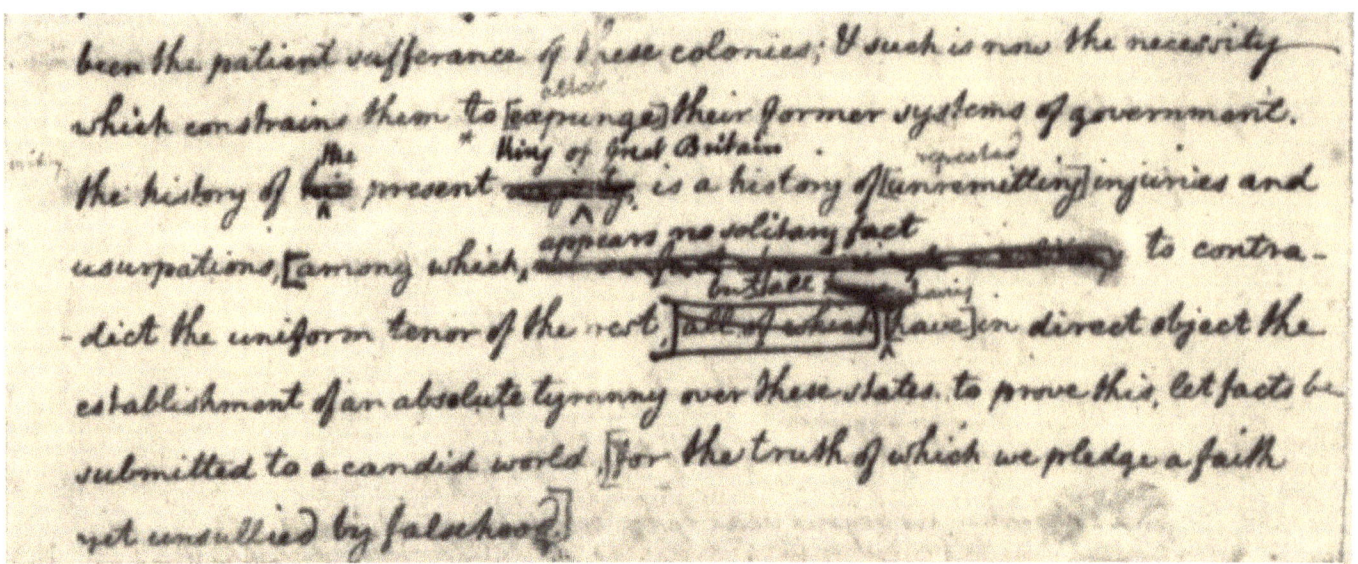

Portion of page 1 of Jefferson's Rough Draft of The Declaration of Independence, courtesy of the Library of Congress

Let Facts Be Submitted to a Candid World

"The history of the present King of Great Britain is a history of repeated injuries and usurpations, all having in direct object the establishment of an absolute tyranny over these States. To prove this, let facts be submitted to a candid world."

Jefferson ends the Preamble with a bold promise: to prove that Britain's rule over the colonies had become tyrannical. These words introduce the long list of wrongs that follow. He wanted the world to see that America's break from Britain wasn't based on emotion, but on evidence—a pattern of repeated abuse that could no longer be ignored or tolerated.

Jefferson's earlier writings, especially his *Summary View of the Rights of British America* (1774), had already outlined these same ideas. In many ways, *The Declaration of Independence* became a clearer, more powerful version of that earlier work.

Breaking Down the Phrases

"The history of the present King of Great Britain is a history of repeated injuries and usurpations, all having in direct object the establishment of an absolute tyranny over these States."

> Jefferson is accusing King George III of abusing his power again and again. Each wrong, he says, was part of a plan to control and dominate the colonies.

"To prove this, let facts be submitted to a candid world."

> Here Jefferson promises that the Declaration will present the evidence—specific facts—to show Britain's guilt. This wasn't a cry of rebellion; it was a case built on proof, reason, and fairness. He wanted the world to see that America's cause was just.

The Indictment: Leading to a List of Grievances

This part of the Declaration marks a turning point. After explaining why the colonies had the right to separate, Jefferson now begins to show how the King violated those rights. (In earlier writings, Jefferson had blamed Parliament or "They." Now he begins to directly blame the king. His language has now becomes treasonous.)

The phrase "let facts be submitted to a candid world" signals that the next section will be factual, not emotional—a list of real abuses that prove the charge of tyranny.

Jefferson's Summary View had already outlined many of the same complaints. By 1776, those ideas had matured into a formal indictment. Each Grievance became a piece of evidence showing why independence was not only justified—but necessary.[34]

> ### This Means
>
> Jefferson wasn't just accusing a king—he was teaching a lesson for all time.
>
> When leaders abuse power, it's not enough to complain; the truth must be proven and written down for the world to see.
>
> By submitting the facts "to a candid world," Jefferson showed that liberty depends on honesty, courage, and evidence—not emotion or anger.
>
> The Constitution would later turn that same principle into law, protecting the right to speak truth and defend freedom through justice, not violence.

Constitutional Safeguards

When the Constitution was written a decade later, it answered Jefferson's Declaration directly. It created a government designed to prevent the same kind of abuses that led to the Revolution.

- **Article III:** Created independent courts to keep justice fair and protect citizens from the kind of one-sided rulings common under the King.

- **Article I, Section 9:** Limited Congress's powers to prevent "injuries and usurpations," including unfair arrests and punishments.

- **The First Amendment:** Guaranteed the right to speak out freely and publish grievances without fear—so that facts could always be "submitted to a candid world."

Together, these protections turned Jefferson's words into law, ensuring that truth and liberty would always have a voice.

Presenting The Grievances

Thomas Jefferson ended the Preamble with these strong words:

> "The history of the present King of Great Britain is a history of repeated injuries and usurpations, all having in direct object the establishment of an absolute tyranny over these States. To prove this, let facts be submitted to a candid world."

With these words, Jefferson began listing the many ways King George III had mistreated the American colonies.

These were not small complaints—they were clear examples of power being used unfairly again and again. The colonists had tried to fix these problems peacefully, but their petitions were ignored.

Now, they were explaining to the world why separation had become necessary.

By this time, fighting had already begun at Lexington and Concord, and Bunker Hill had been fought. The moment for explanation—and for decision—had come.

Understanding the Grievances

The pages that follow help explain each Grievance in a clear and meaningful way.

Many of these ideas come from Thomas Jefferson's earlier writings, especially his 1774 *Summary View of the Rights of British America*, where he first expressed several of the same concerns. The following entries include shorter paraphrases of what he wrote so we can understand his ideas.

More ideas come from his later writings and a historian Benson J. Lossing, who recorded the events of the American Revolution using firsthand accounts and original documents.

Each Grievance is presented with:

- a clear explanation of what happened
- a connection to the ideas behind it
- and a simple summary to show why it mattered

Together, these Grievances reveal a pattern—one that shows why the colonies believed their rights were being taken away, and why they ultimately chose independence.

The Declaration and the Constitution

At the end of each Grievance section, you will see parts of the Constitution that protect against the same kinds of abuses.

This shows how the Declaration identified the problems—and how the Constitution was designed to prevent them.

Grievance 1	He Refuses to Assent to Necessary Laws
Grievance 2	He Forbids Passing Laws of Pressing Importance
Grievance 3	He Suppresses Representation
Grievance 4	He Burdens Legislatures with Fatiguing Measures
Grievance 5	He Dissolves Parliaments & Opposes Rights
Grievance 6	He Endangers Us by Neglecting Elections
Grievance 7	He Controls Settlement of Lands & Naturalization
Grievance 8	He Blocks Local Administration of Justice
Grievance 9	He Has Made Our Judges Dependent on His Will
Grievance 10	He Erected New Offices & Sent Swarms of Officers
Grievance 11	He Keeps Armies Among Us in Times of Peace
Grievance 12	His Military is Superior to Our Civil Authority
Grievance 13	He Subjects Us to Foreign Jurisdiction
Grievance 14	For Quartering Large Bodies of Troops Among Us
Grievance 15	He Protects Foreign Soldiers by Mock Trials
Grievance 16	For Cutting Off from Global Trade
Grievance 17	Taxation Without Representation
Grievance 18	Deprived of Trial by Juries
Grievance 19	Transporting Us Beyond Seas for Trial
Grievance 20	Enlarging the Borders of a Neighboring Province
Grievance 21	Taking Away Charters and Valuable Laws
Grievance 22	Suspends Legislatures & Assumes Power
Grievance 23	Abdicating Governance and Protection
Grievance 24	He Plundered, Ravaged, Burnt & Destroyed
Grievance 25	Foreign Mercenaries Terrorize Our People
Grievance 26	Taken Captive to Bear Arms Against Fellow Citizens
Grievance 27	Inciting Insurrections & Unleashing Merciless Forces
Slavery Clause	The Slavery Clause

Grievance 1
He Refuses to Assent to Necessary Laws

"He has refused his assent to laws the most wholesome and necessary for the public good."

NOTE: Before revolution came frustration. The colonies could not pass even the simplest local laws without royal approval. Britain's king withheld assent again and again, stifling reform and denying self-government.

Thomas Jefferson's 1774 *Summary View of the Rights of British America* (Paraphrased)

The king keeps saying "no" to good laws we make, even when they help the people. Sometimes he gives no reason at all. Because of this, we cannot fix problems or take care of our communities.

From *Our Country, A Household History*, Volume 3, by Benson J. Lossing, 1877

The Colonial Assemblies, from time to time, made enactments touching their commercial operations, the emission of a colonial currency, and concerning representatives in the imperial Parliament, but the assent of the sovereign to these laws was withheld. After the Stamp-Act excitements, Secretary Conway informed the Americans that the tumults should be overlooked, provided the Assemblies would make provision for full compensation for all public property which had been destroyed. In complying with this demand, the Assembly of Massachusetts thought it would be "wholesome and necessary for the public good," to grant free pardon to all who had been engaged in the disturbances, and passed an act accordingly. It would have produced quiet and good feeling; but the royal assent was refused.

Historical Background

During colonial times, the King of England had the final say over every law the colonies tried to pass. Even when those laws were meant to keep people safe, protect trade, or bring peace, the King often said "no." His refusal to approve these laws was not just stubborn—it showed that he wanted control more than fairness.

The colonists believed that good government should serve the people, not rule over them. When the King blocked helpful laws, families suffered and local leaders felt powerless. Thomas Jefferson wrote about this injustice in a pamphlet he wrote two years earlier called, *The Summary View of the Rights of British America*. In it, he explained that the King was rejecting laws that were "wholesome and necessary for the public good."

This constant interference became one of the main reasons the colonies chose to declare their independence.[35]

Modern Interpretation

This Grievance teaches why it's dangerous for one person to hold all the power to approve or stop laws. In America today, no single leader—not even the President—can control everything. Congress makes laws, the President enforces them, and the courts make sure they follow the Constitution.

By dividing power among branches, we prevent tyranny and protect freedom. The colonists wanted that same protection but had to fight for it.

Summary

Grievance 1 shows how angry the colonists became when their local laws were blocked by the King. They wanted a government where laws could be made fairly and for the benefit of the people. This Grievance helped shape the idea that all government power should come from the people, not from one ruler.

> ### This Means
> When one person can stop every good law, the people's voice disappears. The Founders made sure our government would never work that way again. In America, leaders must listen—and laws must serve the public good.

Constitutional Safeguards for Grievance 1

- **Article I, Section 1:** The power to make laws belongs to Congress—a group chosen by the people—not to a king or single ruler.
- **Article I, Section 7:** Explains how a bill becomes a law. If the President says no (a veto), Congress can still pass it with enough votes. That way, no one person has all the power.
- **Article I, Section 8:** Lets Congress passes bill that help everyone—like building roads, protecting trade, and keeping peace.
- **The Bill of Rights (Amendments 1–10):** Lists the basic freedoms of the people and limits what the government can or can't do, making sure leaders listen to citizens.
- **The Tenth Amendment:** Says that powers not given to the national government belong to the states or the people, so local communities can make their own decisions.

Grievance 2
He Forbids Passing Laws of Pressing Importance

"He has forbidden his governors to pass laws of immediate & pressing importance, unless suspended in their operation till his assent should be obtained; and when so suspended, he has neglected utterly to attend to them."

NOTE: Colonial governors could not act without royal permission. Even urgent laws waited months or years for approval from London, leaving local crises unresolved and communities powerless.

Thomas Jefferson's 1774 *Summary View of the Rights of British America* (Paraphrased)

The king makes our governors wait before they can pass important laws. Then he does not act on them at all. Because of this, help comes too late, and problems grow worse.

From *Our Country, A Household History*, Volume 3, by Benson J. Lossing, 1877

In 1764, the Assembly of New York took measures to conciliate the Six NATIONS, and other Indian tribes. The motives of the Assembly were misconstrued, representations having been made to the king that the colonies wished to make allies of the Indians, so as to increase their physical power and proportionate independence of the British crown. The monarch sent instructions to all his governors to desist from such alliances, or to suspend their operations until his assent should be given. He then "utterly neglected to attend to them." The Massachusetts Assembly passed a law in 1770, for taxing officers of the British government in that colony. The governor was ordered to withhold his assent to such tax-bill. This was in violation of the colonial charter, and the people justly complained. The Assembly was prorogued from time to time, and laws of great importance were "utterly neglected."

Historical Background

The King of England made the colonies wait for his approval before their laws could take effect. Even when people needed quick action—like fixing trade problems or protecting towns—the governors couldn't help until messages crossed the ocean to London and back. This long delay often meant nothing got done. Jefferson wrote that such waiting left the colonies "neglected," showing how powerless they had become under distant rule.[36]

Modern Interpretation

This Grievance still fits our world today. When leaders take too long to make decisions, communities can be harmed. During emergencies like funding essential services, wildfires, floods, or disease outbreaks, slow action can lead to government shutdown and even cost lives. Jefferson's complaint teaches that government should act quickly to meet people's needs. It also reminds us that local leaders often understand their communities better than far-away rulers or offices.

Summary

Grievance 2 shows what happens when government becomes too slow and too centralized. The colonists learned that laws must be made by people close to those they serve. The U.S. Constitution was designed so Congress and the states could act promptly, without waiting for royal approval. This grievance helped the Founders see that freedom also means having a government that listens and responds in real time.

> ### This Means
> The King's delays left the colonies stuck and helpless. The Founders decided that in America, leaders must be able to act quickly for the good of the people—without waiting for permission from far away.

Constitutional Safeguards for Grievance 2

- **Article I, Section 1:** Congress makes the laws, not a king or distant ruler. Elected representatives can pass important laws right away.

- **Article I, Section 7:** If the President does not act on a bill within ten days (while Congress is meeting), it becomes law automatically—no endless waiting.

- **Article I, Section 8:** Congress may make any laws needed to carry out its duties, allowing fast action in times of emergency.

- **The 10th Amendment:** States keep the power to handle their own problems, so local governments can respond quickly to their people's needs.

Grievance 3
He Suppresses Representation

"He has refused to pass other laws for the accommodation of large districts of people unless those people would relinquish the right of representation, a right inestimable to them, formidable to tyrants alone."

NOTE: Britain's rulers sought to weaken liberty by silencing local voices. Colonists were told no new laws would pass unless they surrendered their right of representation—the foundation of self-government itself.

Thomas Jefferson's 1774 *Summary View of the Rights of British America* (Paraphrased)

The king will not pass laws for the people unless they give up their right to be represented. This is not fair. The right to choose leaders is what protects their freedom.

From *Our Country, A Household History*, Volume 3, by Benson J. Lossing, 1877

A law was passed by [the British] Parliament in the spring of 1774, by which the popular representative system in the province of Quebec (Canada) was annulled, and officers appointed by the crown had all power as legislators, except that of levying taxes. The Canadians being Roman Catholics were easily pacified under the new order of things, by having their religious system declared the established religion of the province. But "large districts of people" bordering on Nova Scotia felt this deprivation to be a great grievance. Their humble petitions concerning commercial regulations were unheeded because they remonstrated against the new order of things, and Governor Carleton plainly told them that they must cease their clamor about representatives before they should have any new commercial laws. A [British] bill for "better regulating the government in the province of Massachusetts Bay," passed that year, provided for the abridgment of the privileges of popular elections, to take the government out of the hands of the people, and vest the nomination of judges, magistrates, and even sheriffs, in the crown. When thus deprived of "free representation in the Legislature," and the governor refused to issue warrants for the election of members of the Assembly, they called a convention of the freemen, and asked for the passage of "laws for the accommodation of large districts of people." These requests were disregarded, and they were told that no laws should be passed until they should quietly "relinquish the right of representation in the Legislature—a right inestimable to them, and formidable to tyrants only."

Historical Background

Imagine having to travel hundreds of miles just to vote or speak with a leader about a legal matter or your town's problems. That's what some colonists faced. The King refused to let new districts form unless people gave up their right to representation. Western settlers in places that would later become Western New York, Maine, or Ohio had no local voice in government. Jefferson wrote that this was unfair—people far from the cities were still citizens and deserved to be heard.[37]

Modern Interpretation

This Grievance reminds us why fair representation matters. Every person, no matter where they live, should have a voice in government. When leaders ignore large areas or groups, those people lose their influence. Jefferson said that taking away representation is "formidable to tyrants alone"—meaning only tyrants fear the people's voice. In America today, voting and equal representation protect everyone from that kind of rule.

Summary

Grievance 3 showed that the colonists wanted fair and equal representation in all parts of their land. They believed that government must listen to everyone, not just those near the capital. This idea became a foundation of the Constitution and helps us remember that freedom requires participation from every citizen, no matter how far away they live

> ### This Means
> The King didn't want distant settlers to have a say in their own laws. The Founders made sure that every community—big or small—would have a voice in America's government.

Constitutional Safeguards for Grievance 3

- **Article I, Sections 2 and 3:** These parts of the Constitution make sure people in every state have representation in Congress—by population in the House and equally in the Senate.

- **The 14th Amendment:** Guarantees equal protection, making sure all citizens are treated fairly and can be represented in government.

- **The 17th Amendment:** Allows citizens to elect their Senators directly, preventing state leaders from keeping that power for themselves.

Grievance 4
He Burdens Legislatures with Fatiguing Measures

"He has called together legislative bodies at places unusual, and also uncomfortable, and distant from the depository of their Public Records, for the sole purpose of fatiguing them into compliance with his measures."

NOTE: When the King wanted to punish colonial leaders, he made their work as hard as possible. He forced them to meet far away from their records—hoping to wear them down.

Virginia House of Burgesses Resolution (May 24, 1774)

When the British closed Boston's port and punished Massachusetts for resisting unfair taxes, Virginia lawmakers stood with them. As a delegate, Jefferson helped write a resolution expressing sympathy and support.

> "This House, being deeply impressed with the deplorable condition of our sister colony of Massachusetts Bay, whose Assembly is now held in a place at a distance from their records and from the body of their constituents, are desirous to testify their sympathy with their sufferings, and to express their firmest resolve to support them in every constitutional measure for the redress of the grievances under which they labor."

Two days later, the royal governor dissolved the Virginia Assembly. But the delegates refused to stop. Meeting at the Raleigh Tavern in Williamsburg, they called for a general meeting of all the colonies. That led to the formation of the First Continental Congress—the first united step on the road to American independence.[38]

From *Our Country, A Household History*, Volume 3, by Benson J. Lossing, 1877

In consequence of the destruction of tea in Boston harbor in 1773, the inhabitants of that town became the special objects of royal displeasure, The Boston Port Bill was passed as a punishment. The custom-house, courts, and other public operations were removed to Salem, while the public records were kept in Boston and so well guarded by two regiments of soldiers, that the patriotic members of the Colonial Assembly could not have referred to them. Although compelled to meet at a place "distant from the repository of the public records," and in a place extremely "uncomfortable," they were not fatigued into compliance, but in spite of the efforts of the governor, they elected delegates to a general Congress, and adopted other measures for the public good.

Historical Background

The King sometimes forced colonial lawmakers to meet in far-away or uncomfortable places. By doing this, he hoped to wear them down so they would finally give in to his demands.[39]

In 1774, Virginia lawmakers met to support Massachusetts after its Assembly was moved from Boston to Salem. The British governor of Virginia then dissolved the Assembly—but the leaders refused to quit. They met again at a nearby tavern, determined to keep speaking for the people. These actions showed that the colonists would not be silenced, even when the King tried to make governing too difficult to continue.[40]

Legislative Control as a Tool of Power

Tyrants often try to control lawmaking by creating obstacles instead of open attacks. They move meetings, delay sessions, or block access to important places and records. These tactics make it harder for representatives to do their jobs and exhaust them until they give up. Jefferson and his fellow delegates recognized that this kind of quiet control was another way to take away liberty.

Modern Safeguards Against Government Manipulation

Today, laws set clear times and places for when Congress and state legislatures meet. This prevents leaders from using distance or confusion to control decisions. Regular schedules, public access, and open debates protect citizens from the same kind of manipulation the colonists faced under the King.

Summary

Lawmakers must be free to meet without interference. By guaranteeing regular and open legislative sessions, our Constitution ensures that government remains strong, visible, and responsive to the people it serves.

> ### This Means
> King George tried to wear down the colonists by moving their meetings and making it hard to govern. America's Constitution makes sure leaders can meet freely and make decisions without being controlled or delayed.

Constitutional Safeguards for Grievance 4

The Declaration of Independence shows that the King tried to control lawmakers by making it hard for them to meet or do their work. To prevent that from ever happening again, the Constitution created rules that protect both Congress and state legislatures from unfair interference by any leader. These safeguards keep government meetings regular, fair, and free from manipulation.

- **Article I, Section 4:** Each state sets the time and place for elections of Senators and Representatives, ensuring meetings happen by the people's choice—not a ruler's.
- **Article I, Section 5:** Each house of Congress controls its own rules, meetings, and discipline, preventing interference from outside powers.
- **The 20th Amendment:** Sets firm start dates for the President and Congress to stop delays and keep the lawmaking process steady and accountable.

Grievance 5

He Dissolves Parliaments & Opposes Rights

"He has dissolved Representative houses repeatedly & continually, for opposing with manly firmness his invasions on the rights of the people."

NOTE: When colonial leaders spoke up for their rights, the King punished them by shutting down their assemblies. But every time he silenced one, another rose to take its place.

Thomas Jefferson's 1774 *Summary View of the Rights of British America* (Paraphrased)

The king shuts down our lawmaking groups and does not let new ones meet. Because of this, for a long time, there are no leaders to make laws for the people.

From *Our Country, A Household History*, Volume 3, by Benson J. Lossing, 1877

When the British government became informed of the fact that the Assembly of Massachusetts in 1768 had issued a circular to other Assemblies, inviting their co-operation in asserting the principle that Great Britain had no right to tax the colonists without their consent, Lord Hillsborough, the Secretary for Foreign Affairs, was directed to order the governor of Massachusetts to require the Assembly of that province to rescind its obnoxious resolutions expressed in the circular. In case of their refusal to do so, the governor was ordered to dissolve them immediately. Other Assemblies were warned not to imitate that of Massachusetts, and when they refused to accede to the wishes of the king, as expressed by the several royal governors, they were repeatedly dissolved. The Assemblies of Virginia and North Carolina were dissolved for denying the right of the king to tax the colonies, or to remove offenders out of the country for trial. In 1774, when the several Assemblies entertained the proposition to elect delegates to a general Congress, nearly all of them were dissolved.

Historical Background

In colonial times, the King could shut down a legislature whenever it disagreed with him. When that happened, the people lost their voice, and laws could not be passed.

This happened in both England and the colonies. British kings had once faced the same problem with Parliament, which led to the "Glorious Revolution" of 1688. But instead of learning from that event, King George III repeated the same mistake in America—closing colonial assemblies whenever they opposed his policies.[41]

These dissolutions only made the colonies stronger. When their official meetings were canceled, local leaders formed new groups—like Committees of Correspondence and the First Continental Congress—to keep working together for freedom.[42]

Modern Interpretation

Today, no one branch of government can shut down another. The Constitution makes sure that the people's elected representatives can meet, debate, and pass laws without fear of being dismissed by a ruler or president. This protection keeps power balanced and prevents leaders from silencing the voices of the people.

Summary

The Founders built strong safeguards to keep our legislative branch independent. They wanted to be sure that no leader could dissolve or replace the people's representatives for standing up for their rights. Thanks to these safeguards, Congress can always meet and carry out the people's work without royal control or intimidation.

> ### This Means
> The King kept shutting down colonial assemblies whenever they disagreed with him. The Founders made sure that in America, no president or ruler can silence the people's representatives or stop Congress from doing its job.

Constitutional Safeguards for Grievance 5

The Constitution protects the people's right to continuous, stable representation by stopping any leader from unfairly dissolving Congress or state legislatures.

- **Article I, Section 2:** Creates the House of Representatives, elected every two years, so the people always have a voice and can replace leaders peacefully through their vote.
- **Article I, Section 3:** Establishes the Senate as a continuous body—only part of it changes every two years—so it can't be dissolved at once.
- **Article I, Section 5:** Lets each house set its own rules and prevent interference from outside powers.
- **Article I, Section 7:** Describes how a bill becomes a law, ensuring that only Congress—not a king or president—controls the process.
- **The 20th Amendment:** Fixes the start dates for the President and Congress, ensuring that government continues smoothly and cannot be ended by executive will.

Grievance 6
He Endangers Us by Neglecting Elections

"He has refused for a long space of time to cause others to be elected, whereby the legislative powers, incapable of annihilation, have returned to the people at large for their exercise, the state remaining in the mean time exposed to all the dangers of invasion from without, & convulsions within."

NOTE: When the King shut down local elections, he left whole colonies without leaders or laws. Without government, chaos grew—and people had to govern themselves to survive.

Thomas Jefferson's 1774 *Summary View of the Rights of British America* (Paraphrased)

When leaders do not hold elections or choose new representatives, the people have no voice. Then the power goes back to the people, and they must act to keep themselves safe and keep order.

From *Our Country, A Household History*, Volume 3, by Benson J. Lossing, 1877

When the Assembly of New York, in 1766, refused to comply with the provisions of the Mutiny Act, its legislative functions were suspended by royal authority, and for several months the State remained "exposed to all the dangers of invasion from without and convulsions within." The Assembly of Massachusetts after its dissolution in July, 1768, was not permitted to meet again until the last Wednesday of May, 1769, and then they found the place of meeting surrounded by a military guard, with cannons pointed directly at their place or meeting. They refused to act under such tyrannical restrains and their legislative powers "returned to the people."

Historical Background

When the king stopped or delayed elections, the colonies were left without leaders chosen by the people. Without their local assemblies, laws could not be made or enforced, and daily life began to fall apart. Roads went unrepaired, trade slowed, and safety weakened.

In New York, in 1766, the Assembly was shut down for refusing to obey the Mutiny Act. The Mutiny Act was a British law required the American colonies to provide food, housing, and supplies for British soldiers. Many colonists believed this was unfair because it forced them to pay for an occupying army they hadn't invited. When colonial assemblies refused to follow the Act, the king punished them by suspending their right to hold elections. The same thing happened in Massachusetts two years later, which left citizens without any elected lawmakers. These actions created anger and fear that Britain might try to rule the colonies by force.

Without functioning legislatures, the colonies had no way to collect taxes, organize defense, or solve local problems. The people grew restless as British troops filled the streets, enforcing rules no one had voted for. From town halls to taverns, talk of injustice spread, and neighbors began planning how to defend their rights. Shared frustration began to unite the colonies in a common cause.

Jefferson explained that when a king blocks elections, power naturally "returns to the people." This led colonists to form new groups—like Committees of Correspondence and the Continental Congress—so that the people themselves could keep governing.[43]

Modern Interpretation

Today, our Constitution makes sure this can never happen again. The people always have the right to choose their lawmakers. Presidents or governors can't cancel or delay elections to hold onto power. If one branch stops working, others can keep government going so the people's voice is never silenced.

Summary

Grievance 6 was about keeping government in the hands of the people. The colonists wanted fair elections and local control, not distant rule from a king. The Constitution now guarantees that elections must happen regularly and that power can't be taken away by delaying or ignoring them.

> ### This Means
> When leaders refuse to hold elections, they silence the people's voice. America's founders made sure that never happens again—by protecting free, regular elections where the people are always in charge.

Constitutional Safeguards for Grievance 6

- **Article I:** Creates Congress, made up of representatives elected by the people.
- **Article I, Section 2:** Requires elections for the House of Representatives every two years.
- **Article I, Section 4:** Lets Congress set the times and rules for elections so no one can block them.
- **The 17th Amendment:** Allows citizens—not state legislatures—to elect U.S. Senators directly.

Grievance 7

He Controls the Settlement of Lands & Naturalization

"He has endeavored to prevent the population of these states; for that purpose, obstructing the laws for naturalization of foreigners; refusing to pass others to encourage their migrations hither; & raising the conditions of new appropriations of lands."

NOTE: The King wanted to control who could live in America and where they could settle. By blocking land grants and immigration, he slowed the colonies' growth and tried to keep them weak. This was very troubling because the colonies owned western lands that King George III now claimed following the French and Indian War.

Thomas Jefferson's 1774 *Summary View of the Rights of British America* (Paraphrased)

The king makes it hard for people to get land and settle here. He acts like the land belongs to him, but it does not. The land belongs to the people who live in the community.

From *Our Country, A Household History*, Volume 3, by Benson J. Lossing, 1877

Secret agents were sent to America soon after the accession of George the Third to the throne of England, to spy out the condition of the colonists. A large influx of liberty-loving German emigrants was observed, and the king was advised to discourage these immigrations. Obstacles in the way of procuring lands, and otherwise, were put in the way of all emigrants, except from England, and the tendency of French Roman Catholics to settle in Maryland was also discouraged. The British government was jealous of the increasing power of the colonies; and the danger of having that power controlled by democratic ideas, caused the employment of restrictive measures. The easy conditions upon which actual settlers might obtain lands on the Western frontier, after the peace of 1763, were so changed, that toward the dawning of the Revolution, the vast solitudes west of the Alleghanies were seldom penetrated by any but the hunter from the seaboard provinces. When the War for Independence broke out, immigration had almost ceased. The king conjectured wisely, for almost the entire German population in the colonies were on the side of the patriots.

Challenging the Boundaries of Empire and Sovereignty

After the French and Indian War, the King drew new boundary lines through the American colonies. The Royal Proclamation of 1763 sounded like it was meant to keep peace with Native tribes, but it really gave the Crown control over huge areas that had already belonged to the colonies by charter. Lands west of the Appalachian Mountains were now called "royal territory," and colonists were told not to settle there.

To Jefferson and other patriots, this was a shocking power grab. The King was treating land already secured by English settlers, for which they had charters, as if it were newly conquered and his to give away. What had once been the colonists' right to expand had become the King's tool to control them.[44]

Charter Rights Long Preceded French Claims

The colonies' charters—Virginia, Maryland, Connecticut, and Carolina—had promised land stretching far to the west, long before France claimed the same region. These English grants were legal, recognized, and supported by years of settlement. France's "Louisiana" claim, by contrast, was mostly on paper.[45]

When the King later used France's claim as an excuse to redraw America's map, he ignored those older English rights. Jefferson saw this as both dishonest and dangerous.[46]

Legally owned colonial lands could be taken away simply by accepting another nation's later claim for that same land. The colonists believed that the King was changing the rules to tighten his control.

Curtailing Immigration and Colonial Growth

King George III also worried that too many liberty-minded settlers—especially Germans—were moving to America. His ministers began slowing immigration and making it harder for new arrivals to buy land or become citizens. They feared that too much freedom and too many independent farmers would weaken royal authority.

> "The king conjectured wisely," wrote Lossing, "for almost the entire German population in the colonies were on the side of the patriots."

Jefferson condemned this policy as an attempt to keep the colonies small and dependent. By slowing expansion, the Crown could keep tighter control over who owned land and who was loyal. Britain claimed it was protecting order, but the real goal was to limit growth and self-government. The King wanted people to stay where they could be watched and ruled, not where they could build their own free communities.

> "But his majesty has lately taken on him to advance the terms of purchase [of land]… by which means the acquisition of lands being rendered difficult, the population of our country is likely to be checked."

The King wanted the colonies to remain British. He had tolerated enough of German settlement. He now built forts along the frontier and used his soldiers. By slowing expansion and tightening land rules, the Crown hoped to control both the people and the frontier itself, to:

- Stall growth
- Discourage immigration and migration to the frontier
- Keep the frontier under royal supervision

Royal Land Claims and the Loss of Colonial Rights
The King rewarded his soldiers with huge pieces of land after the French and Indian War—but those rewards came from American soil that already belonged to the colonies. Under the Royal Proclamation of 1763, he claimed these western lands as "royal property," handing them out as rewards, ignoring that they already belonged to the colonies.

To Jefferson, his was not generosity—it was a taking of land that already belonged to the colonies. The King was using power no English monarch had ever lawfully claimed: to take land promised to free citizens and give it away at his pleasure. In doing so, he destroyed the colonists' trust and endangered their liberty.

Accepting French Territorial Claims Nullifies Colonial Charters
Britain then accepted France's claim to this land as if it were legitimate. By calling that region "spoils of war," the Crown treated it as newly conquered land already secured by English settlers.

This decision wiped out the rights the colonies held by charter—rights earned through generations of settlement, farming, and defense.

> "The lands which were conquered by the joint arms of Great Britain and America are declared to be their conquest, and subject to their disposal."—Jefferson, 1775

Jefferson and other patriots saw it as the King replacing English law with royal whim. If he could change boundaries at will, no colonial land was truly safe.

The Ohio Company as a Precursor to War
Years before the Revolution, Virginia leaders like George Washington, Lawrence Washington, and George Mason had helped form the Ohio Company to settle lands west of the Alleghenies. Their efforts had been supported by royal grants and based on lawful English charters. But the Proclamation of 1763 erased those promises overnight.

When the King redefined the frontier as royal domain, he made every colonial claim subject to his personal control. This betrayal pushed many of Virginia's leaders to realize that Britain's government no longer respected their rights as Englishmen. What began as a land dispute soon became a fight for independence.[47]

The Fiction of Protection
The King said the Royal Proclamation was meant to "protect" colonists and Native tribes from conflict, but that was only part of the truth. By forbidding settlers to move west, he kept the colonies crowded along the coast—easier to watch, tax, and control.

To Jefferson, this "protection" was a disguise for domination. Britain's actions turned freedom into permission and made colonial progress dependent on royal approval. What had once been their inherited birthright became land they could only use with the King's permission.

Summary
The King's land policies broke centuries of English tradition and denied the colonies their chartered inheritance. He blocked immigration, halted settlement, and claimed the right to decide where free people could live and work. These actions deepened colonial anger and convinced many that true liberty could never exist under royal rule.

Colonial vs Royal Territorial Claims

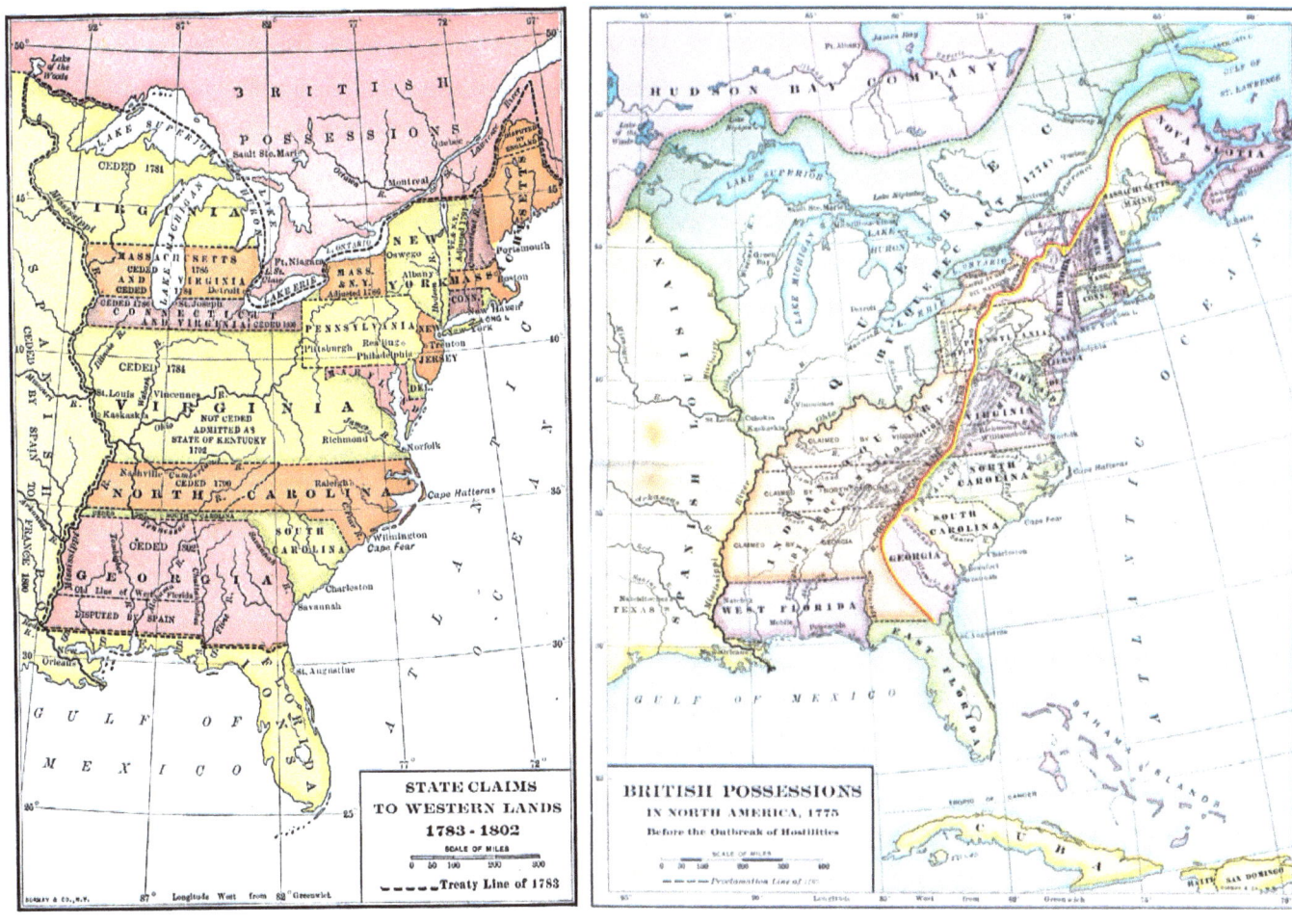

State Claims to Western Lands, 1783–1802. From Matthew H. Bowman, An Atlas of American History (New York: Charles Scribner's Sons, 1911). Map engraved by C. S. Hammond & Company. Public Domain, courtesy of the United States Library of Congress and the Perry-Castañeda Library Map Collection, University of Texas at Austin.

Albert Bushnell Hart, LL.D., The American Nation Vol 14 (New York, NY: Harper and Brothers, 1906)
The red and yellow Proclamation Line of 1763, was colored by the author to represent the new western boundaries of the colonies, as designated by the Royal Proclamation of 1763. (The map on the left approximates accepted colonial claims prior to the 1763 proclamation)

> **This Means**
> The King tried to keep the American colonies small, dependent, and under his control. The founders believed that freedom includes the right to move, build, and prosper without needing royal permission. Their fight for land became a fight for liberty itself.

Constitutional Safeguards for Grievance 7

- **Article IV, Section 3, Clause 2 (Property Clause):** Gives Congress—not a monarch—the power to manage and distribute public lands belonging to the United States.

- **Article I, Section 8, (The Naturalization Clause):** Authorizes Congress to set fair, uniform rules for becoming a U.S. citizen.

- **The Fifth Amendment:** Protects property rights, requiring due process and fair compensation if land is taken for public use.

Grievance 8

He Blocks Local Administration of Justice

"He has suffered the administration of justice totally to cease in some of these colonies, refusing his assent to laws for establishing judiciary powers."

NOTE: When the King blocked local courts and controlled judges, people could no longer rely on fair trials or equal justice. Without independent courts, the law no longer protected the people.

Albemarle County Resolves: Jefferson, July 26, 1774 (Paraphrased)

We keep the power to run our own courts. We will stand against anyone who tries to stop them or keep justice from being done here.[48]

From *Our Country, A Household History*, Volume 3, by Benson J. Lossing, 1877

By an act of Parliament in 1974, the judiciary was taken from the people of Massachusetts. The judges were appointed by the king, were dependent on him for their salaries, and were subject to his will. Their salaries were paid from moneys drawn from the people by the commissioners of customs, in the form of duties. The same act deprived them, in most cases, of the benefit of trial by jury, and the "administration of justice" was effectually obstructed. The rights for which Englishmen so manfully contended in 1688 were trampled under foot. Similar grievances concerning the courts of law existed in other colonies; and throughout the Anglo-American domain there was but a semblance of justice left. The people met in conventions when assemblies were dissolved, and endeavored to establish "judiciary powers," but in vain; and were finally driven to rebellion.

Historical Background

King George III refused to approve colonial laws that created or maintained local courts. This brought justice in many colonies to a stop. Without functioning courts, people could not settle disputes, defend property, or bring criminals to trial.

In 1774, Parliament passed the Massachusetts Government Act, one of the Coercive (Intolerable) Acts. It took away the colony's right to choose its own judges and allowed the King to appoint them instead. Judges now owed their positions and salaries to the Crown, not to the people. Cases that once belonged to local juries were now decided by royal judges.[49]

With justice under royal control, colonists had no fair way to seek justice. Communities began forming their own meetings and temporary courts to fill the gap. These early "shadow governments" showed the people's growing belief that they must govern—and judge—locally when the King would not allow them to do so.[50]

Modern Interpretation

Today, America's judicial system stands independent of both Congress and the President. The Constitution ensures that no ruler or political branch can suspend justice or control the courts for personal power. Judges serve under the law—not under leaders—and trials must remain fair, open, and impartial.

By guaranteeing separate branches of government, the framers made certain that what happened under King George III could never happen again.

Summary

Grievance 8 shows how the King tried to silence justice by keeping the courts under his command. The colonists' stand for fair, local courts led to the principle of an independent judiciary, which became one of the cornerstones of American liberty.

> ### This Means
> When a ruler controls the courts, there is no real justice. America's founders made sure our judges answer only to the law and the Constitution—so justice can never be taken away or paused by politics.

Constitutional Safeguards for Grievance 8

- **Article III:** Establishes the federal government's judicial branch, ensuring an independent court system separate from Congress and the President.

- **The first section of Article III:** States that "The judicial Power of the United States shall be vested in one Supreme Court, and in such inferior Courts as the Congress may from time to time ordain and establish," guaranteeing that the executive branch cannot shut the courts down.

- **The Sixth Amendment:** Guarantees the right to a speedy and public trial, an impartial jury, and legal counsel—ensuring that justice is fair and transparent for everyone.

Grievance 9
He Has Made Our Judges Dependent on His Will

*"He has made our judges dependent on his will alone,
for the tenure of their offices, and amount of their salaries."*

NOTE: The King made judges depend on him for their jobs and pay. This made it hard for them to be fair, because they risked losing everything if they ruled against him.

Thomas Jefferson's 1774 *Summary View of the Rights of British America* (Paraphrased)

Leaders use their power to help themselves, not the people. They make new jobs and give them to their friends, instead of doing what is right.

From *Our Country, A Household History*, Volume 3, by Benson J. Lossing, 1877

As we have observed, judges were made independent of the people. Royal governors were placed in the same position. Instead of checking their tendency to petty tyranny, by having them depend upon the Colonial Assemblies for their salaries, these were paid out of the national treasury. Independent of the people they had no sympathies with the people, and thus became fit instruments of oppression, and ready at all times to do the bidding of the king and his ministers. The Colonial Assemblies protested against the measure, and out of the excitement which it produced, grew that power of the Revolution, the Committees of Correspondence. When, in 1774, Chief Justice Oliver, of Massachusetts, declared it to be his intention to receive his salary from the crown, the Assembly proceeded to impeach him, and petitioned the governor for his removal. The governor refused compliance, and great irritation ensued.

Historical Background

In the colonies, judges were chosen by the King and could be removed whenever he wanted. Their salaries came from the Crown, not the people they served. This made judges afraid to rule against the king, knowing they could lose their jobs and pay.

The danger grew after Parliament passed the Judicature Act of 1761, which confirmed that colonial judges would be paid by the Crown rather than local legislatures. This change tightened royal control over the courts, so decisions generally favored Britain.

Colonial leaders quickly recognized that this system made fair trials almost impossible. They began demanding independent courts where justice could not be controlled or pressured. The U.S. Constitution later fixed this abuse by guaranteeing that judges hold their offices for life (unless impeached for wrongdoing) and that their pay cannot be reduced—so they are free to judge by law, not by fear.[51]

Modern Interpretation

Today, judges in America are independent, meaning they do not answer to political leaders. Federal judges cannot be fired or punished for their rulings, and their pay cannot be lowered while they serve. They answer to the Constitution and can stop other leaders from misusing power of both Congress and the President.

Throughout history, independent courts have protected people from unfair laws and actions by the government. Without that independence, courts could become tools of power instead of guardians of liberty and justice.

Summary

The founders believed that justice should never depend on a ruler's approval. Under the King, judges served at his pleasure; under the Constitution, they serve under the law. Judicial independence became one of the foundations of the republic, protecting every citizen's right to fair and fearless justice.

> ### This Means
> When judges can lose their jobs for making honest decisions, fair justice disappears. The founders made sure America's judges can't be bribed, threatened, or dismissed for doing what's right—so the law always stands above politics.

Constitutional Safeguards for Grievance 9

- **Article III, Section 1:** States that "Judges, both of the supreme and inferior Courts, shall hold their Offices during good Behavior..."

    This means judges can keep their jobs as long as they follow the law—and their pay cannot be reduced to pressure them.

    This contrasts sharply with the colonial system, where judges answered to the Crown for their pay and position—forcing them to rule in favor of royal interests instead of justice.

Grievance 10
He Erected New Offices & Sent Swarms of Officers

"He has erected a multitude of new offices by a self-assumed power, & sent hither swarms of officers to harass our people & eat out their substance."

NOTE: Jefferson uses strong words here to show how upset the colonists are. The King keeps sending more officers to America to collect taxes and control the people. These officers make life harder and take money from the colonists.

Thomas Jefferson's 1774 *Summary View of the Rights of British America* (Paraphrased)

The King sets up many new offices and sends officers to control us. They use their power to take money and make rules that hurt the people.

From *Our Country, A Household History*, Volume 3, by Benson J. Lossing, 1877

After the passage of the Stamp-Act, stamp distributers were appointed in every considerable town. In 1766 and 1767, acts for the collection of duties created "swarms of officers," [unreadable] of whom received high salaries; and when, in 1768, admiralty and vice-admiralty courts who established on a new basis, an increase in the number of officers was made. The high salaries and extensive perquisites [a thing regarded as a special right or privilege enjoyed as a result of one's position (perks)] of all of these, were paid with the people's money, and thus "swarms of officers" "eat out their substance."

Historical Background

Colonists grew angry as Britain created new government offices and filled them with officials loyal to the Crown. These officers worked for the king's interests, not for the colonies. They often misused their power. They demanded taxes, searched homes and ships without good reason, and punished those who resisted.

One of the worst examples came after the Townshend Acts of 1767, which placed taxes on everyday goods like glass, lead, and tea. Britain then sent customs officers to enforce the laws and gave them authority to search anyone's property under "writs of assistance." These open-ended warrants allowed officers to barge in almost anywhere, breaking long-standing rights to privacy and fair treatment.[52]

The British also expanded vice-admiralty courts, which had no juries and often sided with royal officials. Colonists saw these courts as tools of intimidation. Jefferson's words about "swarms of officers" captured how these tax collectors and inspectors became symbols of royal corruption and greed—profiting at the people's expense.[53]

Modern Interpretation

In America today, no branch of government can create endless offices or appoint officials without limits. The Constitution divides that power so it can't be abused. Presidents can nominate officers, but the Senate must approve them. Congress controls funding and decides when offices are created or removed. This balance keeps any single branch from filling government with officials who serve themselves instead of the people.

Summary

Grievance 10 shows the colonists' frustration with a government that created more and more offices and officials to watch, tax, and control them The founders responded by ensuring checks and balances between Congress and the President—so that every appointment of power would require consent and accountability.

> ### This Means
> The King sent "swarms of officers" to take the people's money and limit their freedom. America's founders made sure that never happens again. No leader can now fill offices or create agencies for personal power—the people, through Congress, must always have a say.

Constitutional Safeguards for Grievance 10

The U.S. Constitution prevents any leader from creating offices or appointing officials without limits. It divides that power among the branches of government so no one person can control it alone:

- **Article II, Section 2:** Gives the Senate authority to confirm the President's appointments, including ambassadors, judges, and officers. This ensures one branch cannot appoint officials on their own.

- **Article I, Section 8:** Allows Congress to create or remove federal offices, keeping the power to create offices in the hands of the people's representatives.

- **The Tenth Amendment:** Reserves powers not granted to the federal government for the states or the people, preventing the national government from forcing unwanted officials on local communities.

Grievance 11
He Keeps Armies Among Us in Times of Peace

"He has kept among us, in times of peace, Standing Armies without the Consent of our legislatures."

NOTE: After the French and Indian War, the King began keeping soldiers in the colonies, even when there was no fighting. The colonists did not agree to this. The soldiers were used to enforce rules and scare the people.

Thomas Jefferson's 1774 *Summary View of the Rights of British America* (Paraphrased)

The King sends soldiers here without our permission. They are not chosen by the people or our laws. He has no right to do this, and it puts our freedom in danger.

From *Our Country, A Household History*, Volume 3, by Benson J. Lossing, 1877

After the treaty of peace with France, in 1763, Great Britain left quite a large number of troops in America, and required the colonists to contribute to their support. There was no use for this standing army, except to repress the growing spirit of Democracy among the colonists, and to enforce compliance with taxation laws. The presence of troops was always a cause of complaint; and when, finally, the colonists boldly opposed the unjust measures of the British government, armies were sent hither to awe the people into submission. It was one of those "standing armies" kept here "without the consent of the Legislature," against which the patriots at Lexington, and Concord, and Bunker Hill so manfully battled in 1775.

Historical Background

The colonists grew uneasy seeing British soldiers stationed in their towns when there was no war. Many believed these armies were not for protection but for control—to enforce the King's laws and silence anyone who protested.

After the French and Indian War (1754–1763), Britain left a large army in North America, claiming it was needed for safety. But the colonists suspected the real reason was to keep them obedient. The Quartering Act of 1765 made things worse by forcing colonists to provide housing and supplies for British troops.

Tensions exploded when soldiers fired on an unarmed crowd in the Boston Massacre of 1770, killing five colonists. By 1775, British troops marched to Lexington and Concord to seize colonial weapons. Those confrontations marked the beginning of the Revolutionary War, proving that standing armies in times of peace could be used to threaten, not protect, the people.[54]

Modern Interpretation

Today, the Constitution guarantees that America's military always answers to civilian authority. Congress controls military budgets and laws, while the President commands the armed forces only within those limits. This balance keeps our military strong but never above the people it serves.

Summary

Grievance 11 shows the colonists' fear of permanent armies being used to enforce tyranny. The founders answered this fear by giving Congress—not a king—the power to fund armies, and by protecting citizens' rights through the Second and Third Amendments, which ensure defense is local, lawful, and accountable to the people.

> ### This Means
> The King used his armies to keep people in line. America's founders made sure that could never happen again—our armed forces exist to protect our freedom, not to suppress it.

Constitutional Safeguards for Grievance 11

- **Article I, Section 8:** Gives Congress—not the President—the power to raise and support armies, but limits military funding to two years at a time so civilian control is always maintained.

- **The Third Amendment:** Protects citizens from being forced to house soldiers in peacetime, a direct response to the British Quartering Act.

- **The Second Amendment:** Guarantees the right to a well-regulated militia, ensuring that defense remains local and that the people are never powerless before standing armies.

Grievance 12

His Military is Superior to Our Civil Authority

"He has affected to render the military, independent of & superior to the civil power."

NOTE: The colonists were deeply alarmed when British generals began ruling over civilian leaders. This grievance shows their fear that the army—acting on the King's command—could overrule local laws and take control of everyday life.

Thomas Jefferson's 1774 *Summary View of the Rights of British America* (Paraphrased)

The King has made things even worse by putting the military above the law. Instead of the soldiers obeying the people's laws, he has made the people answer to the soldiers. He cannot place himself above the laws he created. Even if he uses force to do it, force does not make it right.

From *Our Country, A Household History*, Volume 3, by Benson J. Lossing, 1877

General Gage, commander-in chief of the British forces in America, was appointed governor of Massachusetts in 1774: and to put the measures of the Boston Port Bill into execution, he encamped several regiments of soldiers upon Boston Common. The military there, and also in New York, was made independent of, and superior to, the civil power, and this, too, in a time of peace, before the Minute-men were organized.

Historical Background

The colonists grew fearful as Britain placed military leaders above local governments. In 1774, General Thomas Gage, commander-in-chief of all British troops in North America, was appointed military governor of Massachusetts. This gave him both civil and military power, allowing him to enforce laws and punish the people without consent from their elected officials.

Instead of restoring order, Gage's harsh rule and the arrival of British troops in Boston only made tensions worse. Soldiers often ignored local courts, intimidated citizens, and used their authority to enforce the King's will rather than the colony's laws.

In both Boston and New York, the army began acting as if it were above the law—using military trials instead of civil courts and ignoring the rights of the people. The colonists saw this as proof that the King wanted to replace justice with military control, violating long-standing English principles that the military must always answer to civilian authority.[55]

Modern Interpretation

In America today, the military is always under civilian control. The President serves as commander-in-chief, but Congress decides when and how to fund and regulate the armed forces. This balance keeps military leaders accountable and prevents any ruler or general from using the military for personal power.

Summary

Grievance 12 warns what happens when armies rule instead of laws. The founders made sure civilian authority would always come first. Under the Constitution, the armed forces serve the people through their elected government—not the other way around.

> **This Means**
> The King let generals act like rulers over the people. America's founders made sure the military could never rise above civilian authority. Power begins and ends with the people.

Constitutional Safeguards for Grievance 12

- **Article II, Section 2:** Names the President as Commander in Chief, ensuring that military power always answers to an elected civilian leader.
- **Article I, Section 8:** Gives Congress—not the military—the power to raise and fund armies, make rules for the armed forces, and regulate their actions.
- **Posse Comitatus Act of 1878:** Though not part of the original Constitution, this law later reinforced civilian control by restricting the use of the U.S. military in domestic law enforcement.

Grievance 13

He Subjects Us to Foreign Jurisdiction

"He has combined with others to subject us to a jurisdiction foreign to our constitutions and unacknowledged by our laws; giving his assent to their pretended acts of legislation."

NOTE: The colonists were angered when British officials forced them under foreign laws and courts that ignored local rights. They believed this stripped them of justice and placed them under powers they had never agreed to obey.

Thomas Jefferson's 1774 *Summary View of the Rights of British America* (Paraphrased)

These actions are made by people who have no right to rule us. Our laws do not recognize them. We protest these actions and ask the King to stop them, because even small wrongs can cause big problems for the people.

From *Our Country, A Household History*, Volume 3, by Benson J. Lossing, 1877

The establishment of a Board of Trade, to act independent of colonial legislation through its creatures (resident commissioners of customs) in the enforcement of revenue laws, was altogether foreign to the constitution of any of the colonies, and produced great indignation. The establishment of this power, and the remodeling of the admiralty courts so as to exclude trial by jury therein, in most cases rendered the government fully obnoxious to the charge in the text. The people felt their degradation under such petty tyranny, and resolved to spurn it. It was effectually done in Boston, as we have seen, and the government, after all its bluster, was obliged to recede. In 1774, the members of the council of Massachusetts (answering to our Senate), were, by a Parliamentary enactment, chosen by the king, to hold the office during his pleasure. Almost unlimited power was also given to the governor, and the people were indeed subjected to "a jurisdiction foreign to their constitution" by these creatures of royalty.

Historical Background

The colonists believed that Britain's leaders had replaced their local laws with foreign ones. Parliament created new courts and councils that answered only to the King, not to the colonies. These courts followed British maritime law instead of local law, and they took away rights like trial by jury.

Merchants accused of smuggling or violating trade rules could be sent to faraway courts in Nova Scotia or other British ports, where judges were appointed by the Crown and often ruled in favor of Britain. These changes made colonists feel helpless under a foreign system that ignored their own charters and traditions.[56]

The British also formed the Board of Trade and Customs Commissioners to collect taxes and enforce trade laws without colonial approval. These unelected officials could overrule local judges, seize property, and impose fines. Their power to replace local justice with royal authority convinced the colonists that they were being ruled by strangers instead of their own elected leaders.[57]

Modern Interpretation

Today, our system of government ensures that all laws and courts operate under American authority—not foreign influence. Judges are appointed and confirmed through the U.S. process, and every citizen has the right to be tried under U.S. law. This protects our nation from outside interference and guarantees that justice remains accountable to the people.

Summary

Grievance 13 shows how Britain's rulers tried to impose laws and judges not chosen by the colonies. America's founders answered by creating a fully independent legal system—one based on the consent of the governed, where all cases are judged under our own Constitution and laws.

> ### This Means
> The King put colonists under foreign judges and unfair courts. The founders made sure Americans would always be judged by American laws, in American courts, by their fellow citizens.

Constitutional Safeguards for Grievance 13

- **Article III:** Establishes an independent judicial system for the United States, ensuring that all legal matters are decided under American law.

- **The Tenth Amendment:** Reserves powers not given to the federal government for the states, so no outside or unelected power can override local laws.

- **Article II, Section 2:** Requires Senate approval for federal judges and justices, ensuring that those interpreting the law are confirmed by elected representatives.

Grievance 14

For Quartering Large Bodies of Troops Among Us

"For quartering large bodies of armed troops among us."

NOTE: The colonists were upset when British soldiers were placed in their towns and homes without permission. They had to feed and house them, which took away their privacy and felt unfair.

Thomas Jefferson's 1774 *Summary View of the Rights of British America* (Paraphrased)

Each state should decide for itself how many soldiers to have, who they are, and what rules they must follow.

From *Our Country, A Household History*, Volume 3, by Benson J. Lossing, 1877

In 1774 seven hundred troops were landed in Boston, under cover of the cannons of British armed ships in the harbor; and early the following year, Parliament voted ten thousand men for the American service, for it saw the wave of rebellion rising high under the gale of indignation which unrighteous acts had spread over the land. The tragedies at Lexington and Concord soon followed, and at Bunker Hill the War for Independence was opened in earnest.

Historical Background

The Quartering Acts of 1765 and 1774 forced the colonies to house and supply British soldiers. At first, troops were supposed to stay in public inns or empty buildings, but when space ran out, soldiers were often placed in civilian areas—sometimes right inside people's homes. This turned towns into military zones.

In Boston, angry residents refused to make room for soldiers in their shops and factories. In 1768, troops were stationed near Boston's Manufactory House, creating a tense standoff that became a symbol of royal intimidation. Colonists felt these troops were there to control them, not protect them.[58]

The Quartering Acts also revealed deep hypocrisy. England's own laws—like the Bill of Rights of 1689—banned quartering troops in private homes during peace. Yet Britain forced this on the colonies, treating Americans like subjects instead of citizens. The 1774 version of the Act went even further, allowing British officers to house soldiers anywhere they wished, deepening anger and resistance.

Modern Interpretation

This grievance reminds us why the military must never have power over citizens' daily lives. Under the U.S. Constitution, the armed forces are under civilian control, and soldiers cannot be placed in private homes or communities without consent. This protects personal freedom and property rights, ensuring that the military serves the people—not the other way around.

Summary

Grievance 14 shows how Britain's army tried to control the colonies by forcing them to host soldiers against their will. America's founders answered by protecting private homes and limiting military power under the law—so no one would ever again live under occupation in peacetime.

> ### This Means
> The King's soldiers moved into homes, inns, and workplaces without permission. The founders made sure that in America, no soldier can ever demand a place to stay. Our homes belong to the people—not the government.

Constitutional Safeguards for Grievance 14

- **The Third Amendment:** Prohibits soldiers from being housed in private homes without consent—a direct answer to Britain's Quartering Acts.
- **Article I, Section 8:** Gives Congress, not the President or the military, power to raise and fund armies, ensuring civilian control at all times.
- **The Second Amendment:** Guarantees the right to a well-regulated militia, reflecting the founders' belief in local defense rather than standing armies.

Grievance 15
He Protects Foreign Soldiers by Mock Trials

"For protecting them by a mock Trial from punishment for any
Murders they should commit on the Inhabitants of these States."

NOTE: The colonists were angry because British soldiers could avoid punishment for hurting or killing Americans. They were often sent far away to be tried, where justice was less likely.

The Crown's Administration of Justice Act (May 20, 1774) (Paraphrased)
The King protects his soldiers from punishment, even when they harm the people. They are not given fair trials, and justice is not done.

This meant that British criminals could be sent home to England for "mock trials," even for capital offenses.

From Our Country, A Household History, Volume 3, by Benson J. Lossing, 1877

In 1768, two citizens of Annapolis, in Maryland, were murdered by some marines belonging to a British armed ship. The trial was a mockery of justice; and in the face of clear evidence against them, the criminals were acquitted. In the difficulties with the Regulators in North Carolina, in 1771, some of the soldiers who had shot down citizens when standing up in defence of their rights, were tried for murder and acquitted; while Governor Tryon mercilessly hung six prisoners. who were certainly entitled to the benefits of the laws of war if his own soldiers were.

Historical Background

This grievance grew out of anger that British soldiers were rarely held accountable for crimes in the colonies. The worst case was the Boston Massacre of 1770, when British troops fired on a crowd, killing five people. Although some soldiers were tried in Boston, many colonists believed the trials were unfair and that the King's troops were protected from justice.

The problem became worse under the Administration of Justice Act of 1774. It allowed any royal official or soldier accused of murder or other serious crimes to be sent to England for trial—far from colonial witnesses and local juries. Colonists saw this as proof that the King cared more about protecting his soldiers than protecting his people.

This injustice wasn't new. In 1768, British marines in Maryland killed citizens but were acquitted. In North Carolina, Governor Tryon executed colonists who resisted unfair taxes, while British troops who shot unarmed protesters went free. These events convinced Americans that British law no longer offered them any real justice.[59]

Modern Interpretation

This grievance reminds us that everyone—no matter their job, title, or power—must be accountable under the law. In America, soldiers and civilians alike have the same right to a fair trial and due process.

Under today's Uniform Code of Military Justice (UCMJ), members of the armed forces are held to strict standards. Crimes by soldiers, whether in war or peace, must be punished through legal process. The Posse Comitatus Act (1878) also limits the military's role in civilian law enforcement, preventing abuses of power and protecting citizens from intimidation or unequal justice.

Summary

Grievance 15 shows how the King's justice system shielded British troops from punishment, even when they harmed or killed colonists. America's founders made sure that in our system, no one—civilian or soldier—stands above the law.

> ### This Means
> The King's soldiers could hurt or even kill colonists and walk free. America's founders made sure that never happens here—everyone is accountable, and every person has the right to a fair and public trial.

Constitutional Safeguards for Grievance 15

- **The Sixth Amendment:** Guarantees the right to a speedy, public trial by an impartial jury in the place where the crime occurred.
- **The Third Amendment:** Prevents the quartering of soldiers in private homes, avoiding the conflicts that once led to violence.
- **The Fifth Amendment:** Protects everyone—civilian or military—from being deprived of life, liberty, or property without due process of law.

Grievance 16

For Cutting Off Global Trade

"For cutting off our trade with all parts of the world."

NOTE: Britain made rules that stopped the colonies from trading freely with other countries. This made goods more expensive and harder to get. Families across the colonies were hurt, not just merchants.

Thomas Jefferson's 1774 *Summary View of the Rights of British America* (Paraphrased)

We have the right to trade with people all over the world. No one should take that right away or limit it.

From *Our Country, A Household History*, Volume 3, by Benson J. Lossing, 1877

The navigation laws were always oppressive in character: and in 1764, the British naval commanders having been clothed with the authority of custom-house officers, completely broke up a profitable trade which the colonists had long enjoyed with the Spanish and French West Indies, notwithstanding it was in violation of the old Navigation Act of 1660, which had been almost ineffectual. Finally, Lord North concluded to punish the refractory colonists of New England, by crippling their commerce with Great Britain, Ireland, and the West Indies. Fishing on the banks of Newfoundland was also prohibited, and thus, as far as Parliamentary enactments could accomplish it, their "trade with all parts of the world" was cut off.

Historical Background

Britain treated her colonies like suppliers instead of partners. Under the empire's trade laws, colonies could sell only to Britain and had to buy British goods at high prices. This system—called mercantilism—kept wealth and control in the hands of the Crown.

Acts like the Navigation Acts and the Iron Act made things worse. Colonists couldn't ship goods directly to foreign ports, and even local craftsmen risked punishment if they tried to trade on their own. Britain's goal was simple: force the colonies to send raw materials and buy back finished products at inflated prices.[60]

By the 1770s, this unfair system crushed colonial businesses and hurt families who depended on trade for their livelihoods. Jefferson and others saw this as economic slavery—the colonies worked, but the profit went to the Crown.

Modern Interpretation

This grievance warns that when government or big powers control trade, freedom suffers. Jefferson believed people should benefit from their own labor, not be trapped by unfair systems that enrich others.

Today, America's Constitution gives Congress—not the President—control over trade and commerce, protecting citizens from the kind of economic domination Britain once used. Free and fair trade remains one of the cornerstones of liberty.

Summary

Grievance 16 shows how Britain's trade restrictions chained the colonies to royal control. By fighting for open trade, the founders fought for dignity—the right to prosper by their own effort and judgment, not by the permission of a distant king.

> ### This Means
> The King tried to control America's economy and keep colonists dependent on British goods. The founders made sure our freedom to work, trade, and prosper would never again depend on the will of another nation.

Constitutional Safeguards for Grievance 16

- **Article I, Section 8, Clause 3, Commerce Clause:** Gives Congress the power to regulate trade with foreign nations, among the states, and with Native tribes—ensuring that economic power belongs to the people's representatives, not to any monarch.

- **Article I, Section 9:** Prevents Congress from favoring one state's ports or trade over another, guaranteeing equal treatment and opportunity for all.

The Constitution created one fair system for trade under the new federal government, making sure the unfair limits Jefferson described would never happen again in America.

That the exercise of a free trade with all parts of the world, possessed by the American colonists, as of natural right, and which no law of their own had taken away or abridged, was next the object of unjust encroachment... the [British] parliament... assumed upon themselves the power of prohibiting their trade with all other parts of the world, except the island of Great Britain.

"Summary View of the Rights of British America" – Jefferson, 1774

(The British) have raised their commodities, called for in America, to the double and treble of what they sold for before such exclusive privileges were given them, and of what better commodities of the same kind would cost us elsewhere, and at the same time give us much less for what we carry thither than might be had at more convenient ports.

"Summary View of the Rights of British America" – Jefferson, 1774

By one other act, passed in the 23d year of the same reign, the iron which we make we are forbidden to manufacture, and heavy as that article is, and necessary in every branch of husbandry, besides commission and insurance, we are to pay freight for it to Great Britain, and freight for it back again, for the purpose of supporting not men, but machines, in the island of Great Britain.

"Summary View of the Rights of British America" – Jefferson, 1774

By an act passed in the 5th Year of the reign of his late majesty king George the second, an American subject is forbidden to make a hat for himself of the fur which he has taken perhaps on his own soil.

"Summary View of the Rights of British America" – Jefferson, 1774

Grievance 17

Taxation Without Representation

"Or imposing taxes on us without our consent."

NOTE: The colonists were furious when Britain taxed them without letting them have a vote or voice in Parliament. They believed only their own elected assemblies—not a distant king—had the right to decide how they were taxed.

Thomas Jefferson's 1774 *Summary View of the Rights of British America* (Paraphrased)

No one outside our own colonies should have the power to tax or control our property. Only our own governments have that right. But the Royal Governor in Boston has been setting taxes himself—and he can make them as high as he wants.

From *Our Country, A Household History*, Volume 3, by Benson J. Lossing, 1877

In addition to the revenue taxes imposed from time to time and attempted to be collected by means of writs of assistance, the Stamp Act was passed, and duties upon paper, painters' colors, glass, tea, etc., were levied. This was the great bone of contention between the colonists and the imperial government. It was contention on the one hand for the great political truth that taxation and representation are inseparable, and a lust for power and the means for replenishing an exhausted treasury, on the other. The climax of the contention was the Revolution.

Historical Background

This grievance was about fairness and freedom. Britain passed laws like the Sugar Act, Stamp Act, and Townshend Acts that taxed everyday items such as paper, glass, and tea. These taxes were created in London, not in the colonies, and the people who had to pay them had no say in the matter.

Colonists believed this broke the promise of self-government. They began organizing boycotts and protests, declaring, "No taxation without representation!" To them, this wasn't just about money—it was about their right to be heard.[61]

British leaders claimed the taxes were fair because the colonies needed to help pay for the soldiers who had protected them during the French and Indian War. But to the colonists, this was just an excuse. They had already paid their share through local taxes and militias, and they didn't want to fund an army that now seemed to be used against them. Each new tax felt like another chain—and each protest, another step toward independence.

Modern Interpretation

Today, this idea is still central to American government: leaders must answer to the people they tax. The Constitution ensures that taxes are set by elected representatives, so citizens always have a voice in how their money is used.

Summary

Grievance 17 shows how unfair taxes helped spark the American Revolution. The colonists fought not just to lower taxes, but to protect their right to vote on them. That belief—that freedom and representation go hand in hand—became a cornerstone of the United States.

> ### This Means
> The King taxed people who had no voice in government. America's founders made sure that could never happen again—our taxes must be approved by leaders chosen by the people themselves.

Constitutional Safeguards for Grievance 17

The framers of the Constitution remembered how unfair taxes had fueled the Revolution. They made sure only leaders chosen by the people could create or raise taxes. Later, the 16th Amendment updated the system for a modern economy—but it still kept the same core idea: taxes must always answer to the people.

- **Article I, Section 2:** Requires that taxes be based on population and approved by elected representatives in Congress.

- **Article I, Section 8:** Gives Congress—not a King—the power to create and collect taxes, keeping the process accountable to the people.

- **The 16th Amendment:** Allows Congress to levy an income tax while still following the principle that taxation must serve and represent the people fairly.

Grievance 18

Deprived of Trial by Juries

"For depriving us of the benefits of trial by jury."

NOTE: When colonists were accused of breaking a law, they were often not given a fair trial. Instead of a jury of local people, their cases were decided by judges chosen by the King. This meant the people did not have a fair say.

Thomas Jefferson's 1774 *Summary View of the Rights of British America* (Paraphrased)

If a person here is accused of a crime, he can be taken far from home to be tried. He has no friends to help him and no way to prove he is innocent. The people judging him already think he is guilty. This is not fair.

From *Our Country, A Household History*, Volume 3, by Benson J. Lossing, 1877

This was especially the case when commissioners of customs were concerned in the suit. After these functionaries were driven from Boston in 1768, an act was passed which placed violations of the revenue laws under the jurisdiction of the admiralty courts, where the offenders were tried by a creature of the crown, and were deprived "of the benefits of trial by jury."

Historical Background

Trial by jury had long been one of the most trusted rights in English law. It protected ordinary people by letting local citizens—not government officials—decide guilt or innocence. But in the colonies, Britain began to ignore this safeguard. The King's courts used "admiralty courts," where judges chosen by the Crown decided every case. Colonists accused of breaking trade or tax laws were sent far from home, denied lawyers, and often found guilty before their trial even began.

To the colonists, this was more than unfair—it was frightening. They believed the right to a jury trial was a sacred protection that stretched back to the Magna Carta of 1215. When Britain took that away, Americans saw it as proof that the King no longer respected their rights as English citizens. Many colonists realized that only an independent nation could guarantee true justice.

As these abuses continued, word spread through newspapers and town meetings, stirring anger across the colonies. Farmers, merchants, and sailors feared that anyone could be accused and punished without a fair hearing. The cry for justice grew louder, uniting people of all classes around the idea that liberty meant being judged by one's peers—not by the powerful few.[62]

Modern Interpretation

Today, the right to a trial by jury is one of the cornerstones of American freedom. It keeps the government from having too much power and protects each person's voice in the justice system. When a jury decides a case, it represents the community's judgment—not the government's control. This principle reminds us that liberty depends on fair laws and equal treatment for all.

Summary

This Grievance shows how the colonists fought to protect the basic right to a fair trial. They wanted justice to belong to the people, not to the King. Their stand for jury trials helped shape the U.S. Constitution and the Bill of Rights, which still guard our freedoms today.

> ### This Means
> A fair trial protects every person from unfair power. The colonists knew that justice must belong to the people—not the King. By demanding the right to trial by jury, they made sure no one could be punished without proof, and that ordinary citizens—not royal judges—would decide what was fair.

Constitutional Safeguards for Grievance 18

- **Article III, Section 2:** Promises a trial by jury for anyone accused of a crime in federal court.
- **The Sixth Amendment:** Gives every person the right to a speedy, public trial by an impartial jury where the crime was committed.
- **The Seventh Amendment:** Extends the right to a jury trial in civil cases between citizens.

Grievance 19

Transporting Us Beyond Seas for Trial

"For transporting us beyond Seas to be tried for pretended offences."

NOTE: When colonists were accused of crimes against the British government, some were sent all the way to England for trial. They had to leave their families and could not bring witnesses to help them. Far from home, they had little chance of a fair trial.

Thomas Jefferson's 1774 *Summary View of the Rights of British America* (Paraphrased)

The King can send a person far away to England to be tried. Witnesses must travel a long distance, which is hard and costly, so many cannot come. This leaves the accused without help and makes a fair trial almost impossible.

From *Our Country, A Household History*, Volume 3, by Benson J. Lossing, 1877

A law of 1774 provided that any person in the province of Massachusetts, who should be accused of riot, resistance of magistrates or the officers of customs, murder, "or any other capital offence," might, at the option of the governor, be taken for trial to another colony, or transported to Great Britain for the purpose. The minister pretended that impartial justice could not be administered in Massachusetts; but the facts of Captain Preston's case refuted his arguments in that direction. The bill was violently opposed in Parliament, yet it became a law. It was decreed that Americans might be "transported beyond the seas, to be tried for pretended offences," or real crimes.

Historical Background

The colonists were outraged when Britain began sending people across the ocean for trial. The Administration of Justice Act of 1774 allowed British officials and soldiers accused of serious crimes to be tried in England instead of in the colonies. This robbed the accused of local juries, witnesses, and community support. It also made it nearly impossible for them to defend themselves fairly.

To many colonists, this was more than a legal issue—it was a human one. Imagine being thousands of miles from home, facing strangers who already believed you guilty. They saw this as deliberate cruelty meant to silence anyone who dared oppose royal authority. Families were left behind, unable to help or even know what had become of their loved ones.

Newspapers across the colonies condemned these "distant trials" as proof that the King cared more about control than justice. People began to realize that if their rights could be taken away in one colony, they could be taken away everywhere. These experiences pushed Americans closer to believing that independence was the only path to real freedom under law.[63]

Modern Interpretation

Today, Americans understand that justice must happen close to home, where the community can take part and the truth can be tested openly. This Grievance reminds us that being judged by local citizens keeps the justice system honest and accountable. No one should face trial in a distant place where they have no voice or defense.

Summary

The colonists fought against being shipped overseas to stand trial because it stripped them of fairness and dignity. Their struggle led to the constitutional right to local trials and impartial juries—core protections that still safeguard Americans from abuse of power today.

> **This Means**
> The colonists fought against being shipped overseas to stand trial because it stripped them of fairness and dignity. Their struggle led to the constitutional right to local trials and impartial juries—core protections that still safeguard Americans from abuse of power today

Constitutional Safeguards for Grievance 19

The U.S. Constitution and the Bill of Rights address this Grievance by ensuring that trials are held in the state and district where the alleged crime was committed:

- **Article III, Section 2:** Ensures that criminal trials are held in the state and district where the crime occurred.
- **The Sixth Amendment:** Guarantees a speedy, public trial by an impartial local jury where the alleged crime took place.

By writing these protections into the Constitution and Bill of Rights, the Founders made sure that no one could be taken far from home to face trial. These safeguards guarantee that trials happen where the events occurred—among people who understand the place and its circumstances. It was their way of keeping justice fair, local, and connected to the community.

Grievance 20
Enlarging the Borders of a Neighboring Province

"For abolishing the free System of English Laws in a neighboring Province, establishing therein an Arbitrary government, and enlarging its Boundaries to render it at once an example and fit instrument for introducing the same absolute rule into these Colonies."

NOTE: The King redrew maps and changed laws to tighten his control over the colonies. By expanding Canada's borders and replacing English law with royal rule, he sent a warning to the rest of America: Your freedoms can be taken away too.

Jefferson's July 1775 Draft of: *The Declaration of the Causes and Necessity of Taking Up Arms:*

"They have erected in a neighbouring province, **acquired by the joint arms of Great Britain and America,** a tyranny dangerous to the very existence of all these colonies." [64]

Royal Proclamation of 1763

The Proclamation Line of 1763 was a British-produced boundary marked in the Appalachian Mountains at the Eastern Continental Divide. Decreed on October 7, 1763, the Proclamation Line prohibited Anglo-American colonists from settling on lands acquired from the French following the French and Indian War.

Quebec Act of 1774

Eleven years later, the King made things worse with the Quebec Act of 1774. It gave much of the Northwest Territory—land claimed by several colonies—to Quebec and pushed its borders south to the Ohio River. This alarmed leaders like George Washington and George Mason, who had royal permission to settle or invest in that region. It also broke promises made to soldiers who had fought for Britain in the French and Indian War.

The Act was designed to keep French Canadians loyal to Britain. It allowed the Catholic Church to keep its power, restored old French civil laws, and brought back a feudal land system where tenants had to pay dues to wealthy landowners. These changes pleased some French leaders but angered English-speaking settlers who wanted elected government, English law, and private land ownership. Instead, the King placed Quebec under a 23-member council he appointed himself.

To many Americans, this Act was a warning. If the King could change borders and laws in Canada without consent, he could do the same in the Thirteen Colonies. The Quebec Act became a symbol of how far Britain was willing to go to replace freedom with royal rule.[65]

From *Our Country, A Household History*, Volume 3, by Benson J. Lossing, 1877

This charge is embodied in an earlier one. The British ministry thought it prudent to take early steps to secure a footing in America so near the scene of inevitable rebellion as to allow them to breast, successfully, the gathering storm. The investing of a legislative council in Canada with all powers except levying of taxes, was a great stride toward that absolute military rule which bore sway there within eighteen months afterward. Giving up their political rights for doubtful religious privileges, made them willing slaves, and Canada remained a part of the British empire when its sister colonies rejoiced in freedom.

Historical Background—Proclamation Line of 1763 and the 1774 Quebec Act

When the Revolution began, the French foreign minister Vergennes proposed that America's independence should extend only to the Appalachian Mountains. Everything beyond—including the Ohio River Valley—would belong to Quebec or be placed under Spanish control. If that plan had succeeded, the United States would have remained trapped between the mountains and the sea.

Fortunately, American negotiators Benjamin Franklin, John Jay, and John Adams refused. At the Treaty of Paris in 1783, they secured recognition of full independence and extended the western boundary to the Mississippi River. The new treaty overturned the Quebec Act and the Proclamation Line of 1763, restoring the colonists' right to their land and self-government.

The result was more than just new borders—it was the return of principle. By winning control of their own territory, Americans proved that liberty and lawful ownership were stronger than royal decrees.[66]

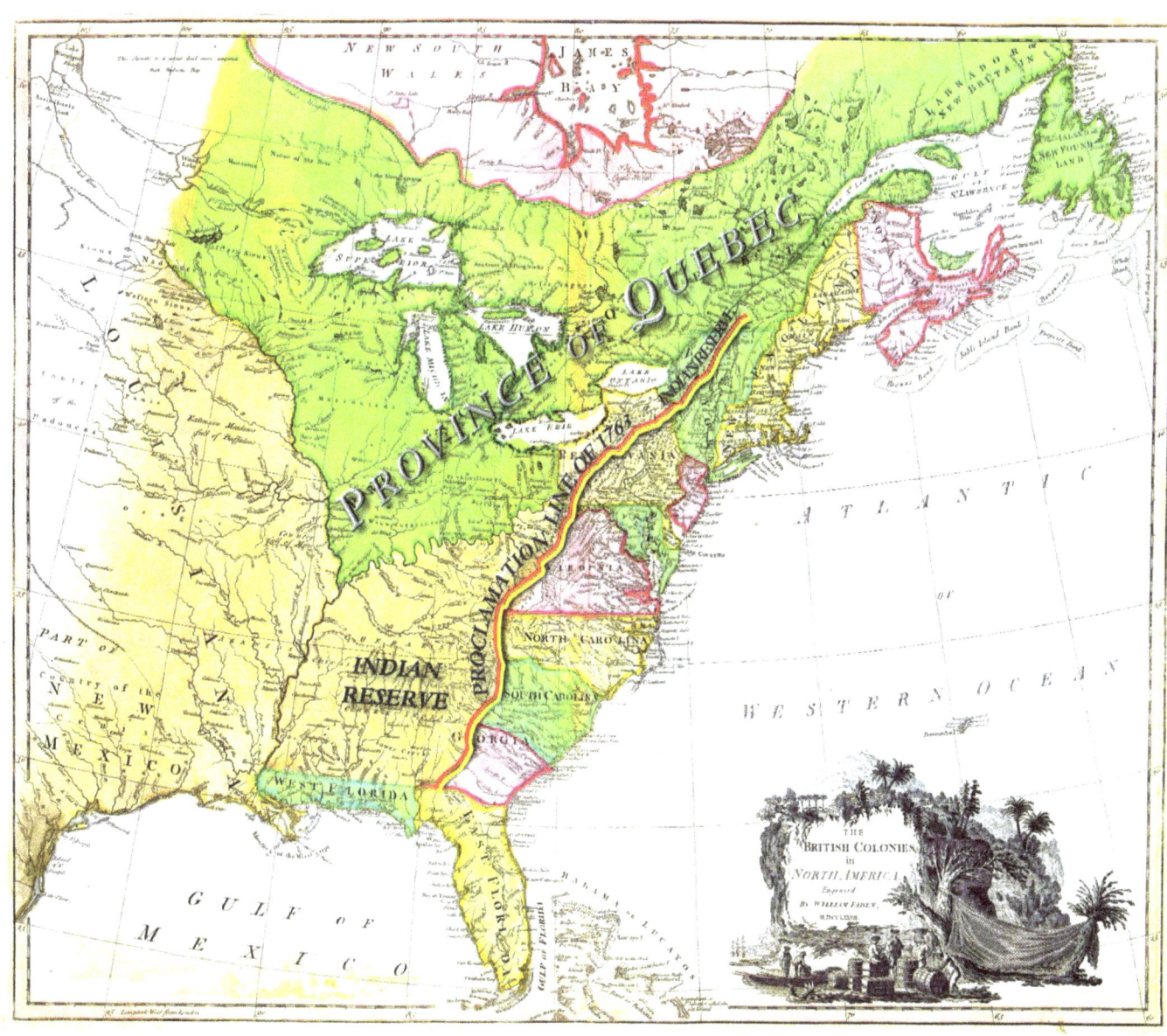

British colonies in North America; Lawrence H. Slaughter Collection of English maps, charts, globes, books and atlases / Charts and maps, 1777, Engraved by William Faden, 1750?–1836
[Proclamation Line of 1763 and enlarged titles of Province of Quebec and Indian Reserve added by author]

French Proposal at The Treaty of Paris

MAP OF
NORTH AMERICA
Showing the Boundaries of
THE UNITED STATES, CANADA, AND
THE SPANISH POSSESSIONS
according to the proposals of the Court of France in 1782

English	Red (Ohio Country and Canada)
United States	Green (Eastern Seaboard)
Spanish	Yellow (Alabama, Mississippi, Tennessee)
Uncolored	Indian Territory

Under Spanish (yellow) or American (white) protection, according as it lies West or East of the Yellow intersecting line.

In September 1782, the French Foreign Minister proposed that the United States gain independence but limit it to the area east of the Appalachian Mountains. In his proposal, Britain would retain the land north of the Ohio River (the future Northwest Territory) as part of its Province of Quebec. An independent Indian state was to be established, with the southern part designated as Indian Territory under Spanish control. This would have constrained the United States from the Eastern Seaboard to the crest of the Appalachian Mountains.[67]

Treaty of Paris, September 3, 1783

John Adams, Benjamin Franklin, and John Jay rejected the French proposal and negotiated peace terms directly with the British, resulting in the Treaty of Paris, officially ending the Revolutionary War. Important points included:

1. Great Britain recognized independence for the United States of America.
2. It placed vast Western territories to the Mississippi River within the United States of America, and America recognized British colonies in Canada and Florida.
3. The treaty overturned boundaries of the Proclamation of 1683 and the Quebec Act of 1774.
4. Provisions were made for Loyalists to have their properties returned and prewar debts repaid.
5. America was awarded fishing rights in the waters off of Newfoundland.
6. Britain and the United States each had access to the Mississippi River.
7. The British were to surrender of all posts within the territory of the United States.[68]

Historical Background

The Proclamation Line of 1763 forbade colonists from settling on lands gained from France after the French and Indian War (which belonged to the colonies before France had claimed it). It was meant to prevent conflict with French Canadians and Native nations but instead angered settlers whose colonial charters already claimed that land. Many saw it as a royal land grab—an effort by a king to profit from trade and the rich Ohio Territory.

The King broke promises made to war veterans and ignored long-standing colonial charters. Instead of rewarding those who had fought for Britain, he recognized old French claims and declared the western lands his own royal domain. It was like saying, "This land is mine, and anyone who wants to use it must pay me."

This Grievance also includes the Quebec Act of 1774, which extended Quebec's boundaries south to the Ohio River and blocked westward expansion. To many colonists, it set a dangerous example—if Britain could change laws and borders in Quebec, it could do the same everywhere. The act threatened self-government, legal rights, and religious freedom, becoming one of the most hated laws before the Revolution.[69]

Modern Interpretation

This Grievance reminds us that freedom includes the right to govern and protect one's own land. When Britain redrew colonial borders and replaced local law with foreign rule, it denied Americans the ability to manage their future. The U.S. Constitution prevents that kind of arbitrary power by ensuring that only Congress—representing the people—can make territorial or legal changes within the United States.

Summary

The colonists saw the Quebec Act and the Proclamation Line as threats to both liberty and identity. They fought not just for property but for the principle that self-government and faith could not be rewritten by distant rulers. Their victory at the Treaty of Paris reclaimed both land and liberty—and set the boundaries of a nation where the people, not a king, would decide their own future.

> ### This Means
> Britain tried to control America by redrawing its map and its laws. The colonists saw through the plan: if a king could erase borders and freedoms once, he could do it again. Standing for self-rule ensured that Americans would never live under shifting boundaries or foreign authority. What began as a protest against unfair borders ended with a peace treaty that tripled the size of the United States—proving that the fight for liberty could redraw maps not only in America, but across the world.

Constitutional Safeguards for Grievance 20

The Constitution says that no government can make new laws or redraw boundaries without the consent of the people and their representatives. This protects self-government and religious freedom from the kind of rules in the Quebec Act.

- **Article IV, Section 3:** Gives Congress—not a King—the sole authority to create new states or alter their boundaries, preventing any unilateral changes.
- **Article IV, Section 4:** Guarantees a republican form of government in every state, ensuring that no arbitrary or authoritarian rule can take hold.
- **The First Amendment:** Protects freedom of religion and prevents the government from favoring or establishing any faith.
- **The Tenth Amendment:** Reserves all powers not given to the federal government to the states and the people, ensuring local autonomy to protect our rights and our lands.

Grievance 21

Taking Away Charters and Valuable Laws

"For taking away our Charters, abolishing our most valuable Laws, and altering fundamentally the Forms of our Governments."

NOTE: The King took away the colonies' charters and changed their laws. This took away their right to govern themselves. Governments that had been free were now controlled by the King.

Thomas Jefferson's 1774 *Summary View of the Rights of British America* (Paraphrased)

The people settled and built America with their own work, so the land belongs to them. The King has no right to take it, divide it, or change their governments.

From *Our Country, A Household History*, Volume 3, by Benson J. Lossing, 1877

This is a reiteration of a charge already considered, and refers to the alteration of the Massachusetts charter, so as to make judges and other officers independent of the people, and subservient to the crown. The governor was empowered to remove and appoint all inferior judges, the attorney generals, provost-marshals, and justices of the peace, and to appoint sheriffs independent of the council. As the sheriffs chose jurors, trial by jury might easily be made a mere mockery. The people had hitherto been allowed, by their charter, to select jurors; now the whole matter was placed in the hands of the creatures of government.

Historical Background:

Jefferson chose his punctuation in this Grievance with care. Each clause—taking away charters, abolishing valuable laws, and altering governments—describes a separate attack on the colonies' rights. Together, these actions show how Britain used royal power to erase American self-rule:

GRIEVANCE CLAUSES	CONSTITUTIONAL OFFENSE	HISTORICAL EXAMPLE & CONTEXT
Clause 1: For **TAKING** away our Charters,	Revoked territorial and constitutional rights guaranteed by colonial charters.	*Royal Proclamation of 1763 and Quebec Act (1774) erased long-standing colonial boundaries, seizing the Ohio Country as royal domain secured for the Crown.*
Clause 2: ABOLISHING our most valuable Laws,	Nullified colonial self-legislation and the right of local consent.	Parliament's repeated disallowance of colonial acts and veto of assemblies' laws placed governance above local will.
Clause 3 and **ALTERING** fundamentally the Forms of our Governments.	Substituted representative government with royal authority.	*The Massachusetts Government Act (1774) replaced elected councils and judges with Crown appointees, ending jury independence and local self-rule.*

Britain's actions turned free, self-governing colonies into territories ruled by royal power. The King claimed this as his "right of conquest," even though the same lands had already been lawfully settled under earlier English charters.

Jefferson called this a direct attack on liberty. In his *Declaration of the Causes and Necessity of Taking Up Arms* (1775), he warned that Parliament had "assumed a right of altering our charters and established laws." To the colonists, this proved that Britain no longer saw them as citizens with rights but as subjects to be controlled—people to be ruled, not represented.

This Grievance captures the colonists' anger over Britain's decision to cancel charters and rewrite their governments without consent. Charters were the colonies' founding documents, giving them the right to govern themselves and make their own laws. When the British government altered or revoked these charters, it was seen as an assault on freedom and an attempt to centralize power under royal rule.[70]

The Massachusetts Charter had been revoked as early as 1684, but tensions reached a breaking point with the Massachusetts Government Act of 1774. This law stripped the colony of its ability to elect its own leaders, making judges and sheriffs answer only to the Crown. It destroyed the right to fair trials because those same sheriffs—appointed by royal governors—controlled jury selection. The Act also restricted town meetings, silencing the people's voice in local government.

Colonists viewed these actions as a betrayal of their English rights, breaking traditions that reached back to the Magna Carta of 1215. They feared that if Britain could take away one colony's charter, it could dismantle them all. Representative assemblies could be replaced overnight by royal councils loyal only to the King. The loss of these self-governing rights united the colonies in resistance and strengthened their demand for independence. Britain's earlier acts—the Royal Proclamation of 1763 and the Quebec Act of 1774—only deepened that fear by redrawing borders and violating the boundaries promised in colonial charters.[71]

The Keystone Grievances

Three Grievances stand at the center of America's complaints against Britain, with this 21st perhaps the most important of all. Together, they trace the full pattern of royal overreach—from the taking of land once protected by charters, to the twisting of colonial law, to the destruction of the governments that guarded those laws. Together, these three wrongs show how the King's reach grew—from the land itself to laws, and the very governments that protected them.

A Triad of Tyranny

These Grievances work like three links in a chain—tightening the King's control until self-government was gone.

Grievance 7—Land and Population
The Crown blocked westward settlement, raised the price of land, and limited who could own it. The *Proclamation Line of 1763* declared western lands the "bounty of war," reserved for royal profit, not for the colonists who had fought for them.

Grievance 20—Law and Boundaries
The *Quebec Act of 1774* replaced English law in the Ohio region with French civil law and royal authority. It wasn't protection—it was conversion. The King's power stretched into new territories, replacing local rule and setting a precedent for arbitrary control across the continent.

Grievance 21—Charters and Constitutions
This was the final blow—**the Crown's seizure of constitutional authority** itself. By "taking away our charters," Britain erased the legal foundation of the colonies. The very governments that had built and defended America now existed only by royal permission, not by the people's consent.

In these three acts—controlling land, changing laws, and destroying liberty—the King made himself master over what had once been free.

Jefferson's Moral Logic of Rebellion

Jefferson reminded Parliament that the Crown had done nothing to plant or build America. The colonies were founded by private effort, not royal funds—by settlers, tradesmen, and farmers who paid their own way and worked the land with their own hands.

> "America was conquered, and her settlements made, and firmly established, at the expense of individuals; for themselves alone they have a right to hold, and to dispose of as they please."   —*A Summary View*

Jefferson argued that if the King had not planted the seed, he could not claim the harvest. A government that neither paid for the soil nor defended it had no right to its fruits. To be ruled and taxed under those conditions was, in Jefferson's words, "slavery in everything but name."

The Ancestral Precedent

Jefferson traced this idea of independence back to England's own past.

> "Our ancestors, before their emigration to America, were the free inhabitants of the British dominions in Europe, and possessed a right which nature has given to all men, of departing from the country in which chance, not choice, has placed them…"   —*A Summary View* (1774)

He reminded his readers that the Saxons had once crossed the sea from Germany to Britain, carrying their laws and liberties with them. When they left their homeland, they owed no tribute to the rulers they had left behind. So too, Americans owed no obedience to a king who neither financed their journey nor defended their rights.

The Law of Life and Liberty

To Jefferson, independence wasn't rebellion—it was renewal. He believed that the spread of new societies was part of the natural order, like the growth and division of living things. Life continues by separation, not by servitude. A new nation carries forward the best of the old, but it lives by its own strength.

Britain's great mistake was treating the colonies not as partners in civilization but as plantations—property to control instead of people to respect. Jefferson saw liberty as the law of creation itself: the right to live free, to grow, and to govern oneself.

Just as the Angles and Saxons had once left Europe to build a new England, so the English crossed the Atlantic to build new communities in America. Their right to leave, to build, and to govern was not rebellion against kings—it was obedience to the natural laws of liberty.

The Restoration of Law

In this 21st Grievance, Jefferson unites all three wrongs into one clear message::

- **Taking land** (Grievance 7)
- **Corrupting law** (Grievance 20)
- **Destroying government** (Grievance 21)

These were not simply political mistakes—they were constitutional thefts, robbing people of their right to exist as a free nation. When Americans declared independence, they didn't destroy their governments; they restored them. They reclaimed what the Crown had taken away—the right to govern by consent and under law. What Britain called rebellion was, in truth, restoration: a return to the oldest truth of all—that law, not power, is the rightful ruler of mankind.

> "Just as the Saxons once became English, the English now became American."

Summary

Grievance 21 shows how the colonists resisted Britain's attempts to erase their laws and charters. The Founders believed liberty required lawful self-government—not control from a distant ruler. The U.S. Constitution protects these principles by guaranteeing a republican form of government, ensuring that states keep power over their own affairs and that no law can unfairly change or cancel existing rights.

> ### This Means
> The King tried to erase America's freedom at its foundation—its laws, charters, and self-government. The colonists fought back, proving that liberty can't be canceled by royal decree. When they restored their own governments, they weren't rebelling; they were reclaiming what was already theirs. Their victory turned Britain's tyranny into America's renewal—and ensured that power in this new nation would forever belong to the people, not a king.

Constitutional Safeguards for Grievance 21

The Constitution guards against any ruler or government changing state laws or charters without consent. These provisions keep our system of self-government stable and fair:

- **Article IV, Section 4:** Guarantees every state a republican form of government, protecting it from arbitrary changes or control.
- **Article I, Sections 9 and 10:** Prevent both Congress and the states from passing unfair or retroactive laws that would cancel contracts or rewrite charters.

The Tenth Amendment: Reserves all powers not given to the federal government to the states and the people, including the authority to establish and maintain their own laws within the Constitution's limits.

Grievance 22

Suspends Legislatures & Assumes Power

"For suspending our own legislatures & declaring themselves invested with power to legislate for us in all cases whatsoever."

NOTE: When colonial leaders spoke up, the King shut down their meetings. He took away their power to make laws and made decisions for them instead. This meant the people no longer had a voice in their own government.

Thomas Jefferson's 1774 *Summary View of the Rights of British America* (Paraphrased)

One government has no right to shut down another that is free. The King's leaders try to take away our lawmaking power, even though we did not choose them and cannot control them. This is not right.

From *Our Country, A Household History*, Volume 3, by Benson J. Lossing, 1877

This, too, is another phase of the charge just considered. We have noticed the suppression of the Legislature of New York, and in several cases, the governors, after dissolving Colonial Assemblies, assumed the right to make proclamations stand in the place of statute law. Lord Dunmore assumed this right in 1775, and so did Sir James Wright of Georgia, and Lord William Campbell of South Carolina. They were driven from the country in consequence.

Historical Background

In 1767, Britain suspended the New York Assembly after it refused to obey the Quartering Act, which forced colonists to house and supply British troops. This was more than punishment—proof that the King and Parliament could shut down colonial self-government whenever they wished.

Soon after, royal governors in other colonies tried the same. The Massachusetts Government Act of 1774 ended that colony's legislative independence. Governors like Lord Dunmore in Virginia, Sir James Wright in Georgia, and Lord William Campbell in South Carolina took even greater power, issuing royal orders that replaced local laws. As resistance spread, many of these governors fled their posts—driven out by citizens who refused to surrender their right to govern themselves.

To the colonists, these acts broke one of England's oldest constitutional traditions—that laws should come from representatives chosen by the people. If Britain could silence one legislature, it could silence them all. This Grievance convinced Americans that only complete independence could protect their freedom of self-government.[72]

Modern Interpretation

This reminds us that representative government cannot exist if elected legislatures can be suspended or replaced by unelected rulers. In today's terms, it defends the principle that no single branch of government may seize another's authority. America's system of checks and balances grew from this very lesson, ensuring that power stays divided between state and federal governments—and always accountable to the people.

Summary

This Grievance shows how Britain tried to destroy colonial self-rule by silencing elected assemblies and claiming all power for itself. The Founders answered by designing a government where power would never again rest in one place. Through the U.S. Constitution, they created a system that guarantees local self-government, shared authority, and laws made only by elected representatives.

> **This Means**
>
> Britain tried to rule by shutting down America's voice. When colonial assemblies were silenced, liberty itself was silenced too. The Founders made sure that could never happen again—our legislatures, both state and national, answer to the people alone, not to any ruler who claims absolute power.

Constitutional Safeguards for Grievance 22

The U.S. Constitution directly addresses this Grievance by establishing a clear framework for federalism and the separation of powers:

- **Article IV, Section 4:** Guarantees every state a republican form of government, meaning no federal or executive power can suspend a state's legislature.

- **Article I:** Establishes a Congress made up of elected representatives, ensuring that lawmaking power always remains with the people—not with a ruler or appointed authority.

- **The Tenth Amendment:** Reserves powers not given to the federal government for the states and the people, securing state independence and preventing federal overreach.

Grievance 23

Abdicating Governance and Protection

"He has abdicated Government here, by declaring us
out of his Protection and waging War against us."

NOTE: When Britain called the colonies rebels, the King stopped protecting them. Instead, he sent armies to fight against them. By doing this, he gave up his duty to govern and protect the people.

Thomas Jefferson's 1774 *Summary View of the Rights of British America* (Paraphrased)

When leaders lose the trust of the people and use power the wrong way, it becomes dangerous for them to stay in charge. Then the people have the right to remove them.

From *Our Country, A Household History*, Volume 3, by Benson J. Lossing, 1877

In his message to Parliament early in 1775, the king declared the colonists to be in a state of open rebellion; and by sending armies hither to make war upon them, he really "abdicated government," by thus declaring them "out of his protection," He sanctioned the acts of governors in employing the Indians against his subjects, and himself bargained for the employment of German hirelings. And when, yielding to the pressure of popular will, his representatives (the royal governors) fled before the indignant people, he certainly "abdicated government."

Historical Background

In 1775, King George III declared that the colonies were in open rebellion. Instead of seeking peace, he sent troops to fight them, issued a Proclamation of Rebellion, and encouraged harsh punishments for those supporting independence. Parliament followed with the Prohibitory Act, cutting off trade, seizing ships, and hiring foreign soldiers to fight Americans. These actions proved to the colonists that Britain no longer saw them as citizens but as enemies.

The colonists viewed this as an abdication of government—when a ruler stops protecting his people and wages war against them, he forfeits the right to rule. To them, this was not treason but self-defense. By 1776, many believed the King had broken the bond between Britain and America forever.[73]

Many colonists who had once hoped for reconciliation now saw the war as a fight for survival. Britain's declaration made it clear that peace could no longer come through loyalty but only through liberty. The King's war against his own people became proof that the colonies must govern and defend themselves.

Modern Interpretation

Government must protect its citizens and states. When leaders ignore their duty or use force against the people they serve, they lose moral authority to govern. The Founders built the U.S. system so that responsibility and accountability can never again be abandoned.

Summary

Grievance 23 shows how King George III gave up his role as protector and turned into a tyrant. The U.S. Constitution answered this betrayal by creating a government that cannot abandon its citizens. Through checks and balances, divided powers, and elected leadership, America ensured that no ruler could ever again declare war on the very people he was meant to defend.

> ### This Means
> When Britain turned its armies against the colonies, it proved that power without duty becomes tyranny. The founders formed a nation where government must always serve and protect the people—never attack them. Our leaders hold power only so long as they keep their promise to defend our rights and safety.

Constitutional Safeguards for Grievance 23

The U.S. Constitution ensures that government can never abandon its duties to the states or the people:

- **Article II:** Establishes the presidency to guarantee executive leadership that cannot abdicate its responsibilities.
- **Article IV, Section 4:** Guarantees every state protection against invasion and domestic violence, fulfilling the protective duty Britain refused.

Together, these principles ensure a government that cannot forsake its citizens or wage war against them—one that remains bound by service, protection, and the consent of the governed.

Grievance 24

He Plundered, Ravaged, Burnt & Destroyed

"He has plundered our seas, ravaged our coasts, burnt our towns & destroyed the lives of our people."

NOTE: When British forces attacked American towns, they didn't just target soldiers—they targeted everyone. Homes, ships, and even churches were burned, leaving families with nothing. The King's armies brought war into civilian streets, proving that Britain's goal was not peace or order, but punishment. These fires turned loyal subjects into determined patriots.

From Jefferson's July 1775 draft of *The Declaration of the Causes and Necessity of Taking Up Arms*:

"General Gage, by proclamation bearing date the 12th day of June, after reciting the grossest falsehoods and calumnies against the good people of these colonies, proceeds to declare them all, either by name or description, to be rebels & traitors…burning the town of Charlestown, attacking & killing great numbers of the people residing or assembled therein; and is now going on in an avowed course of murder & devastation, taking every occasion to destroy the lives & properties of the inhabitants."

From Benson J. Lossing's, *Our Country*

When naval commanders were clothed with the powers of custom-house officers, they seized many American vessels; and after the affair at Lexington and Bunker Hill, British ships of war "plundered our seas" wherever an American vessel could be found. They also "ravaged our coasts and burnt our towns." Charlestown, Falmouth (now Portland, in Maine), and Norfolk were burnt, and Dunmore and others "ravaged our coasts." and "destroyed the lives of our people." And at the very time when this Declaration was being read to the assembled Congress, the shattered fleet of Sir Peter Parker was sailing northward, after an attack upon Charleston, South Carolina.

Bombarded and Burned by the British
- Falmouth, MA (Now Portland, Maine) October 18, 1775
- Charles Town, MA June 17, 1775
- Bristol, RI October 7, 1775
- Norfolk, VA, January 1, 1776

Historical Background

British troops treated Americans terribly, bombarding and burning many of their cities and towns. They attacked places like Falmouth, Massachusetts (now Portland, Maine), Charlestown, Massachusetts, and Norfolk, Virginia. These were not just battles—they were acts of punishment meant to scare the colonies into giving up. Whole neighborhoods, businesses, and farms were destroyed.

If you look at the map, you'll see that many of these attacks happened even before *The Declaration of Independence* was signed. British warships raided harbors, burned homes, and struck in the dead of winter—proving that the King's goal was not peace but total control. In Virginia, Lord Dunmore's raids ruined coastal towns and plantations, and in the Carolinas and Georgia, British troops targeted key ports and supply routes. It became clear that Britain wasn't just fighting an army—it was attacking ordinary people. These events pushed more colonists to unite for independence.[74]

Modern Interpretation

This Grievance teaches that military power must always stay under the control of the people. Soldiers must protect—not harm—civilians. The Founders believed that freedom could survive only if armies were led by elected governments, not rulers acting alone.

Summary

The colonists' anger toward British destruction shaped the way America's government handles military power. Because of this experience, the Constitution guarantees that the military will always be under civilian control, protecting citizens' homes, property, and freedom from abuse.

Additional Considerations

Leaders like Lord Dunmore in Virginia and other royal governors made things worse by seizing ships, forcing sailors into service, and attacking coastal settlements. These abuses convinced the founders that strong civilian control of the military was essential. That's why the Constitution and Bill of Rights guarantee both military accountability and the protection of personal rights.

> ### This Means
> Britain's soldiers didn't just fight armies—they attacked homes, towns, and families. These brutal raids showed that power without limits leads to abuse. The Founders made sure that in America, the military would never rule the people again. Our troops serve under civilian leaders, and the rights of families and property are protected by law.

Constitutional Safeguards for Grievance 24

The Constitution includes specific safeguards to protect citizens and property:

- **The Third Amendment:** No soldier can live in someone's home without permission, even in wartime. This came from the colonists' experience of being forced to house British troops.

- **Fourth Amendment:** Protects people from unreasonable searches and seizures, keeping personal property and privacy safe from abuse.

- **Article I, Section 8:** Gives Congress—not the President or the military—the power to declare war, raise armies, and provide for a navy. This ensures that all military actions must answer to elected representatives, not to rulers or generals.

Grievance 25

Foreign Mercenaries Terrorize Our People

"He is at this time transporting large armies of foreign mercenaries to complete the works of death, desolation & tyranny, already begun with circumstances of cruelty & perfidy unworthy the head of a civilized nation."

NOTE: Britain hired soldiers from other countries to fight the colonists. These soldiers were paid to fight, not to protect the people. This made the colonists feel that the King's war was unfair and cruel.

Thomas Jefferson's 1774 *Summary View of the Rights of British America* (Paraphrased)

Bringing in foreign soldiers without the people's permission is dangerous. If this can happen, then the people's freedom is not safe.

From *Our Country, A Household History*, Volume 3, by Benson J. Lossing, 1877

This charge refers to the infamous employment of German troops, known here as Hessians.* Their presence in the colonies was regarded as the final outrage—a refinement of cruelty in which a Christian king made war upon his own people with the swords of strangers.

* One of the committee members, most likely Benjamin Franklin, made an entry on Jefferson's Rough Draft, listing Scottish soldiers as being foreign mercenaries.

Historical Background

In 1776, King George III hired about 30,000 German soldiers, known as Hessians, to fight the colonists.

To the Americans, this was more than just a military act—it was a betrayal. The King had chosen to pay outsiders to destroy his own people instead of seeking peace. Stories of Hessian cruelty spread quickly, convincing many colonists that Britain would never treat them as citizens again.

Jefferson condemned this as a moral crime, proof that Britain had lost its humanity. He believed that a ruler who brings foreign armies against his own people loses the right to rule them.[75]

Modern Interpretation

This Grievance reminds us that leaders must never hire outsiders to use violence against their own citizens. Power must always answer to the people it governs. America's founders made sure that no foreign force could ever decide our nation's battles or shape its future.

Summary

When the King sent foreign armies to fight Americans, he crossed a line that could never be repaired. The colonies now saw independence not as rebellion, but as survival. Jefferson's warning still echoes today: liberty cannot be defended by those who fight only for pay or power.

> ### This Means
> Britain hired strangers to attack Americans—people with no loyalty to justice or freedom. The colonists realized that a king who would pay foreigners to kill his own people could never be trusted to protect their rights. That's why the U.S. made sure its armies would always serve the people, never rule over them.

Constitutional Safeguards for Grievance 25

The Constitution prevents any ruler from using foreign or private armies to harm Americans:

- **Article I, Section 8:** Gives Congress the power to raise and support armies. This means the government cannot hire outside forces without the people's consent.

- **The Third Amendment:** Place defense under elected representatives, ensuring citizen control of the military.

- **The Militia Clauses (Article I, Section 8, Clauses 15–16):** Place defense under elected representatives, ensuring citizen control of the military.

- **The Logan Act (1799):** Later reinforced Jefferson's warning by outlawing private or foreign interference in American diplomacy.

Grievance 26

Taken Captive to Bear Arms Against Fellow Citizens

"He has constrained our fellow Citizens taken Captive on the high Seas to bear Arms against their Country, to become the executioners of their friends and Brethren, or to fall themselves by their Hands."

NOTE: British ships captured American sailors and forced them to join the Royal Navy. These men were made to fight against their own friends and country. They were treated harshly and had no choice in what happened to them.

Jefferson's Perspective

The King forces captured sailors to fight against their own country. They must harm their friends or be harmed themselves. This is cruel and wrong.[76]

From *Our Country, A Household History*, Volume 3, by Benson J. Lossing, 1877

An act of Parliament passed toward the close of December, 1775, authorized the capture of all American vessels, and also directed the treatment of the crews of armed vessels to be as slaves and not as prisoners of war. They were to be enrolled for "the service of his majesty," and were thus compelled to fight for the crown, even against their own friends and countrymen. This act was loudly condemned on the floor of Parliament as unworthy of a Christian people, and "a refinement of cruelty unknown among savage nations."

Historical Background:

Before the Revolution, British press gangs roamed American ports, seizing merchants, sailors, and fishermen to serve aboard British warships. Families watched in horror as husbands and sons were dragged away, never to return. By the 1770s, these kidnappings had become symbols of tyranny and slavery at sea.

When reports reached Philadelphia in 1776 describing the abuse of captured sailors, Jefferson turned outrage into accusation. He wrote that Britain's actions proved a nation ruled by cruelty, not conscience. Forcing Americans to fight their own countrymen—"to become the executioners of their friends and brethren"—was, to him, the ultimate act of moral corruption.

Modern Interpretation

This Grievance reminds us that governments must never force anyone to fight for a cause they know is wrong. True freedom requires both liberty of action and liberty of conscience. America's founders believed that no government has the right to command citizens to betray what is right or just.

Today, these principles live on in laws that protect conscience and forbid coerced service. They remind every generation that power must be guided by morality—not fear or force.

Summary

Grievance 26 turns the suffering of captured sailors into a lesson for all time: freedom cannot exist without conscience. Jefferson's words became a warning to future nations that obedience without justice is slavery. America was founded on the belief that no ruler can compel a person to act against truth or conscience.

> ### This Means
> Britain forced captured sailors to fight against their own country. Jefferson called this "enslaving their consciences." The Founders built a nation where no one could ever be forced to fight for tyranny or punished for refusing to do wrong. True liberty means the freedom to obey what is right.

Constitutional Safeguards for Grievance 26

- **Article I, Section 8:** Grants Congress exclusive authority to define and punish piracy and felonies on the high seas. This ensures that the law of nations—not the whim of monarchs—governs maritime justice and protects individuals from coerced service.

- **The Eighth Amendment:** Prohibits "cruel and unusual punishments," standing as a constitutional rebuke to the brutal coercion and dehumanization condemned in this grievance.

- **The Thirteenth Amendment:** Abolishes involuntary servitude in all forms, enshrining in law the principle that no citizen can be compelled to labor or fight against conscience under threat or force.

- **The Uniform Code of Military Justice (Article 92):** In the modern era, affirms that soldiers and sailors are bound by lawful orders only—a living reflection of Jefferson's doctrine that obedience to dark and unjust causes ends in the light of conscience.

Grievance 27

Inciting Insurrections & Unleashing Merciless Forces

"He has excited domestic insurrections amongst us, and has endeavored to bring on the inhabitants of our frontiers, the merciless Indian Savages whose known rule of warfare, is an undistinguished destruction of all ages, sexes, and conditions."

NOTE: The King tried to turn people against each other. He encouraged uprisings and attacks to bring fear and violence to the colonies. This made the colonists feel he would use any means to keep control.

From Jefferson's Preamble to the Virginia Constitution (Paraphrased from what he wrote in Philadelphia just a week or so before):

The King tries to cause fighting among us and bring attacks to our towns. This brings fear and harm to people of all kinds.

From *Our Country, A Household History*, Volume 3, by Benson J. Lossing, 1877

This was done in several instances, [Royal Governor of Virginia] Dunmore, was charged with a design to employ the Indians against the Virginians as early as 1774; and while ravaging the Virginia coast in 1775 and 1776, he endeavored to excite the slaves against their masters. He was also concerned with Governor Gage* and others, under instructions from the British ministry, in exciting the Shawnoese, and other savages of the Ohio country, against the white people. Emissaries were also sent among the Cherokees and Creeks for the same purpose; and all of the tribes of the Six Nations, except the Oneidas, were found in arms with the British when war began. Thus excited, dreadful massacres occurred on the borders of the several colonies.

* From the Massachusetts Historical Society: Thomas Gage, a decorated war hero in the French and Indian War, served as the commander in chief of the British Forces in North America from 1763–74. He arrived in Boston in May 1774 to replace Thomas Hutchinson as royal governor of Massachusetts.

Historical Background

During the Revolution, British officers promised freedom to enslaved people who would fight for the Crown and armed Native allies to raid frontier settlements. Instead of defending his people, the King turned their neighbors into weapons of war.

In Virginia, Lord Dunmore's 1775 proclamation to free enslaved men who joined the British army inflamed tensions and spread terror along the coast and frontier. At the same time, royal agents encouraged Native attacks against American towns. To Jefferson, this was the ultimate betrayal—a ruler who would destroy his own subjects rather than lose control of them.

Jefferson's words condemned not any people but the abuse of power itself: when rulers use division, fear, or race to keep control, they lose all moral authority to govern.

Modern Interpretation

This Grievance warns that governments must never turn citizens against one another or use outside groups to create fear. True leadership protects unity through justice, not manipulation.

America's founders believed that freedom depends on trust between the governed and their leaders. When leaders divide their people to keep control, liberty itself is in danger.

Summary

Grievance 27 exposes the moment when Britain's rule turned from order to cruelty. By trying to incite rebellion and unleash violence, King George III lost all claim to moral rule. The colonies realized that independence was no longer rebellion—it was survival.

> ### This Means
> When the King tried to make Americans fight each other, he proved that tyranny will destroy its own people to stay in power. The Founders built a republic where leaders must unite, not divide—where government protects every citizen equally and never uses fear as a weapon.

Constitutional Safeguards

The Constitution and later laws ensure that no ruler can ever divide or endanger Americans for political gain:

- **The Preamble:** Commits the Republic to "insure domestic Tranquility," forbidding any government from turning citizens against one another.

- **Article I, Section 8:** Gives Congress authority over relations with Native nations, guaranteeing peace through lawful diplomacy instead of manipulation.

- **Article II, Section 2:** Places the power to make treaties in the people's representatives, requiring consent before foreign or tribal conflicts can be escalated.

- **The Fourteenth Amendment:** Guarantees equal protection under the law, rejecting all divisions of race, birth, or class that tyranny was once used to justify oppression.

Jefferson's Lost Clause
The Slavery Clause

NOTE: In his first draft of The Declaration of Independence, Jefferson spoke strongly against the slave trade. He said it was wrong to take people from their homes, sell them, and treat them as property. He believed this was a serious injustice that went against human rights.

JEFFERSON'S CLAUSE DELETED BY CONGRESS:

"He has waged cruel war against human nature itself, violating its most sacred rights of life & liberty in the persons of a distant people who never offended him, captivating & carrying them into slavery in another hemisphere, or to incur miserable death in their transportation thither. this piratical warfare, the opprobrium of infidel powers, is the warfare of the Christian king of Great Britain. **determined to keep open a market where MEN should be bought & sold**, he has prostituted his negative for suppressing every legislative attempt to prohibit or to restrain this execrable commerce: and that this assemblage of horrors might want no fact of distinguished die, he is now exciting those very people to rise in arms among us, and to purchase that liberty of which he has deprived them, & murdering the people upon whom he also obtruded them; thus paying off former crimes committed against the liberties of one people, with crimes which he urges them to commit against the lives of another."

Thomas Jefferson's 1774 *Summary View of the Rights of British America* (Paraphrased)

Ending slavery is a great and important goal in the colonies, where it was wrongly brought long ago. But we must first stop bringing more people from Africa, or freeing others will do no good if more take their place. Yet our efforts to stop this trade are blocked. This is a shameful misuse of power, and if it is not changed, it must be limited by law.

Analysis of the Lost Clause

Including the Slavery Clause in the Declaration would have been a brave stand against the slave trade. But slavery was part of the Southern way of life, so ending it would not have been easy. If it had stayed in, America might have solved the issues of slavery much sooner.

So what did Jefferson mean when he wrote… "**We hold these truths to be self-evident, that all men are created equal**, that they are endowed by their Creator with certain unalienable Rights, that among these are Life, Liberty and the pursuit of Happiness," whom did he mean?

Many people today think he meant only White men, because the Declaration doesn't mention slaves, women, or Native Americans. But Jefferson's first draft did include a section condemning slavery. That part was taken out when South Carolina and Georgia refused to sign. **Jefferson's lost words clearly called enslaved people "MEN," written big and bold!**[77]

> **Jefferson's Draft To Revise Virginia's Constitution, May–June 1783**
>
> After serving as governor under Virginia's 1776 Constitution, Jefferson believed changes were needed and drafted an updated version. One of his most radical proposals dealt with slavery:
>
> …*"nor to permit the introduction of any more slaves to reside in this state, or the continuance of slavery beyond the generation which shall be living on the 31st. day of December 1800; all persons born after that day being hereby declared free."*[78]

In his initial draft of the Declaration of Independence, Jefferson blamed Britain's King George III for his role in creating and perpetuating the Transatlantic Slave Trade — which he describes, in so many words as essentially, a crime against humanity

Jefferson's Lost Words Against Slavery

Jefferson's first draft of the Declaration spoke out boldly against slavery. He called it a cruel war against human nature itself. If Congress had kept his words, it would have been the longest Grievance in the Declaration—a clear stand that slavery was wrong. But slavery was deeply rooted in the Southern economy, and some colonies refused to sign if this section stayed in. To keep unity, Congress removed it.

When Jefferson wrote that "all men are created equal," he meant everyone—men, women, and children of every race and background. In the rough draft, his "Slavery Clause" even used the word MEN in large letters to show that enslaved people were included. His lost words prove that the promise of equality was meant for all humanity.

A Nation Divided Over Conscience

Removing the Slavery Clause exposed the painful divide among the colonies. Some wanted to end slavery; others feared losing wealth and power if it disappeared. Many hoped the issue would fade on its own, but Jefferson knew it couldn't. How could a nation built on "life, liberty, and the pursuit of happiness" allow people to be bought and sold?

Even though Jefferson himself owned slaves, his writings show a man torn between his world and his conscience. He believed slavery was wrong and that the new nation's freedom would be incomplete until every person could share in it.

Jefferson's Fight Didn't End Here

Jefferson never gave up on trying to stop the slave trade. As governor of Virginia, he worked to limit the importation of enslaved people. On December 2, 1806, he encouraged Congress to ban America's participation in the trade entirely, using much of the same language he had written in his deleted clause from 1776. Congress did so, passing the legislation on March 2, 1807—three weeks before England passed their first such legislation.

He Tried Again to End Slavery

In later years, Jefferson pushed to end slavery in new territories and proposed that no child born after 1800 should remain enslaved. The plan failed by just one vote in Congress, but it showed that Jefferson was still fighting for the freedom he had declared was every person's natural right.

Proof of the King's Role

Jefferson and other leaders accused Britain's King George III of blocking every attempt to limit the slave trade. British merchants made huge profits from selling enslaved Africans, and the King used his power to protect that system. Colonial leaders even passed resolutions urging an end to the trade, but the King vetoed them all—choosing greed over justice:

> "Resolved that it is the Opinion of this Meeting, that during our present Difficulties and Distress, no Slaves ought to be imported into any of the British Colonies on this Continent, and We take this Opportunity of declaring our most earnest Wishes to see an entire Stop for ever put to such a wicked cruel and unnatural Trade."[79]

The King's Own Actions Are Further Exposed

Evidence later showed that British officials encouraged uprisings among enslaved people and promised them freedom if they fought for the Crown. In Virginia, Royal Governor Lord Dunmore issued a "Proclamation of Emancipation," calling the enslaved to rise against their American masters. Jefferson saw this not as mercy, but as proof that Britain would use human lives as weapons to hold power:

> This is further illustrated by events in Virginia in the fall of 1775. The Royal Governor, Lord Dunmore, who had retreated to a British frigate off the Virginia coast, issued a *Proclamation of Emancipation* on Nov. 7, 1775 in order to call the enslaved to arms against their masters. The governor's proclamation and reaction to it were published in Dixon & Hunter's Gazette on November 25, 1775, page three.

The King *"Prostituted His Negative"*

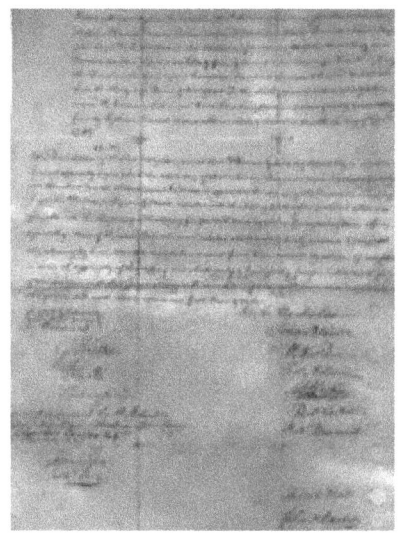

Patrick Michael McFadden of Bucks County, Pennsylvania, is a historical document collector and author of *An American Tale of Freedom's Promise*. Recently, he acquired a rare document revealing how King George III bound the right to collect duties on liquor and enslaved people in Virginia for £100,000 (equivalent to approximately $25 million today). This transaction paints the king as a profiteer, perhaps even "prostituting himself," as Thomas Jefferson suggested in the slavery clause of his rough draft of *The Declaration of Independence*. This performance bond provides direct evidence of the king's personal involvement in the slave trade.

Notably, the document bears the signature of George Wythe—Jefferson's close friend and legal mentor from 1762–67.[80] Wythe witnessed the bond on behalf of the lieutenant governor. A portion of the bond reads:

> Know all men by these Presents that we, Robert Carter Nicholas, John Blair, William Nelson, Thomas Nelson, … Esquires are held & firmly bound to our Sovereign Lord King George the third in the Sum of one hundred thousand pounds to be paid to our said Lord the King, his heirs & successors … Sealed with our Seals and dated this Tenth–day of April–1767.…Robert Carter Nicholas is appointed treasurer of the Revenues arriving from the Duties on Liquors & Slaves imported into this Colony.

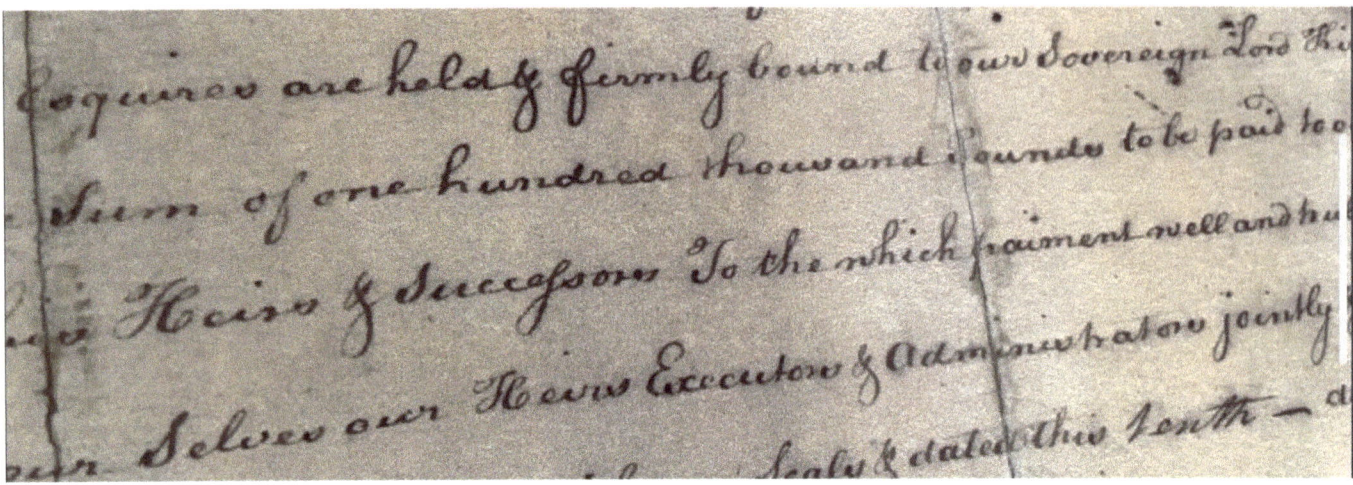

This passage shows that Robert Carter Nicholas and a group of prominent Virginians—including future signers of *The Declaration of Independence*—agreed to be bound to pay £100,000 to the king and his heirs in exchange for the right to collect duties on imported liquor and enslaved people. Such arrangements likely influenced Jefferson's later critique of George III in the Slavery Clause, where he condemned the king for "prostituting his negative" to block colonial efforts to restrict the "execrable commerce" of slavery.

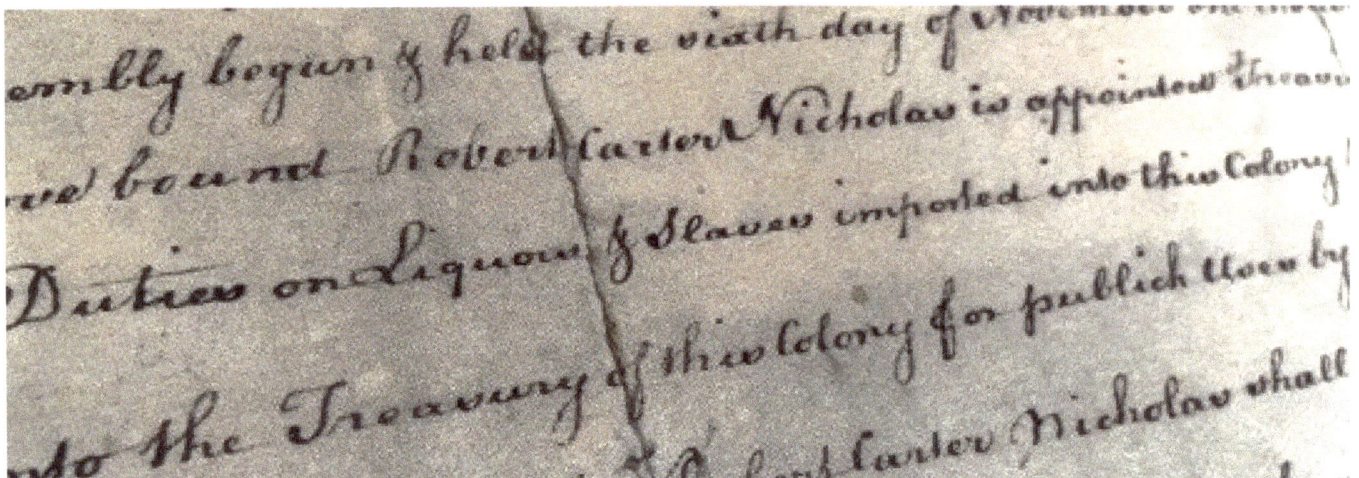

Historical Background
The King Forced Slavery on the Colonies and Blocked Efforts to Stop It

Imagine if a principal forced your school to keep an unfair rule even though the students and teachers wanted to change it, just because certain kids were making money from it. That wouldn't be right, would it?

That's kind of what happened to the American colonists with slavery. Many of them wanted to stop bringing enslaved people from Africa into the colonies. They tried passing laws to end the slave trade, but King George III blocked every single attempt because he and British merchants were making money from it. Worse, he made sure there was always a market where people could be bought and sold like objects. Thomas Jefferson called this "piratical warfare"—meaning the King was treating human beings like stolen goods.

Jefferson originally included a strong statement against slavery in *The Declaration of Independence*, calling it an "assemblage of horrors" and blaming King George III for keeping the cruel practice alive. But this passage—the longest Grievance in his original draft—was removed because South Carolina and Georgia refused to support independence unless it was taken out.

How Did This Shape America?

The removal of Jefferson's Slavery Clause was one of the biggest compromises of the American Revolution. If it had stayed in *The Declaration of Independence*, slavery might have ended much sooner. Instead, the fight against slavery would take almost 90 more years—and it would take a Civil War to finally abolish it.

Although his words were cut from the Declaration, Jefferson didn't stop fighting against slavery. As governor of Virginia, he spearheaded efforts to ban the importation of enslaved people—one of the first laws of its kind. Later, as president, he convinced Congress to pass a law banning U.S. participation in the transatlantic slave trade in 1807, using some of the same words from his original draft of the Declaration.

Ending the slave trade was not the same as ending slavery itself—and the numbers proved it. According to the 1790 census, 694,207 people remained in bondage. That number would grow to 4 million by 1860. While the Constitution laid a foundation for justice, African Americans and Native American tribes endured stolen land, denied rights, and generations of oppression. This history left deep scars on America and serves as a reminder that achieving justice requires action—not just words.

> **Ben Franklin**, who had previously owned house slaves, began to champion the cause of abolition. His 1790 petition, to the House of Representatives and Senate, called for decisive action to abolish slavery and the transatlantic slave trade. The petition urged Congress to **"devise means for removing this inconsistency from the character of the American people"** and to **"promote mercy and justice toward this distressed race."**
>
> In Franklin's 1770 article, **'A Conversation Between an Englishman, a Scotchman, and an American,'** the American observes, '**Several laws heretofore made in our Colonies to discourage the importation of slaves, by laying a heavy duty…have been disapproved and repealed by your Government.**'[81]

Summary

"The Rough Draft of the Declaration included a powerful statement against slavery, but it was removed to keep all 13 colonies united in the fight against Britain. This decision delayed justice, but it did not end the fight for freedom. Over time, Americans fought—and still fight—to fulfill the promise that "all men are created equal."

Modern Interpretation

Jefferson's lost words remind us that freedom and equality don't always come easily. It takes courage to stand up for what is right, even when others try to silence the truth. By learning from history, we can continue striving for a future where liberty and justice are a reality for everyone.

Constitutional Safeguards

- **The 13th Amendment (1865)**: Officially abolished slavery in the United States.
- **The 14th Amendment (1868):** Granted citizenship and equal protection under the law to formerly enslaved people and their children.
- **The 15th Amendment (1870):** Gave African American men the right to vote.

Indictment
The King is Disqualified by His Tyranny

"In every stage of these Oppressions We have Petitioned for Redress in the most humble terms: Our repeated Petitions have been answered only by repeated injury. A Prince whose character is thus marked by every act which may define a Tyrant, is unfit to be the ruler of a free people."

NOTE: After listing all the wrongs, Jefferson gave a final judgment. The colonies had asked again and again for fairness, but were only met with more harm. They came to see that a ruler who will not listen cannot be trusted. Because of this, the King lost his right to rule them.

From Jefferson's *Declaration of the Causes and Necessity of Taking Up Arms* (1775)

We have asked the King for help many times, as politely as we can. We have explained our concerns and even stopped trading with Britain to show we are serious. We hoped this would bring peace, but it did not. These events show that we can no longer trust the King to act fairly.

Our Country: A Household History For All Readers. Volume 1, Lossing, 1878

Thus closed that immortal instrument—an arraignment of a monarch unparalleled in the world's history. With calm logic and moral strength the representatives of the people declared that the king had forfeited every claim to their allegiance. He was no longer their sovereign; he was a tyrant, and, as such, unfit to be the ruler of a free people. It was not rebellion but revolution—an act of justice long delayed.[82]

Historical Background

Before America declared independence, the colonies spent years trying to reason with the King. They sent letters, petitions, and peaceful appeals, asking him to treat them fairly. But every time they reached out, the King either ignored them or punished them for speaking up. Jefferson's final statement in the Declaration wasn't written in anger—it was written in truth. The King had broken the sacred trust between ruler and people. A leader who refuses to listen is no longer a protector—he becomes the problem.

Jefferson wanted the world to understand that this was not a fight for power, but for principle. The colonists believed that real authority comes from fairness, honesty, and respect for the people. When those things vanish, so does the right to rule.

Modern Interpretation

Jefferson's warning still matters today. Freedom survives only when people have the courage to question authority and speak the truth, even when it's unpopular. Governments should serve the people—not silence them.

When leaders stop listening, liberty begins to fade. But when citizens use their voices with wisdom and courage, they keep tyranny from creeping back. Every generation must guard that balance, because freedom doesn't protect itself.

Summary

The Founders didn't rush to rebellion. They tried peace first—again and again. When every lawful path failed, they finally stood for their rights. The Declaration's last words weren't about hate or revenge. They were about responsibility: a duty to defend liberty when all other options were gone.

Jefferson's closing line declared that a tyrant is "unfit to be the ruler of a free people." It was both a judgment and a lesson. Freedom demands self-government—and self-government demands courage.

> ### This Means
> When the King tried to make Americans fight each other, he proved that tyranny destroys its own people just to stay in power. The Founders built a republic where leaders must unite, not divide—where government protects every person equally and never uses fear as a weapon.

Constitutional Safeguards

- **First Amendment:** Protects the right of every person to speak, write, and gather freely, so truth can challenge power.

- **Fifth Amendment:** Ensures that no one can lose liberty without fair legal process.

- **Ninth Amendment:** Affirms that freedom doesn't come from government—it belongs to the people.

- **Tenth Amendment:** Keeps power in the hands of the people and the states, not a distant ruler.

Enemies in War, in Peace Friends

"Nor have we been wanting in attentions to our British brethren. **We have warned them**, from time to time, of attempts by their legislature to extend an unwarrantable jurisdiction over us. We have reminded them of the circumstances of our emigration and settlement here. We have appealed to their native justice and magnanimity, and we have conjured them by the ties of our common kindred to disavow these usurpations, which would inevitably interrupt our connections and correspondence. **They, too, have been deaf to the voice of justice** and of consanguinity. We must, therefore, acquiesce in the necessity, which denounces our separation, and **hold them, as we hold the rest of mankind, enemies in war, in peace friends**."

NOTE: After listing all the wrongs, Jefferson ended with calm words, not hate. The colonists had asked for peace many times, but were not heard. They would fight only because they had to—and still hoped for friendship when peace returned.

From Jefferson's *Declaration of the Causes and Necessity of Taking Up Arms* (1775)

"But that this declaration may not disquiet the minds of our Friends & fellow subjects in any part of the empire, we do further assure them that we mean not in any wise to affect that union with them in which we have so long & so happily lived, and which we wish so much to see again restored."

Thomas Jefferson's 1774 *Summary View of the Rights of British America* (Paraphrased)

We seek peace and friendship with all people. But we will not flatter out of fear. We will not give up what is right or make peace with wrong.

Historical Background

Before the Revolution, the colonists tried many times to reason with Britain. They sent letters, petitions, and delegates asking for fairness. Britain and the King ignored every appeal. The colonists were family—connected by blood, language, and faith—but those bonds were broken when justice was denied.

Jefferson's phrase "Enemies in War, in Peace Friends" reminded the world that Americans would defend their freedom without hatred. Even in declaring war, they hoped for reconciliation. They wanted independence built on honor, not revenge.

Modern Interpretation

Jefferson's words still matter today. Real strength isn't shown by anger but by courage and fairness. True freedom means standing for what's right while treating others with dignity.

America's founders believed peace must be pursued wherever possible. Fighting for liberty does not mean hating an enemy—it means loving freedom enough to defend it and hoping that peace will one day return.

Summary

This final grievance closes the Declaration with heart and humility. The colonists had tried every peaceful way to be heard. When all those efforts failed, they stood together as one people to defend liberty. Yet even then, Jefferson's words promised forgiveness and friendship once freedom was secured.

America's birth was not about revenge—it was about responsibility. The Founders believed liberty must always walk hand in hand with peace.

> ### This Means
> When the King tried to make Americans fight each other, he proved that tyranny destroys its own people just to stay in power. The Founders built a republic where leaders must unite, not divide—where government protects every person equally and never uses fear as a weapon.

Constitutional Safeguards

- **First Amendment:** Protects the right to speak, write, and gather freely so that truth can be heard without violence.

- **Treaty Clause (Article II, Section 2):** Lets the President and Senate make peace and form alliances—continuing Jefferson's vision of friendship among nations.

- **Foreign Relations Powers:** Ensures America seeks peace through diplomacy, carrying forward the Declaration's promise of "peace and friendship with all mankind."

They Pledged Their Lives

"We, therefore, the Representatives of the United States of America, in General Congress assembled, appealing to the Supreme Judge of the world for the rectitude of our intentions, do, in the name, and by the authority of the good people of these Colonies, solemnly publish and declare, that these United Colonies are, and of right ought to be, free and independent States; that they are absolved from all allegiance to the British crown, and that all political connection between them and the State of Great Britain is, and ought to be, totally dissolved; and that as free and independent States, they have full power to levy war, conclude peace, contract alliances, establish commerce, and to do all other acts and things which independent States may of right do. And for the support of this declaration, **with a firm reliance on the protection of Divine Providence, we mutually pledge to each other our lives, our fortunes, and our sacred honour.**"

Note: Jefferson's final words gave the Declaration its heart. After all the wrongs were listed, the colonies ended with unity and faith. They knew they were risking their homes, families, and lives—but they believed freedom was worth it. By promising their "lives, fortunes, and sacred honor," they showed courage, trust in God, and their resolve to stand as free and independent states.

From Jefferson's *Declaration of the Causes and Necessity of Taking Up Arms* (1775)

We make this promise before God and the world. No matter the cost, we will keep fighting to protect our freedom. We will use all our strength to defend our lives and our homes, and to live as a free and independent people.

Historical Background

By July 1776, the colonies had tried every peaceful path. Letters, petitions, and appeals for fairness had all been rejected. Signing the Declaration was not just a political act—it was a life-and-death decision. It was treason. Each signature was a vow of faith and loyalty to one another and to their new nation.

Many of the delegates hesitated before signing, knowing that capture meant death for treason. Yet courage spread across the room as each man stepped forward. The moment was not only political—it was sacred. They were sealing their faith with their lives.

When Jefferson wrote of "firm reliance on the protection of Divine Providence," he meant that America's hope rested not on kings or armies but on God. It was both a statement of independence and a prayer for guidance.

Modern Interpretation

The Founders' pledge still speaks across time. Their courage was not about anger—it was about moral strength. "Sacred honor" meant honesty, faithfulness, and the promise never to betray the truth.

Today, freedom continues only when people protect it with integrity. Each generation must decide whether liberty is something to be inherited—or something to be earned again through faith, unity, and courage.

Summary

These final words were more than the end of the Declaration—they were the beginning of the American spirit. The signers showed that freedom lives through sacrifice, loyalty, and trust. Their signatures became a symbol of hope that liberty, once claimed, would be defended by every generation to come.

> **This Means**
> Freedom was not just declared—it was pledged.
> Those who signed the Declaration risked everything so that others could live free.
> Keeping that promise now belongs to us.

Constitutional Safeguards

- **First Amendment:** Ensures the right to speak, publish, and worship freely, preserving the same liberty of conscience that the Founders appealed to as they signed their names beneath Jefferson's words.

- **The Right to Petition**: Empowers citizens to seek redress before resorting to resistance—the very principle the colonies exhausted before pledging their lives to independence.

- **The Oath of Office Clause (Article II, Section 1):** Requires every president to swear before God to preserve, protect, and defend the Constitution—a living echo of the Founders' sacred pledge.

- **The Treaty Clause (Article II, Section 2):** Grants power to make peace and alliances, ensuring that the Republic born in war would seek its permanence in peace.

Signing the Declaration

On August 2, 1776, in Philadelphia, fifty-six delegates of the Second Continental Congress took a bold and dangerous step—they signed *The Declaration of Independence*. This happened a month after the Congress had approved the Declaration on July 2, 1776, when they voted to officially break away from Great Britain.

A group of five men—John Adams, Roger Sherman, Robert Livingston, Benjamin Franklin, and Thomas Jefferson—made up the committee to draft of the Declaration. It was written by Jefferson. Adams and Franklin suggested minor edits. Then, after much debate and a few changes (one major), Congress approved a final version.

Once it was finished, a printer named John Dunlap was given the job of making the first copies, called the Dunlap Broadside. About 200 copies were printed, but only 26 survive today. On July 8, 1776, Colonel John Nixon stood in front of a crowd in Philadelphia's Independence Square and read the Declaration out loud for the first time.

The official copy of the Declaration—the engrossed version—was ready for signatures on August 2, 1776. Delegates signed on behalf of their states, beginning with New Hampshire and ending with Georgia. John Hancock, the President of Congress, signed first. His signature was so large and bold that it became famous—people today still say **"Put your John Hancock"** when they mean **"Sign your name!"**

Not everyone signed on August 2. Some signed later, including Henry Lee, George Wythe, Elbridge Gerry, Oliver Wolcott, Lewis Morris, Thomas McKean, and Matthew Thornton. Seven men who had been in Congress on July 2nd never signed at all.[83]

Keeping It a Secret

At first, the names of the signers were kept secret. Britain saw them as traitors, and if the colonies lost, they faced grave danger. In early 1777, Mary Katherine Goddard printed a new version revealing all their names.

Five signers of the Declaration were captured and brutally tortured. Nine fought in the war and died from wounds or hardship. Two lost sons in battle, while two others had sons taken captive. At least a dozen saw their homes pillaged and burned.[84]

A Dangerous Decision

Signing the Declaration was an act of incredible bravery. These men weren't just writing their names on a piece of paper—they were risking everything. By putting their names on this document, they were openly defying King George III and the British government. If they lost the war, they could be arrested, imprisoned, or even executed for treason. John Hancock said at the signing on August 2nd, "There must be no pulling different ways," he declared. "We must all hang together." Franklin replied, "Yes, we must, indeed, all hang together, or most assuredly we shall all hang separately."[85]

> "All that I have, and all that I am, and all that I hope, in this life, I am now ready here to stake upon it; and I leave off as I begun, that live or die, survive or perish, I am for the Declaration. It is my living sentiment, and by the blessing of God it shall be my dying sentiment, Independence now, and Independence forever."
> —John Adams[86]

Who Signed the Declaration?

The 56 signers came from all 13 colonies. Here's the order in which they signed:[87]

1. **Delaware**: George Read, Caesar Rodney, Thomas McKean
2. **Pennsylvania**: George Clymer, Benjamin Franklin, Robert Morris, John Morton, Benjamin Rush, George Ross, James Smith, James Wilson, George Taylor
3. **New Jersey**: Abraham Clark, John Hart, Francis Hopkinson, Richard Stockton, John Witherspoon
4. **Georgia**: Button Gwinnett, Lyman Hall, George Walton
5. **Connecticut**: Samuel Huntington, Roger Sherman, William Williams, Oliver Wolcott
6. **Massachusetts**: John Adams, Samuel Adams, John Hancock, Robert Treat Paine
7. **Maryland**: Charles Carroll, Samuel Chase, William Paca, Thomas Stone
8. **South Carolina**: Thomas Heyward, Thomas Lynch, Arthur Middleton, Edward Rutledge
9. **New Hampshire**: Josiah Bartlett, William Whipple, Matthew Thornton
10. **Virginia**: Carter Braxton, Benjamin Harrison, Thomas Jefferson, Richard Henry Lee, Francis Lightfoot Lee, Thomas Nelson Jr., George Wythe
11. **New York**: William Floyd, Francis Lewis, Philip Livingston, Lewis Morris
12. **North Carolina**: Joseph Hewes, William Hooper, John Penn
13. **Rhode Island**: Stephen Hopkins, William Ellery

Summary

The men who signed *The Declaration of Independence* knew the risks—but they signed anyway. They believed so strongly in freedom that they pledged their lives, their fortunes, and their sacred honor to the cause. Their courage helped create a new nation, and their signatures became a powerful symbol of the fight for liberty.[88]

The Price They Paid

Have you ever wondered what happened to the men who signed *The Declaration of Independence*?

Five signers were captured by the British and held as prisoners. Twelve had their homes ransacked and burned. Two lost sons in the war; another had two sons captured. Nine fought in the Revolution and died from wounds or war-related hardships.

What kind of men were they?
- Twenty-four were lawyers and jurists.
- Eleven were merchants,
- Nine were farmers and plantation owners—men of means and education.

Yet they signed the Declaration knowing that if caught, they could be executed for treason. They pledged their lives, their fortunes, and their sacred honor.

Their Sacrifices
- **Carter Braxton (VA),** a wealthy planter and trader, lost his shipping fleet to the British navy. He sold his properties to pay debts and died in financial ruin.
- **Thomas McKean (DE)** was pursued by the British, forcing his family into hiding. He served in Congress without pay and lost much of his fortune.
- **Thomas Nelson Jr. (VA)** saw the British take over his home in Yorktown. He urged Washington to fire on it. The home was destroyed, and he died bankrupt.
- **Francis Lewis (NY)** had his home and properties destroyed. His wife was captured and later died from mistreatment.
- **John Hart (NJ)** fled his home while his wife was dying. His children scattered, his land was ruined, and he spent a year in hiding. He returned to find his wife dead and died soon after.
- **Richard Stockton (NJ)** was imprisoned for his role in the Revolution. He never fully recovered from mistreatment.
- **Edward Rutledge, Arthur Middleton, and Thomas Heyward Jr. (SC)** were captured at the Siege of Charleston and held prisoner for over a year.

The Truth Behind the Legends
While no signer was executed, their sacrifices were real. Some suffered financially, others endured imprisonment or the loss of loved ones. They were not reckless rebels but principled men willing to risk everything for liberty.[89]

As they pledged in 1776: *"For the support of this Declaration, with a firm reliance on the protection of Divine Providence, we mutually pledge to each other our lives, our fortunes, and our sacred honor."*

These men gave us an independent America. Can we keep it?

Comparing the Grievances

Thomas Jefferson's grievances in *The Declaration of Independence* is a slight expansion to the grievances proclaimed in the Preamble to the Virginia Constitution, which he wrote during mid-May to early June 1776.

Each charge against King George III appears in both documents, often with identical wording. Jefferson was not merely influenced by the Virginia grievances—but was their sole author. The complaints outlined in his Virginia draft were not confined to the concerns of a single colony; they served as a sweeping indictment of British rule, articulating frustrations shared throughout all thirteen colonies.

When tasked with drafting the Declaration, Jefferson did not need to construct a new case for independence—he had already done so for Virginia. Instead, he refined and expanded his well-established arguments, elevating them from a regional protest to a unifying call to the colonies. The striking similarities between the two documents confirm the ideological foundation for American independence was firmly in place before the Second Continental Congress acted. Jefferson's work for Virginia was not merely a precursor—it was the foundation of America's clarion call for independence.

From "A Summary View" to the Grievances

These grievances did not emerge in isolation; they distilled the essence of Jefferson's complaints first laid out in *A Summary View of the Rights of British America*, written two years earlier in July 1774. That document, delivered to Virginia delegates in session at Williamsburg, was Jefferson's bold attempt to define the American colonies' rights and to condemn British oppression.

His 1776 grievances generally follow the same sequence as those in his *Summary View*, beginning with the king's obstruction of colonial laws, his refusal to approve necessary reforms, and his interference with representative government. Jefferson denounced the king's dissolving of colonial legislatures, his failure to call new assemblies, and his restrictions on westward expansion—issues that also appear at the forefront of both the Virginia grievances and his Rough Draft of the Declaration. Condemning standing armies, foreign mercenaries, controlling our trade, and taxation without representation all appeared in his 1774 arguments.

By the time he wrote the Virginia grievances and the Declaration, Jefferson was not merely reacting to recent events—he was reinforcing a well-established case for independence that he had been refining for years.

Final Edits to the Grievances in The Declaration of Independence

As Jefferson copied the grievances from his Virginia document into the Rough Draft of *The Declaration of Independence*, he made very few changes. All the complaints stayed, with small tweaks to make them stronger. Some were expanded, like the King sending soldiers, and trifling with courts. Later, the clause blaming King George for promoting slavery was cut because southern colonies refused to sign if it remained. Other parts were reworked, showing how difficult it was for delegates to unanimously agree on content and phrasing. Referring to edits and deleting the Slavery Clause, Jefferson wrote that Congress had mangled it.[90]

The Table of Grievances

The grievances that follow are not the product of passion, but of patience worn thin. Jefferson organized them like a lawyer drafting an indictment—each charge precise, supported by precedent, and escalating in moral force. Together they transform a list of colonial complaints into a sweeping legal and philosophical case for independence. The table that follows traces this evolution, comparing Jefferson's Virginia arguments to his final Declaration text and showing how his earlier logic matured into America's charter of accountability. Grievances highlighted in gray indicate that were added after the Rough Draft had been presented to Adams and Franklin.

Refining the Grievances

#	Declaration of Independence Final June 15+/- – 28, 1776	Declaration of Independence, Rough Draft June 11 – 14+/-, 1776	Jefferson's Preamble to the Virginia Constitution Mid-May – June 10+/-, 1776
1	He has refused his Assent to Laws, the most wholesome and necessary for the public good.	he has refused his assent to laws the most wholesome and necessary for the public good:	by putting his negative on laws the most wholesome & necessary for ye public good;
2	He has forbidden his Governors to pass Laws of immediate and pressing importance unless suspended in their operation till his Assent should be obtained; and when so suspended, he has utterly neglected to attend to them.	he has forbidden his governors to pass laws of immediate & pressing importance, unless suspended in their operation till his assent should be obtained; and when so suspended, he has neglected utterly to attend to them.	by denying to his governors permission to pass laws of immediate and pressing importance, unless suspended in their operations for his assent, and, when so suspended, neglecting to attend to them for many years;
3	He has refused to pass other Laws for the accommodation of large districts of people unless those people would relinquish the right of Representation in the Legislature, a right inestimable to them and formidable to tyrants only.	he has refused to pass other laws for the accomodation of large districts of people unless those people would relinquish the right of representation, a right inestimable to them, formidable to tyrants alone:	by refusing to pass certain other laws, unless the person to be benefited by them would relinquish the inestimable right of representation in the legislature.
4	He has called together legislative bodies at places unusual, uncomfortable, and distant from the depository of their public Records, for the sole purpose of fatiguing them into compliance with his measures.	*Not in the Rough Draft, but comes from the Virginia House of Burgesses Resolution (May 24, 1774) where Jefferson was a delegate:* "This House, being deeply impressed with the deplorable condition of our sister colony of Massachusetts Bay, whose Assembly is now held in a place at a distance from their records and from the body of their constituents."	
5	He has dissolved Representative Houses repeatedly, for opposing with manly firmness his invasions on the rights of the people.	he has dissolved Representative houses repeatedly & continually, for opposing with manly firmness his invasions on the rights of the people:	by dissolving legislative assemblies repeatedly and continually for opposing with manly firmness his invasions on the rights of the people;
6	He has refused for a long time, after such Dissolutions, to cause others to be elected; whereby the Legislative Powers, incapable of Annihilation, have returned to the People at large for their exercise; the State remaining, in the meantime, exposed to all the Dangers of Invasion from without, and convulsions within.	he has refused for a long space of time to cause others to be elected, whereby the legislative powers, incapable of annihilation, have returned to the people at large for their exercise, the state remaining in the mean time exposed to all the dangers of invasion from without, & convulsions within:	when dissolved, by refusing to call others for a long space of time, thereby leaving the political system without any legislative head;

7	He has endeavored to prevent the population of these States; for that purpose obstructing the Laws for Naturalization of Foreigners; refusing to pass others to encourage their migrations hither, and raising the conditions of new Appropriations of Lands.	he has endeavored to prevent the population of these states; for that purpose obstructing the laws for naturalization of foreigners; refusing to pass others to encourage their migrations hither; & raising the conditions of new appropriations of lands:	by endeavoring to prevent the population of our country, & for that purpose obstructing the laws for the naturalization of foreigners & raising the condition lacking appropriations of lands;
8	He has obstructed the Administration of Justice, by refusing his Assent to Laws for establishing Judiciary powers.	Albemarle County Resolves: Jefferson, July 26, 1774: "We will ever maintain the legal and constitutional power of our own courts of justice, and protest against any attempt by the King or Parliament of Great Britain to suspend their operation or prevent the due course of justice within this colony."	
9	He has made Judges dependent on his Will alone, for the tenure of their offices, and the amount and payment of their salaries.	While no direct precedent appears in Jefferson's earlier writings, this grievance evolved naturally from colonial outrage over one of the Intolerable Acts, the 1774 Massachusetts Government Act, which made judges dependent upon royal will and salaries—widely condemned as the destruction of judicial independence.	
10	He has erected a multitude of New Offices, and sent hither swarms of Officers to harrass our people, and eat out their substance.	he has erected a multitude of new offices by a self-assumed power, & sent hither swarms of officers to harrass our people & eat out their substance:	This was not in the Virginia Preamble. Later, Jefferson added it by squeezing the words "Erected swarms of officers" between the lines—right above Grievance 11.
11	He has kept among us, in times of peace, Standing Armies without the Consent of our legislatures.	he has kept among us in times of peace standing armies & ships of war:	by keeping among us, in times of peace, standing armies and ships of war;
12	He has affected to render the Military independent of and superior to the Civil Power.	he has affected to render the military, independant of & superior to the civil power:	by affecting to render the military independant of & superior to the civil power:
13	He has combined with others to subject us to a jurisdiction foreign to our constitution, and unacknowledged by our laws; giving his Assent to their Acts of pretended Legislation:	he has combined with others to subject us to a jurisdiction foreign to our constitutions and unacknoleged by our laws; giving his assent to their pretended acts of legislation,	by combining with others to subject us to a foreign jurisdiction, giving his assent to their pretended acts of legislation.
14	For quartering large bodies of armed troops among us:	for quartering large bodies of armed troops among us;	for quartering large bodies of troops among us;
15	For protecting them, by a mock Trial, from punishment for any Murders which they should commit on the Inhabitants of these States:	The Administration of Justice Act allowed any Crown official accused of murder or other capital crimes in Massachusetts to be removed from the colony and tried elsewhere—often in England—by courts sympathetic to the Crown. In practice, it placed royal officers above colonial law, ensuring that even the gravest abuses could escape local justice under the guise of a "lawful" trial.	
16	For cutting off our Trade with all parts of the world	for cutting off our trade with all parts of the world;	for cutting off our trade with all parts of the world;
17	For imposing taxes on us without our consent:	for imposing taxes on us without our consent;	for imposing taxes on us without our consent;
18	For depriving us in many cases, of the benefits of Trial by Jury:	for depriving us of the benefits of trial by jury;	for depriving us of the benefits of trial by jury;

19	For transporting us beyond Seas to be tried for pretended offenses:	for transporting us beyond seas to be tried for pretended offences:	for transporting us beyond seas to be tried for pretended offences;
20	For abolishing the free System of English Laws in a neighbouring Province, establishing therein an Arbitrary government, and enlarging its Boundaries so as to render it at once an example and fit instrument for introducing the same absolute rule into these Colonies:	From: Jefferson's July 1775 draft of: *The Declaration of the Causes and Necessity of Taking Up Arms:* "They have erected in a neighbouring province, acquired by the joint arms of Great Britain and America, a tyranny dangerous to the very existence of all these colonies." *He drafted this as a delegate to the Second Continental Congress in Philadelphia. His draft was considered a bit too harsh, so it was modified by John Dickinson to tone down the rhetoric.*	
21	For taking away our Charters, abolishing our most valuable Laws, and altering fundamentally the Forms of our Governments:	for taking away our charters, & altering fundamentally the forms of our governments;	This Grievance is not in Jefferson's Virginia Preamble. He added it later while working on his drafts, and it appears in both, showing that he moved ideas back and forth as he wrote.
22	For suspending our own Legislatures, and declaring themselves invested with power to legislate for us in all cases whatsoever.	for suspending our own legislatures & declaring themselves invested with power to legislate for us in all cases whatsoever:	for suspending our own legislatures & declaring themselves invested with power to legislate for us in all cases whatsoever;
23	He has abdicated Government here, by declaring us out of his Protection and waging War against us.	he has abdicated government here, withdrawing his governors, & declaring us out of his allegiance & protection:	and finally, by abandoning the Helm of Government, and declaring us out of his Allegiance and Protection;
24	He has plundered our seas, ravaged our coasts, burnt our towns, and destroyed the lives of our people.	he has plundered our seas, ravaged our coasts, burnt our towns & destroyed the lives of our people:	by plundering our seas, ravaging our coasts, burning our towns and destroying the lives of our people;
25	He is at this time transporting large Armies of foreign Mercenaries to complete the works of death, desolation, and tyranny, already begun with circumstances of Cruelty & Perfidy scarcely paralleled in the most barbarous ages, and unworthy the Head of a civilized nation.	he is at this time transporting large armies of foreign mercenaries to compleat the works of death, desolation & tyranny, already begun with circumstances of cruelty & perfidy unworthy the head of a civilized nation:	by transporting at this time a large army of foreign mercenaries to compleat the works of death, desolation & tyranny already begun with circumstances of cruelty & perfidy so unworthy the head of a civilized nation;
26	He has constrained our fellow Citizens taken Captive on the high Seas to bear Arms against their Country, to become the executioners of their friends and Brethren, or to fall themselves by their Hands.	On June 5, 1776, The Philadelphia Gazette reported that American sailors had been captured or impressed into British service—men forced to man the very guns turned against their countrymen. Between June 8 and 10, Congress received additional dispatches describing the abuse of American prisoners aboard British ships. Jefferson, seething at these reports, transformed outrage to ink by adding this to the Fair Copy of *The Declaration of Independence* after he had completed the Rough Draft. The Fair Copy was lost after delivery for printing the Declaration.	

	Final Declaration of Independence	Rough Draft of the Declaration of Independence	Preamble to the Virginia Constitution
27	He has excited domestic insurrections amongst us, and has endeavored to bring on the inhabitants of our frontiers, the merciless Indian Savages whose known rule of warfare, is an undistinguished destruction of all ages, sexes, and conditions. *(Another number was later entered on the Composition Draft. It shows Jefferson changing them to be combined into a single Grievance)*	he has endeavored to bring on the inhabitants of our frontiers the merciless Indian savages, whose known rule of warfare is an undistinguished destruction of all ages, sexes, & conditions of existence: *(A number on the Composition Draft shows Jefferson instructing himself to move the text in the Declaration)* he has incited treasonable insurrections in our fellow-~~subjects~~ **citizens**, with the allurements of forfeiture & confiscation of our property:	*(This is two clauses higher in Virginia Constitution's Preamble)* by inciting insurrections of our fellow **subjects**, with the allurements of forfeiture and confiscation; *(These are two separate grievances in the Virginia Preamble)* by endeavouring to bring on the inhabitants of our Frontiers the merciless Indian savages, whose known rule of Warfare is an undistinguished Destruction of all Ages, Sexes, and Conditions of Existance;

Jefferson's Lost Clause—The "Slavery Clause"

Final Declaration of Independence	Rough Draft of the Declaration of Independence	Preamble to the Virginia Constitution
The Slavery Clause in Jefferson's Rough Draft was removed at the insistence of representatives from Georgia and South Carolina. Those delegates refused to sign the Declaration if this clause remained. Eleven states were in favor of this clause. It was imperative that all of the colonies were united in this effort or it was doomed to fail. Jefferson blamed not only Southern interests for its removal, but also Northern slave merchants, "for tho' their people have very few slaves themselves yet they had been pretty considerable carriers of them to others." [91] In the end, Jefferson was dejected, feeling Congress had "mangled it."	he has waged cruel war against human nature itself, violating its most sacred rights of life & liberty in the persons of a distant people who never offended him, captivating & carrying them into slavery in another hemisphere, or to incur miserable death in their transportation thither. this piratical warfare, the opprobrium of infidel powers, is the warfare of the <u>*CHRISTIAN*</u> king of Great Britain. determined to keep open a market where **MEN** should be bought & sold, he has prostituted his negative for suppressing every legislative attempt to prohibit or to restrain this execrable commerce: and that this assemblage of horrors might want no fact of distinguished die, he is now exciting those very people to rise in arms among us, and to purchase that liberty of which he has deprived them, & murdering the people upon whom he also obtruded them; thus paying off former crimes committed against the liberties of one people, with crimes which he urges them to commit against the lives of another.	by prompting our negroes to rise in arms among us; those very negroes whom he hath from time to time by an inhuman use of his negative he hath refused permission to exclude by law;

Indicting King George III

In every stage of these Oppressions We have Petitioned for Redress in the most humble terms: Our repeated Petitions have been answered **only** by repeated injury.	in every stage of these oppressions we have petitioned for redress in the most humble terms; our repeated petitions have been answered by repeated injury.	by answering our repeated petitions for redress with a repetition of injuries;
A Prince whose character is thus marked by every act which may define a Tyrant, is unfit to be the ruler of a free people.	**a prince whose character is thus marked by every act which may define a tyrant, is unfit to be the ruler of a people** who mean to be free. future ages will scarce believe that the hardiness of one man, adventured within the short compass of 12 years only, on so many acts of tyranny without a mask, over a people fostered & fixed in principles of liberty.	Jefferson's First Draft of his Proposed Virginia Constitution: "From all which premises it appears that the sd. George Guelp, not only for his criminal abuses of the high duties of the kingly office, but also by his own free & voluntary act of abandoning & putting us from his allegiance subjection & dominion, may now lawfully, rightfully, & by consent of both parties be divested of the kingly powers:"[92]

Jefferson's introduction to the Virgina grievances was introduced in the Virginia Constitution with these words:

> "Whereas George Guelf king of Great Britain and Ireland and Elector of Hanover, heretofore entrusted with the exercise of the kingly office in this government hath endeavored to pervert the same into a detestable and insupportable tyranny;"[93]

The Welf family—also spelled Guelf in old English—is one of the oldest noble families in Europe. The family originated in what is now southern Germany, and were part of the House of Hanover, a German royal dynasty.[94]

When Jefferson called King George III "George Guelf," he was invoking the king's German ancestry. The name served as a subtle but pointed reminder that George was not truly British. Not only was he a tyrant, but, as Jefferson implied, "he's not even—really—one of us." The word Guelf is derived from the Old High German word Welf, which literally means "whelp" or "wolf."

Jefferson's indictment of King George III was not an act of rebellion but was the result of two years of reasoning and writing. It began with his ***Albemarle County Resolves***, which he wrote in May-June 1774 because of Boston's suffering under tyrannical royal rule, where he first connected local injustice to universal rights. Jefferson followed with his ***Summary View of the Rights of British America*** in June-July 1774—a long argument that the colonies were independent by nature, joined to Britain only by mutual consent. The following year, in the ***Declaration of the Causes and Necessity of Taking Up Arms***, Jefferson transformed protest into principle, asserting that liberty justified resistance. By May 1776, his ***Preamble to the Virginia Constitution*** refined these ideas into a compact series of grievances—becoming, in essence, the pre–Rough Draft of *The Declaration of Independence*.

The Grievances of 1776 were not spontaneous outrage but the polished result of years spent thinking about tyranny and contradiction. Each stage of Jefferson's writing was brought both insight and clarity to America's moral purpose. The final Declaration did more than indict a king—it completed a philosophical journey that began in Albemarle and ended in Philadelphia. **Liberty was declared. Principle became law. Jefferson's words captured the voice and conscience of a nation.**

Grievances Added After the Rough Draft

After Jefferson shared his Rough Draft with Adams and Franklin and incorporated their suggestions, he prepared a new "Fair Copy." In it, he refined the wording of several Grievances and added six more—not simply at the end, but placed deliberately within the document's structure. The full extent of Jefferson's revisions before presenting this copy to Congress is unknown, but the language and placement of these added Grievances reflect his distinctive style. The Fair Copy itself, along with any edits made by Congress, was lost after being sent to the printer.

#	Added After the Rough Draft	Source Text
4	He has called together legislative bodies at places unusual, uncomfortable, and distant from the depository of their public Records, for the sole purpose of fatiguing them into compliance with his measures.	Virginia House of Burgesses Resolution (May 24, 1774): Jefferson, present as a delegate, described Massachusetts' Assembly as removed to a distant place—separated from its records and constituents to force compliance.
8	He has obstructed the Administration of Justice, by refusing his Assent to Laws for establishing Judiciary powers.	Drawn from Jefferson's Albemarle County Resolves (July 26, 1774), which condemned parliamentary interference with "our internal polity and administration of justice." Jefferson later charged that the King obstructed justice by refusing assent to judicial laws.
9	He has made Judges dependent on his Will alone, for the tenure of their offices, and the amount and payment of their salaries.	No direct precedent appears in Jefferson's earlier writings. The Grievance reflects colonial outrage over the Massachusetts Government Act (1774), which made judges dependent on royal will and salaries—undermining judicial independence. Jefferson expanded this into a broader indictment of executive control over justice.
15	For protecting them, by a mock Trial, from punishment for any Murders which they should commit on the Inhabitants of these States.	The Administration of Justice Act (May 20, 1774) allowed royal officials accused of capital crimes to be tried outside the colony—often in Great Britain—shielding them from local accountability.
20	For abolishing the free System of English Laws in a neighbouring Province, establishing therein an Arbitrary government, and enlarging its Boundaries so as to render it at once an example and fit instrument for introducing the same absolute rule into these Colonies.	Source: Jefferson's June 1775 draft of *The Declaration of the Causes and Necessity of Taking Up Arms*. He warned that Britain had established arbitrary rule in a neighboring province—dangerous to the liberties of all the colonies.
26	He has constrained our fellow Citizens taken Captive on the high Seas to bear Arms against their Country, to become the executioners of their friends and Brethren, or to fall themselves by their Hands.	Reports in June 1776 described American sailors captured and impressed into British service—forced to fight against their own country. Jefferson transformed these accounts into this Grievance. Here, he also employs the term "citizens," reflecting his shift from subjects of the Crown to members of a political community.

Working Composition Draft

Above: Jefferson wrote notes to move ideas into better places. Some numbers show where a complaint should be moved or added in the final version.

Below: Jefferson first wrote "subjects," then crossed it out and wrote "citizens." This small change showed a big idea—Americans were no longer ruled by a king. They were becoming citizens of a new nation.

The Working Composition Draft

Thomas Jefferson did not write the *Declaration of Independence* all at once. He used earlier writings to help him, like the "Working Composition Draft" on the left.

One of those writings was Jefferson's introduction, or preamble, to a plan he wrote for Virginia's government. He worked on it in the same room, over the weeks before writing the Declaration.

He used that page as a guide. Many of the same ideas and complaints appear again in the Declaration.

Jefferson made notes on the page to move ideas around and improve them. These were not random edits. They were part of his process—helping him build the Declaration step by step.

A Repeated Method from 1775

Jefferson used this same method before. In 1775, he helped write a document explaining why the colonies were fighting.

He would write a first version, then copy it again more carefully, making changes as he worked.

Instead of starting over, he improved what he had already written.

This shows that Jefferson was not making up ideas at the last minute. He was shaping ideas he had been working on for years.

One of the most important changes he made was crossing out "subjects" and writing "citizens."

Jefferson's Epiphany
No longer Subjects, but Citizens

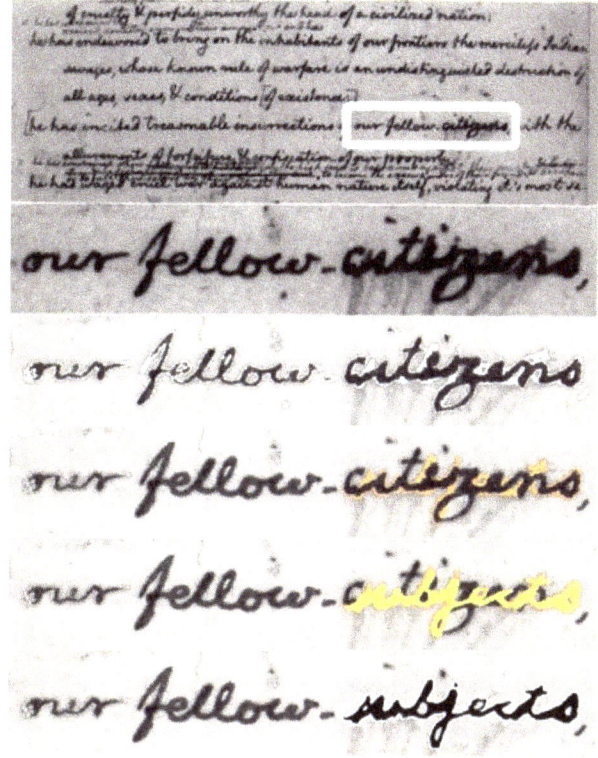

In his first draft of the Declaration of Independence, Thomas Jefferson first wrote the word "subjects."

That word meant people who were ruled by a king.

But then something changed. Jefferson stopped, wiped out the word, "subjects," while the ink was wet. Then he wrote, "citizens" over the smudged ink."

This was an important moment. "Subjects" obey a king. "Citizens" are in charge of the country.

With that one change, Jefferson helped show Americans what they would become.

A Hidden Change, Discovered Centuries Later

For a long time, no one noticed this change.

Years later, scientists used special tools to study Jefferson's writing. They were able to see the word he had first written underneath.

They discovered that Jefferson had first written "subjects," and then changed it to "citizens." This showed that the change was not a mistake. It was a careful choice.

Then Jefferson wrote "citizens" above "subjects" on the preamble—a sign that his thinking had changed.

Before the Declaration

By the summer of 1776, many Americans were making up their minds. The British government had failed them. The question now was what would happen next—who would govern them once the King's authority was gone. The Declaration would explain their decision to the world, but it did not begin it. The war had already been underway for more than a year.

The Exhaustion of Reconciliation

For more than a year, the colonies had tried to make peace. They sent careful appeals to the King, including the Olive Branch Petition and the *Declaration of the Causes and Necessity of Taking Up Arms*. These documents protested injustice while still claiming loyalty.

Nothing changed. Instead, the King declared the colonies in rebellion and sent more troops. By early 1776, peace was no longer possible.

Give Me Liberty or Give Me Death

March 23, 1775: Just before the fighting began, Patrick Henry delivered a powerful speech in Virginia. The room was filled with leaders, including George Washington, Thomas Jefferson, and Richard Henry Lee. His words captured the urgency of the moment:

"There is no peace… give me liberty or give me death!" [95]

April 1776: Adams's Thoughts on Government

By April, the crisis was no longer just talk—it required action. Royal authority had collapsed, and new governments were taking shape.

In *Thoughts on Government*, John Adams explained how Americans could govern themselves. He outlined key ideas for new state constitutions, like Separation of Powers, a Two-Part Legislature, and a separate executive like a President.[96]

May 10, 1776: Permission to Govern

Congress recommended that each colony form its own government, based on the authority of the people. It did not yet declare independence—but it made self-government official.

May 15, 1776: Authority Transferred

Congress declared that royal authority had failed and must be set aside. All powers of government were to come from the people. Independence was no longer theoretical—it was already happening.

May 15th Virginia Proposes Independence

That same day in Williamsburg, Virginia's leaders declared their government dissolved and instructed their delegates to propose independence in Congress—what became known as the Lee Resolution.

June 7-11: The Lee Resolution

On June 7, Richard Henry Lee made an important proposal in Congress. He said the colonies should be free and independent.did

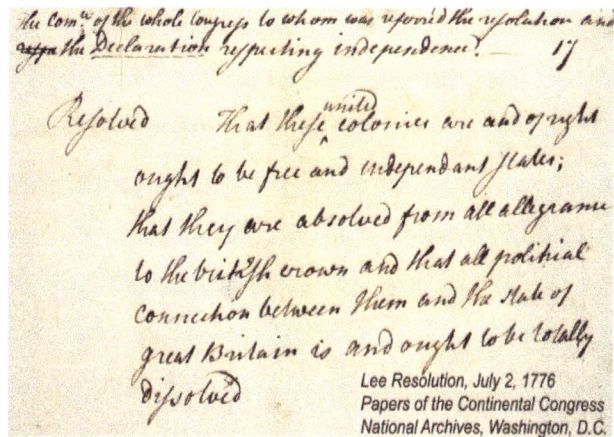

Lee Resolution, July 2, 1776
Papers of the Continental Congress
National Archives, Washington, D.C.

Congress did not vote right away. On June 11, they chose three committees:

1. To draft a declaration of independence
2. To prepare foreign alliances
3. To create a plan for the colonies to work together as one nation

Some colonies were not ready yet. They needed time to get approval from their assemblies. So the vote was delayed.

Even so, the work continued. A draft of *The Declaration of Independence* was prepared so it would be ready.

Leaders knew they had to be careful. If they rushed, the colonies might divide. They needed to stand together.

Liberty and Order

By the end of May 1776, independence was already beginning. Congress was meeting, Washington was leading the army, and new governments were forming. Royal authority was fading.

The Declaration of Independence did not start these changes—it explained them.

Freedom required more than agreement. It required careful planning.

John Adams worked on building governments that could last. Thomas Jefferson explained why the colonies were separating. Together, they helped make sure liberty would bring order—not chaos.

Why This Matters

These events help us understand the purpose of *The Declaration of Independence*.

When Congress chose a committee on June 11, they had not yet voted for independence—but they were getting ready.

If independence was approved, they would need to explain it right away—to other nations and to their own people.

Even so, the work continued. A draft of *The Declaration of Independence* was prepared so it would be ready when the time came.

Journey to Philadelphia

For nearly a year before the Declaration, Thomas Jefferson had been working in Congress. He spent much of his time writing reports, helping make decisions, and solving problems.

In late March 1776, Jefferson returned home to Virginia. His mother was very ill, and he needed to take care of family matters. He asked for a short leave, but he planned to return soon.

On May 7, Jefferson left Monticello and began his journey north to Philadelphia. He traveled about 300 miles, stopping in small towns along the way.[97]

- May 7 – Monticello to Orange Court House (30 mi)
- May 8 – Orange Court House to Culpeper Court House (15 mi)
- May 9 – Culpeper Court House to Fairfax Court House (55 mi)
- May 10 – Fairfax Court House to Leesburg and Potomac crossing (20 mi)
- May 11 – Potomac crossing to Frederick Town and Taneytown (55 mi)
- May 12 – Taneytown to Wright's Ferry on the Susquehanna (40 mi)
- May 13 – Wright's Ferry to Lancaster (15 mi)
- May 14 – Lancaster to central Philadelphia (60 mi)

On May 14, 1776, his carriage rolled into it final destination—seven days after leaving Monticello. The man who had gone home to bury his mother returned to the Congress of the colonies, travel-worn but resolute, ready to lend his pen to the cause of independence.

When Jefferson arrived, he learned that John Adams was preparing to ask each colony to create its own government. Jefferson may have wanted to return to Virginia to help write its constitution, but he stayed in Philadelphia because he had an important duty. He later explained:

> "I had been elected a delegate to the Convention of Virginia, but was detained in Congress by the duty of preparing a Declaration of Independence. I prepared a Constitution for my native State, and sent it to the Convention."[98]

Refining the Language of Liberty

Thomas Jefferson is sometimes described as young and quiet, but he was a strong writer. For years, he had been thinking about freedom, government, and the rights of the people. By 1776, he was ready.

These ideas did not come all at once. He built them step by step, across several important writings.

A Succession of Jefferson's Revolutionary Documents

1. July 1774: *Albermarle County Resolves*   705 Words

Jefferson wrote this in response to British actions that punished the colonies. He argued that the colonies should not be forced to obey unfair laws.

He believed that when people are treated unjustly, they have the right to act.

> "We will ever be ready to join with our fellow subjects... in exerting all those rightful powers, which God has given us, for the re-establishing and guaranteeing such their constitutional rights, when, where, and by whomsoever invaded."[99]

Other leaders saw how strong his words were and encouraged him to write more. So, within a week or so, he expanded his ideas by writing, *A Summary View of the Rights of British America*.

2. August 1774: *A Summary View of the Rights of British America*   7,017 words

Thomas Jefferson, *A Summary View of the Rights of British America* 1774. Library of Congress.

This work made Jefferson well known across the colonies. It clearly explained the colonies' complaints against the King.

John Adams later said Jefferson had a "masterly pen," because he explained his ideas so clearly.

The Summary View was printed and shared widely in America and England. It helped people see Jefferson as an important voice for colonial rights.[100]

3. June 1775: *Declaration of the Causes and Necessity for Taking Up Arms*   2,390 words

Jefferson helped write this document for Congress.

It explained why the colonies were fighting. It was not a call for independence yet—but it made clear that the colonies were defending their rights.

Congress later used a different final version, but Jefferson's ideas were still important. He believed freedom was worth defending, and that giving in to tyranny was wrong.

4. May & Early June 1776: *Jefferson's Proposed Virginia Constitution*   1,250+/- words

When Jefferson returned to Philadelphia, Congress was already talking about independence. John Adams had urged each colony to form its own government.

This pushed Jefferson to begin writing a plan for Virginia's government.

He worked in rented rooms on High Street, now called Market Street, drafting a Virginia constitution. This is where he would soon write *The Declaration of Independence*.[101]

Grievances as a Constitutional Preamble

Jefferson wrote that King George III had ruled with "tyranny." He listed many grievances against the King. This list was copied into the Declaration just a few days later.

In addition to grievances, Jefferson wrote a complete constitutional framework for government. His plan included:

- **No** person coming into Virginia could be held as a slave
- **Fair** inheritance laws
- **Freedom** of religion
- **Protection** from soldiers living in private homes
- **Fair** purchase of Native lands
- **Right** to bear arms

The ideas Jefferson wrote in this constitution were not just ideas—they came from real experience. He believed that rights come from God, and that government exists to protect them.

Drafting the Declaration

1,337 words

When Congress decided to move toward independence, Thomas Jefferson turned big ideas into clear words. He was chosen to write the Declaration, not by chance, but because he had been preparing for years.

> John Adams later said Jefferson had a **"masterly pen,"** and trusted him to do it well. [102]

Jefferson worked in rented rooms in Philadelphia. He wrote carefully and with purpose.

The Declaration followed a clear plan:

- A beginning that explained natural rights
- A list of Grievances against the King
- A final statement saying the colonies should be free

Jefferson did not make up these ideas all at once. He had been developing them for years in earlier writings.

After finishing his draft, he showed it to John Adams and Benjamin Franklin. They made a few small changes to make the wording clearer and stronger.

Jefferson then prepared a clean copy, "Fair Copy," to present to Congress.

Presented to Congress

Congress read the Declaration and worked through it line by line. They made some changes, but the main ideas—especially the Grievances—remained.

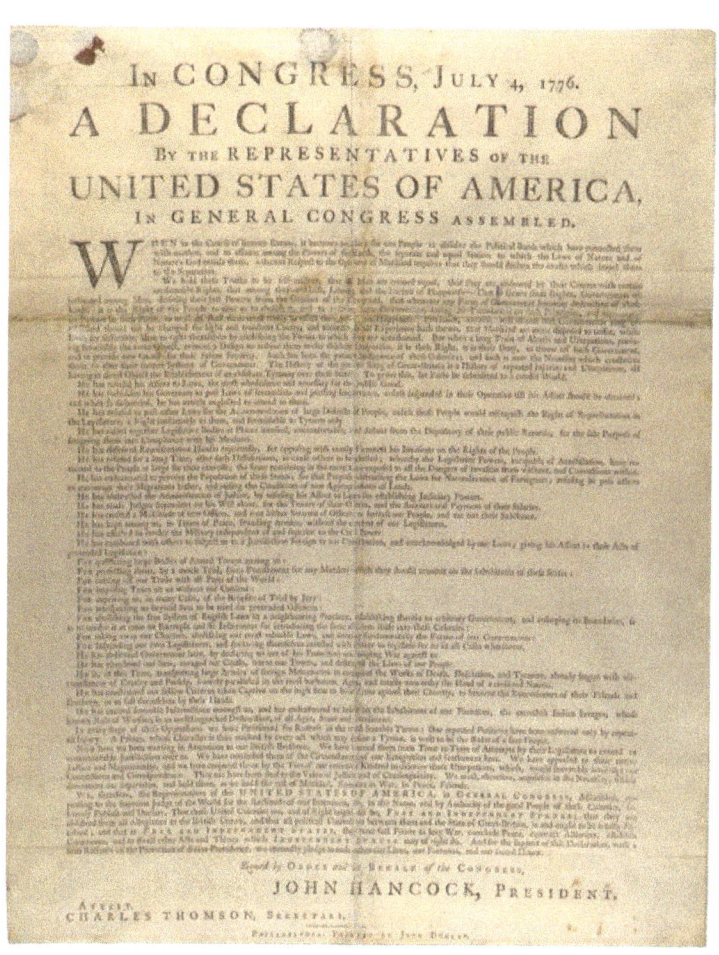

The biggest change was removing the section about slavery. Because of this, Jefferson later said that "Congress mangled it."

The final version was printed so people across the colonies could read it. The document shown here is what the Declaration looked like when it was first shared with the public.

After the printer set the type, the original handwritten copy was never seen again.

This printed version is called the Dunlap Broadside, and it can be seen today at the National Archives in Washington, D.C.

June 28–July 2: The Declaration was Tabled as Congress Debated Independence

While Congress debated independence, Jefferson's Declaration sat on the table, waiting. The colonies were close—but not all were ready.

One delegate, Caesar Rodney of Delaware, rode through the night to Philadelphia—even though he was very sick—to cast the deciding vote on July 2. When the vote for independence was finally secured, Congress turned to the Declaration—not to decide if they would be free, but to explain why.

For several days, the Fair Copy waited. Now it would be read, debated, and revised.

July 2–4: Congress Debates and Edits

Congress met as a group and worked through Jefferson's document line by line. They made a few changes. Jefferson later said Congress had "mangled it," especially when they removed the section about slavery.

Even so, the main ideas—including the Grievances—remained strong. This was not the end of Jefferson's work—it was the final step before it was shared with the world.

Congress at work—debating, revising, and approving the Declaration before it was sent to the printer.

Evening of July 4: To the Printer

After approving the final version, Congress sent the Declaration to printer John Dunlap. That same night, the words were set in type and printing began. The original handwritten Fair Copy was never seen again.

July 5: The Dunlap Broadsides

About 200 copies were printed overnight. They were quickly sent to General Washington and leaders in other places. Now people could read the Declaration for themselves.

July 19–August 2: The Engrossed Parchment

Congress ordered a formal handwritten copy on parchment. Timothy Matlack carefully wrote the version we know today.[103] Fifty-six delegates signed it, beginning on August 2.

January 18, 1777: The Goddard Broadside

When the British threatened Philadelphia, Congress moved to Baltimore. There, printer Mary Katharine Goddard printed a new version of the Declaration—the first to include all the names of the signers.[104]

American Scripture

Jefferson later said he was not trying to create something new, but to express what Americans already believed. In about a week, he had written a draft built from ideas he had been developing for years.

Over the next days, he refined the language—carefully shaping each line. For more than 250 years, the Declaration of Independence has continued to inspire people around the world. It has become America's founding message—its *"Psalms of Liberty."*

Classical Ear and Architectural Prose

Thomas Jefferson was not just a thinker—he was trained to write beautifully. He studied Greek and Roman writers who taught that good writing should be clear, balanced, and strong.

In *The Declaration of Independence*, his words move almost like music. His sentences have rhythm, and his ideas are carefully built—one part leading to the next.

Building Ideas Like a Pattern

Jefferson often used a simple pattern:

- First, he made a statement
- Then, he explained it
- Then, he returned to it with even more power

This helped his writing feel steady and strong, not rushed or confusing.

A Mirror Effect

Jefferson also used a special technique where ideas are repeated in reverse order—like looking in a mirror. This helped his writing feel balanced and complete. His ideas connect and answer each other, instead of just piling up.

Writing with Rhythm

Jefferson wrote with a "musical ear." Some sentences are long, some are short—but they fit together.

This keeps the writing interesting and easy to follow. Even when he is listing Grievances, his tone stays calm and controlled. His writing persuades—not by shouting, but by being clear, steady, and powerful.

When Jefferson Dined Alone

In 1962, President John F. Kennedy welcomed a group of Nobel Prize winners to the White House. He said:

> "I think this is the most extraordinary collection of talent, of human knowledge, that has ever been gathered together at the White House—with the possible exception of when Thomas Jefferson dined alone."[105]

This was partly a joke—but also true. Jefferson was not just a leader. He was a scholar, a musician, an architect, and a writer who understood how to shape ideas.

Three Great Voices

Some people think Adams, Jefferson, and Mason worked separately—but they were really working together in different ways.

- John Adams helped build strong governments
- George Mason helped define rights
- Thomas Jefferson shared those same ideas and provided a clear and powerful voice

Jefferson helped the nation speak. His words helped people understand what they were fighting for.

Notes on the State of Virginia
Including Observations on Slavery and Africans
Jefferson, 1785

Why Jefferson Wrote This

Notes on the State of Virginia began as answers to questions from a French official named François Marbois. He asked Jefferson about life in Virginia—its land, people, and government.

Jefferson later turned his answers into a book. Because of this, the ideas in the book come from different questions—and sometimes they do not match each other.

This section does not try to excuse Jefferson or hide his mistakes. It shows him as he really was—careful and thoughtful in some ways, but wrong in others.

Slavery and Its Effects

When Jefferson wrote about slavery, he strongly criticized it.

He said slavery teaches people to be cruel—one group to command, and another to obey. He also warned that children growing up in slavery could learn these habits

Jefferson believed slavery harmed everyone. It hurt those who were enslaved, but it also damaged the character of those who owned slaves. He warned that a society built on slavery could lose its sense of fairness and put freedom at risk.

These were not casual ideas. Jefferson took this seriously. He believed slavery was dangerous to Virginia and to the future of the country.

A Confusing Contradiction

But later in the same book, Jefferson wrote very different things about race.

Instead of blaming slavery for the harm he described, he suggested that some differences were natural. This did not match what he had already written. This is important to understand: Jefferson was answering different questions, one after another. His answers about slavery showed deep concern. His answers about race showed serious mistakes.

Even in his own writing, his stronger ideas—about how slavery harms people—stand against his weaker ones.

Race, Error, and Limits

Jefferson tried to explain differences between people using the science of his time. But his ideas were based on limited knowledge and were wrong.

What makes this especially troubling is that he already understood how slavery harmed people. His claims about race ignored what he already knew.

His situation also mattered. Jefferson was deeply in debt. Under Virginia law, enslaved people were treated as property and could be taken to pay debts. This made it harder for him to act, even when he knew what was right.

Sometimes, when he had to sell enslaved people, he tried to keep families together or sell them to people they knew. These actions did not make slavery right—but they show how difficult and painful the system was.

Understanding these limits helps explain Jefferson's actions—but it does not excuse them.

Benjamin Banneker Speaks Up

In 1791, a free Black man named Benjamin Banneker wrote to Jefferson.

Benjamin Banneker sent Jefferson his almanac and reminded him of the words in the Declaration—that all people have rights. He also challenged Jefferson to live up to those ideas.

Jefferson replied more carefully than before. He praised Banneker's abilities and admitted that slavery's conditions had harmed people. But he did not fully correct his earlier views.

Still, something important happened—when faced with real evidence and a real person, Jefferson listened.

A Struggle Not Yet Finished

Jefferson's writings on slavery and race are difficult to read—and they should be.

They show a man who understood some truths clearly, but did not fully act on them.

History does not ask us to ignore this or excuse it. It asks us to learn from it—and to think carefully about what is right.

A Wolf by the Ears

Jefferson's Lament

In 1820, Thomas Jefferson wrote, "We have the wolf by the ears."[106]

He meant that slavery was a terrible problem. If they held on to it, it was wrong. But if they let go too quickly, it could bring danger and chaos.

Jefferson believed slavery should end. But he also believed it had to be done carefully, with a plan.

He thought people needed to prepare—by ending the slave trade, teaching the next generation, and building a society ready for freedom.

Jefferson could see the goal clearly—but he knew it would take time to reach it.

Trying to End the Slave Trade

Jefferson worked to stop the importation of enslaved people.

- In 1778, Virginia passed a law to end the slave trade
- In 1783, Jefferson proposed a plan that children born after a certain date would be free

That plan did not pass—but it showed what he was trying to do: stop bringing slaves to America first, then end slavery over time.

President Jefferson's Message to Congress

When Jefferson became president, he again asked Congress to end the slave trade.

In 1807, Congress passed a law banning the importation of enslaved people, starting in 1808. This was an important step—but slavery itself still continued. Jefferson knew the problem was not solved.

Jefferson and Sally Hemmings

Sally Hemings was an enslaved woman who lived at Jefferson's home, Monticello.

History tells us that Jefferson and Sally Hemings had children together. Some of their children were later freed. One of them said Jefferson had promised that his children "should be free."

This part of Jefferson's life is complicated, and people still study and discuss it today.

A Nation Divided

As the country grew, the question of slavery became more serious. In 1820, the Missouri Compromise tried to keep balance between free states and slave states.

But many people saw the problem clearly: How could a nation built on freedom continue to allow slavery? Jefferson worried that the issue could divide the nation—and he was right.

A Long Struggle

Slavery did not end in Jefferson's lifetime.

But the ideas in the Declaration—that all people have rights—continued to grow. Over time, more Americans saw that those words had to apply to everyone.

The struggle to live up to those ideas would continue for many years.

Afterword

⚠ Teacher & Family Note

The following pages introduce some very hard parts of our past—slavery and the unfair treatment of people in the New World. These stories aren't meant to scare, but to help you understand what can happen when freedom is taken away. You may want to read these pages with a parent or teacher so you can ask questions and talk about what you learn.

Even in the hardest times, brave men and women stood up for what was right. Their courage and kindness helped move our country toward liberty and equality. As we celebrate 250 years of America's story, we can look back with honesty—and look forward with hope. America isn't perfect, but its people have always found the strength to answer the call of liberty for all.

Jefferson's Struggle with Slavery and the Slave Trade

Thomas Jefferson, a man both celebrated and criticized, embodied the contradictions of America's founding. In 1776, as he wrote *The Declaration of Independence*, he boldly stated that all men are created equal and have unalienable rights to life, liberty, and the pursuit of happiness. Yet, at the same time, he was a slave owner.

Jefferson originally included a powerful statement condemning the transatlantic slave trade in his first draft of the Declaration. However, delegates from Southern states demanded its removal, as they depended on slavery for their economies. Even so, Jefferson continued to push for change.

As governor of Virginia in 1778, he signed a law banning the importation of enslaved people into the state. Later, as president, he urged Congress to outlaw American participation in the transatlantic slave trade. In 1807, Congress passed a law banning the importation of slaves, taking effect on January 1, 1808—the earliest date allowed by the Constitution. The United States was only the second country to pass such a law, following Denmark's 1792 ban, which took effect in 1803.[107]

Although Great Britain passed a similar law in 1807, it did not fully enforce the ban in its Caribbean colonies for decades. In fact, British ships transported more than 25,000 enslaved Africans to the West Indies even after the trade was technically outlawed. Denmark and Great Britain did not abolish slavery in their colonies until 1848 and 1833, respectively.[108]

Indentured Servitude and Its Brutality

Even after slavery was abolished in British territories, many former slaves were placed into indentured servitude. Indentured laborers were typically bound by contracts that required them to work for four to eleven years in exchange for passage to a new land. In theory, they would be free after their contracts ended, but in reality, they were often trapped in brutal conditions.

Indentured servitude was especially common after Britain ended slavery in its Caribbean colonies in 1833. To replace enslaved labor, plantation owners brought millions of workers from India, China, and Africa to work in sugar plantations and mines across the British, French, Dutch, and Danish empires. Between 1834 and 1917, over 1.3 million Indian laborers were sent to distant colonies, creating large Indian diaspora communities in places like Jamaica, Trinidad, Mauritius, and Fiji.[109]

Although indentured servitude was not the same as chattel slavery—where enslaved people were considered property for life—many indentured laborers suffered terrible mistreatment. Some were tricked or kidnapped into signing contracts they could not read. Others faced extreme punishment for trying to escape. Their struggle is an important but often overlooked part of history.[110]

The "Duty Boys" of 1619

The story of slavery in North America did not begin with the arrival of Africans in Jamestown. It began in England with the **Project of 1619**—the transporting of **White, adolescent indentured servants to Jamestown**.

Duty Boys

In the spring of 1619, two English ships, the *Jonathan* and the *Duty*, arrived in Jamestown carrying 140 children who had been taken from the streets of England. Many of these **"Duty Boys"** had been held in London's Bridewell Prison, generally for vagrancy, since 1617

These children were **sent to the colonies to "learn a trade."** The Duty Boys were from eight to sixteen years of age, and forty percent were young girls. None of these children was of age to sign legal contracts of indenture. **Of the first 300 children brought to Jamestown, 12 remained alive after three years.** [111]

The planters had these servants for a finite period of time and tended to get as much out of them as they could. These servants often worked between twelve to sixteen hours a day. In 1619 John Rolfe, the man responsible for the tobacco industry wrote that there was a wanton "buying of men and boys." The historian Edmund Morgan wrote this was "a system of labor that treated men as things."[112]

The White Lion

A few months after the Duty Boys arrived, another ship landed near Jamestown in August of 1619—the **White Lion. This British ship traded "twenty and some odd" Africans for food**. This was recorded by John Rolph, whose wife was Pocahontas. John Rolph wrote that the Africans were traded for "victuals."

First Recorded African Slaves in Mainland North America
Presented over a graph representing the entire 364 years of the Trans-Atlantic Slave Trade

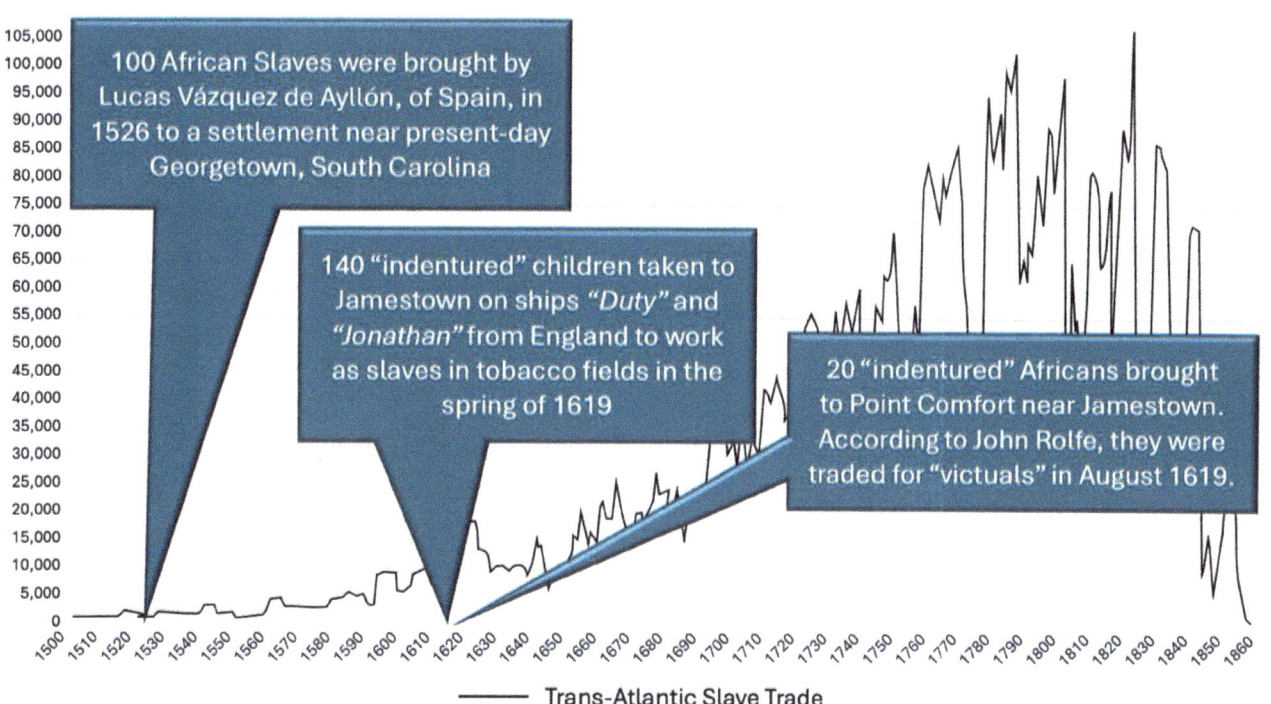

The Origins of Slavery in America

The Project of 1619 wasn't the beginning of slavery in the Americas. More than a century earlier, Portugal and Spain had already transported thousands of African slaves to South and Central America. By the time the English established Jamestown in 1607, slavery was already firmly entrenched in the Spanish and Portuguese colonies.

The First African Slaves in Mainland North America

The idea that African slavery in America began in 1619 is not accurate. Nearly a century earlier, in 1526, Spanish explorer Lucas Vázquez de Ayllón brought 100 enslaved Africans to a settlement called San Miguel de Gualdape, likely near present-day Georgetown, South Carolina. When Ayllón died, a mutiny broke out among the Spanish settlers. In a twist of fate, the African slaves helped suppress the rebellion. Soon after, the struggling colony collapsed. The Spanish survivors fled back to Hispaniola, but the Africans reportedly remained, integrating with local Indigenous tribes—perhaps the first free Black community in what would become the United States.[113]

Indentured Servants: The Forgotten Majority

Before the American Revolution, over two-thirds of European immigrants arrived in the colonies as indentured servants, working off the cost of their passage. Between the 16th and 18th centuries, around 320,000 indentured servants—primarily from England, Scotland, and Ireland—crossed the Atlantic to labor under harsh contracts. Many endured grueling conditions, but they were promised freedom, and often land, once their service ended.[114]

Transported Convicts: Criminals or the Desperate Poor?

Not all indentured servants came voluntarily. British authorities emptied jails, sending convicts—many guilty of minor offenses like stealing bread or failing to pay debts—to the colonies. Though treated as slaves and outcasts during their term of indenture, they still retained the hope of eventual freedom.[115]

A Stark Contrast: Indentured Servitude vs. Slavery

Of 500,000 European immigrants to America prior to the Revolution, around 320,000 were indentured servants, compared to about 269,300 enslaved Africans imported during the same period. Yet, their experiences were vastly different. While indentured servants faced brutality, they had a contractual path to freedom. African slaves, by contrast, were trapped in a system that condemned them—and their descendants—to lifelong bondage under laws that denied them even the faintest hope of liberty.

The Project of 1619 tells a more complex story than the simplified narrative of slavery's origins. It reveals that forced labor in America took many forms, but only one group—enslaved Africans—was permanently stripped of their humanity and future.[116]

How Slavery Became the Law

While both indentured servitude and slavery existed in early America, the defining difference became law. In the mid-1600s, colonial legislatures began passing statutes that codified lifelong slavery. In 1662, Virginia declared that children inherited the status of their mother, ensuring that slavery became hereditary. By the end of the 17th century, race-based chattel slavery had fully replaced indentured servitude as the dominant labor system in the American colonies.[117]

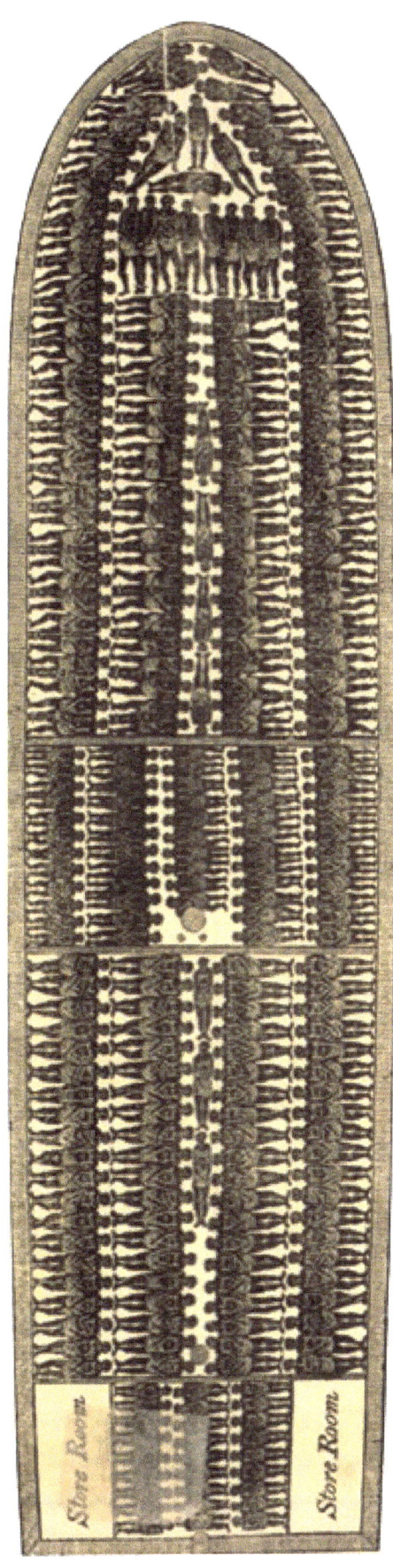

Slave Ship Brookes

The image on this page is one of the most famous drawings ever made about slavery. It shows how enslaved people were packed tightly into the British slave ship Brookes in 1788. The ship was designed to carry cargo, not people, but enslaved Africans were crammed in like supplies—stacked in rows with almost no space to move. This drawing was created by abolitionists (people who wanted to end slavery) in England to show the world the cruelty and inhumanity that defined the transatlantic slave trade.[118]

Britain was responsible for transporting about 2.5 million enslaved Africans to the New World—including over 300,000 to the British colonies in North America. These ships took people from Africa and forced them to work on plantations, mostly in the Caribbean and the American South. The people on board were treated not as human beings, but as property.

How Cramped Were the Conditions?

The Brookes was not supposed to carry more than 470 people, but slave traders ignored those limits. At one point, it carried 609 enslaved men, women, and children—more than the ship was built to hold.

How much space did each person have?

- **Men** – 6 feet long, 1 foot 4 inches wide (but crammed together, often with only 9 inches of width, forcing them to lay on their sides, or on top of each other).

- **Women** – 5 feet 10 inches by 1 foot 4 inches.

- **Boys** – 5 feet by 1 foot 2 inches.

- **Girls** – 4 feet 6 inches by 1 foot.

The space between decks was only 2 feet 7 inches high, meaning most people could not even sit up. They were forced to lie on top of each other for weeks at a time.

The reality of life below deck was horrifying. People were chained together at the wrists and ankles, packed so tightly that they could barely move. The heat, lack of fresh air, and terrible sanitation caused disease to spread quickly. Twenty-percent died.

A Picture That Changed the World

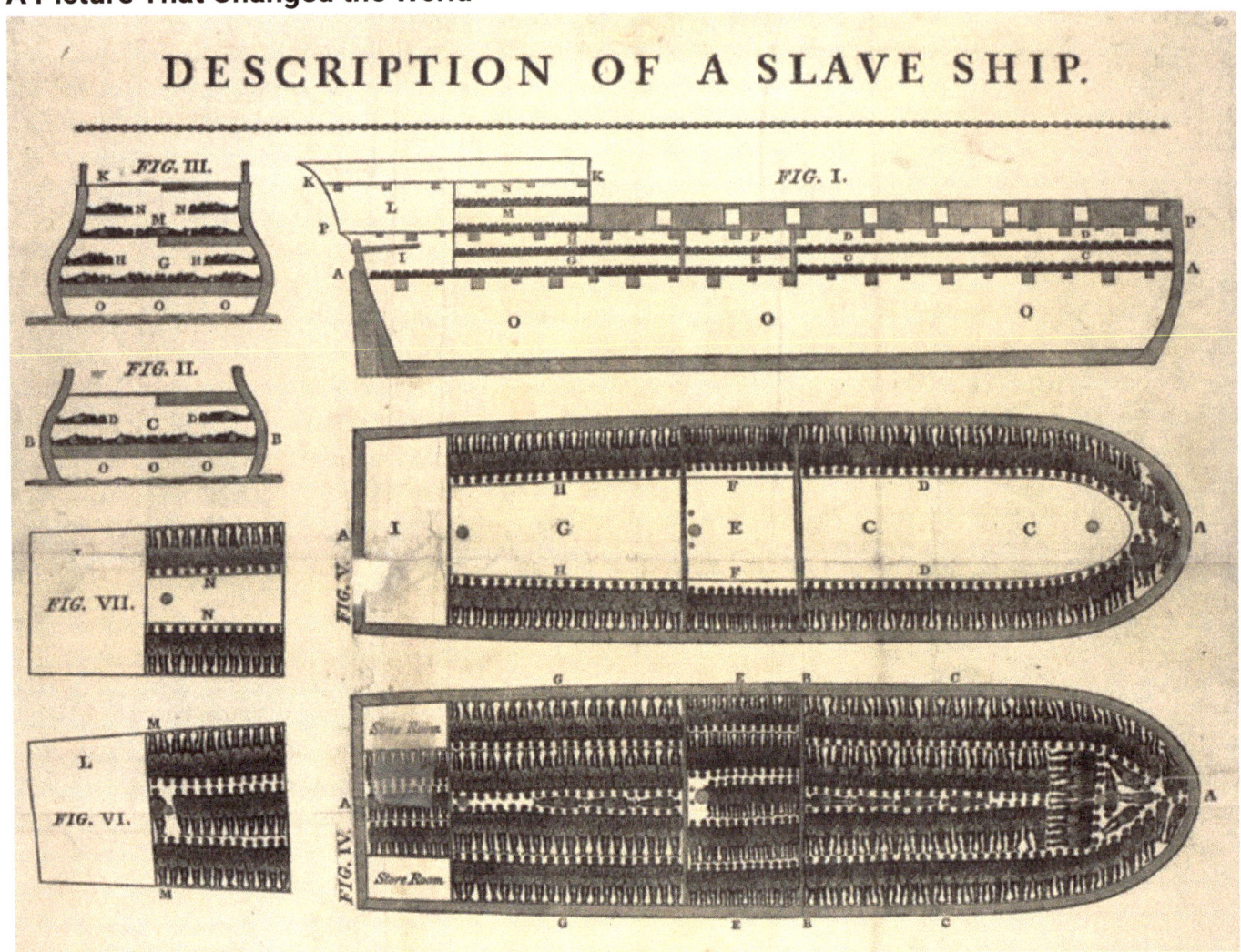

Life Aboard a Slave Ship

A survivor of the slave trade later described the suffering:

> **"The men, instead of lying on their backs, were placed on their sides, or on each other. In the morning, some were found dead."**

Slave traders forced the enslaved to come up on deck for "exercise," which they called "dancing"—but it was really just a way to keep them alive long enough to be sold. If the weather was bad, people stayed below deck for days or weeks, causing sickness to spread even faster.

One witness reported that during a storm:

> **"Fifty slaves perished in that small space of time."**

Even the sailors on board suffered from the stench and disease. Some people claimed the slave trade helped train new sailors, but in reality, many died from the conditions on board.

Ending the Slave Trade

The Brookes drawing became one of the most powerful tools in the fight to end slavery. Abolitionists in Great Britain used it to show how inhumane the slave trade was, helping to convince people that it needed to stop. People who had never seen the inside of a slave ship were shocked.

The movement to end the transatlantic slave trade gained momentum, and in 1807, two major nations took action. **The United States passed a law banning participation in the slave trade on March 2, 1807**, but it couldn't take effect immediately until the 20-year limit ended in 1808. The law was written with a "trigger clause," making it **officially take effect on January 1, 1808**.

William Wilberforce was inspired by revelations of the Slave Ship Brooks and lead the fight against the slave trade in England. Three weeks after the U.S. law was passed, **Britain passed its law on March 25, 1807**.[119] Though these laws stopped the legal importation of enslaved people, both nations remained involved in slavery—Great Britain being primarily involved in the Caribbean. The fight for full abolition was far from over.

The images and descriptions of the Brookes represent one of the darkest aspects of human history. They serve as a stark reminder of the atrocities committed and the suffering endured. Yet, they also reflect the power of truth and exposure to spur social change. The horrors revealed in the Brookes engraving galvanized the abolitionist movement, ultimately challenging the moral conscience of a nation and the world.

DESCRIPTION OF A SLAVE SHIP.

The PLAN and SECTIONS annexed exhibit a slave ship with the slaves stowed.* In order to give a representation of the trade against which no complaint of exaggeration could be brought by those concerned in it, the *Brooks* is here described, a ship well known in the trade, and the first mentioned in the report delivered to the House of Commons last year by Captain Parrey, who was sent to Liverpool by Government to take the dimensions of the ships employed in the African slave trade from that port. These plans and sections are on a scale of the 8th of an inch to a foot.

DIMENSIONS OF THE SHIP

	Feet	Inches
Length of the Lower Deck, gratings, bulk-heads, included At AA	100	0
Breadth of *Beam* on the *Lower Deck* inside, BB	25	4
Depth of *Hold*, OOO from ceiling to ceiling	10	0
Height between decks from deck to deck	5	8
Length of the *Men's Room*, CC on the lower deck	46	0
Breadth of the *Men's Room*, CC on the lower deck	25	4
Length of the *Platforms*, DD in the men's room	46	0
Breadth of the *Platforms* in men's rooms on each side	6	0
Length of the *Boys Room*, EE	13	9
Breadth of the *Boys Room*	25	0
Breadth of *Platforms*, FF in boy's room	6	0
Length of the *Women's Room*, GG	28	6
Breadth of the *Women's Room*	23	6
Length of the *Platforms* in women's room	6	0
Breadth of the *Platforms* in women's room	10	6
Length of the *Gun Room*, II on the lower deck	10	6
Breadth of the *Gun Room* on the lower deck	12	0
Length of the *Quarter Deck*, KK	33	6
Breadth of the *Quarter Deck*	19	6
Length of the *Cabin*, LL	14	0
Height of the *Cabin*	5	2
Length of the *Half Deck*, MM	16	6
Height of the *Half Deck*	6	2
Length of the *Platforms*, NN on the half deck	16	6
Breadth of the *Platforms* on the half deck	6	0
Upper deck, PP:		
Nominal tonnage	297	
Supposed tonnage by measurement	320	
Number of Seamen	45	

The number of slaves which this vessel actually carried appears from the accounts given to Capt. Parrey by the slave-merchants themselves as follows:

Men	351	
Women	127	Total
Boys	90	609
Girls	41	

The room allowed each description of slaves in the plan is:
- To the Men, 6 feet by 1 foot 4 inches.
- Women, 5 feet 10 in. by 1 foot 4 in.
- Boys, 5 feet by 1 foot 2 in.
- Girls 4 feet 6 in. by 1 foot

* This is the usual manner of placing the slaves, but it varies according to the position of the ship, and the practice of the different commanders.

With this allowance of room, the utmost number that can be stowed in a vessel of the dimension of the *Brooks*, is as follows, (being the number exhibited in the plan) and is less than 1 1/2 to a ton, viz. †

			On the Plan	Actually carried
Men - on the lower deck, at	CC		124	
Ditto on the platform of ditto,	CC	DD	66	190	351
Boys - lower deck EE	--	--	46		
Ditto - platform FF	--	--	24	70	90
Women - lower deck, GG	--	--	83		
Ditto - platform, HH	--	--	40	183	127
Women Half deck, MM	--	--	36		
Ditto Platform ditto, NN	--	--	24		
Girls Gun room, II	--	--	27	41	
General Total			470	609	

The principal difference is in the *men*. It must be observed, that the *men*, from whom only insurrections are to be feared, are kept continually in irons, and must be stowed in the room allotted for them, which is of a more secure construction than the rest.

In this ship the number of men actually carried was ——— 351
The number of men stated in the plan at 1 foot 4 inches each ——— 190
Difference 161

As the ship on this plan would stow 42 women, boys and girls in the places here allotted to them than she did carry, supposing that number of men taken from the men's room, and placed in their stead, this will reduce the number of men to 309 in the men's room; of course the room allowed them, instead of being 16 inches as in the plan, was in reality only 10 inches each; but if the whole number of 351 were stowed in the men's room, they had only 9 inches each to lay in.

The men therefore, instead of lying on their backs, were placed, as is usual, in full ships, on their sides, or on each other. In which last situation they are not unfrequently found dead in the morning.

The longitudinal section, fig. I. shews the manner in which the slaves were placed on all the decks and platforms, which is also further illustrated by the transverse sections, fig. II. & III. By which it appears, that the height between the decks is 5 feet 8 inches, which, allowing 2 inches for the platform and its bearers, makes the height between the decks and the platform 2 feet 9 inches; but the platform and their knees, with the carlings, taking 4 inches on an average, this space is unequally divided, and above or under the platforms cannot be estimated at more than 2 feet 7 inches; so that the slaves cannot, when placed either on or under the platform, relieve themselves by sitting up; the very short ones excepted, nor can *they*, except on board the larger vessels. The average of 9 vessels measured by Captain Parrey, being mostly large ships, was only 5 feet 2 inches. The height of the Venus between decks was 4 feet 2 inches; of the Kitty 4 feet 4 inches, both of which had platforms. In these smaller vessels therefore, they have not 2 feet under or upon the platforms.

In fig. I. under the upper deck PP, and the lower deck AA, the beams and intervening carlings are represented by shaded squares. The beams are also introduced on one side of the transverse sections II and III, in order to shew the space which a slave placed under a beam has to lie and breathe in.

† It must be noted, that every possible advantage of stowing is allowed in the plan. There are or ought to be in each apartment one or more poopoo tubs; there are also stanchions to support the platforms and decks; for which no deduction is made; but the deck is supposed clear of every incumbrance whatever.

Transatlantic Slave Trade

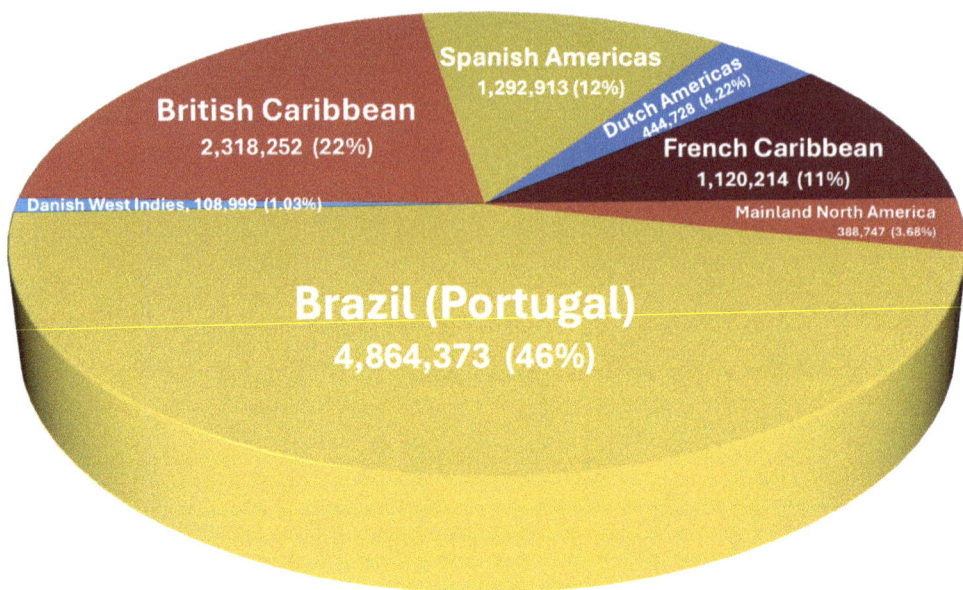

Above: Six civilized European nations were heavily involved in the Trans-Atlantic Slave Trade. Portugal, which had been given permission by the Pope in 1450 to place Africans into perpetual slavery, was by far the greatest offender, with nearly five million. Great Britain was next, with about 2.5 million. The Spanish and French each brought over a million. The Netherlands brought 444 thousand to the Dutch Americas, and Denmark shipped 109,000 slaves to the Danish West Indies.[120]

Breakdown of Mainland North America African Slave Imports

British Flag Merchants	264,912	France	8,876
New England Colonial Merchants under British Rule	37,013	Spain	1,851
Total under British Rule	**301,925**	Denmark/Baltic	1,489
		Netherlands	1,212
U.S.A. (Under 20 year clause, 1789-1808)	**63,927**	Portugal/Brazil	382
During the Articles of Confederation	5,086		
Illegal Smuggling after constitutional ban until 1860	4,505	**Total North America Slave Imports**	**388,747**

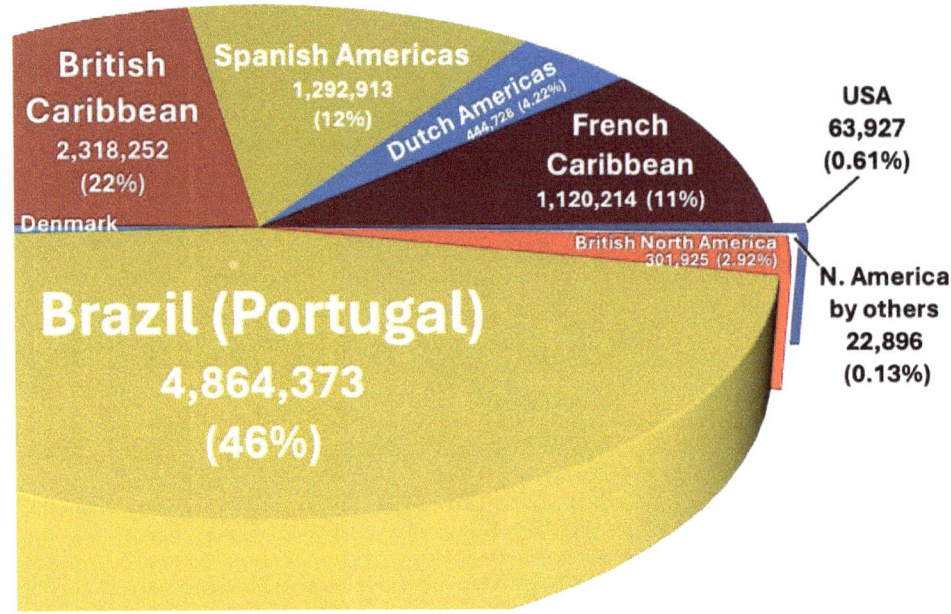

Of the 10.5+ million African Slaves brought to the Americas, **388,747** landed in Mainland North America.

Of those, **301,925 were brought by British and New England ships sailing under the British crown prior to 1776.**

American ships brought 5,086 under the Articles of Confederation and **63,927 that were allowed by the 20 year compromise** in the U.S. Constitution when America could finally regulate the trade.

Horrors of Slavery in Africa

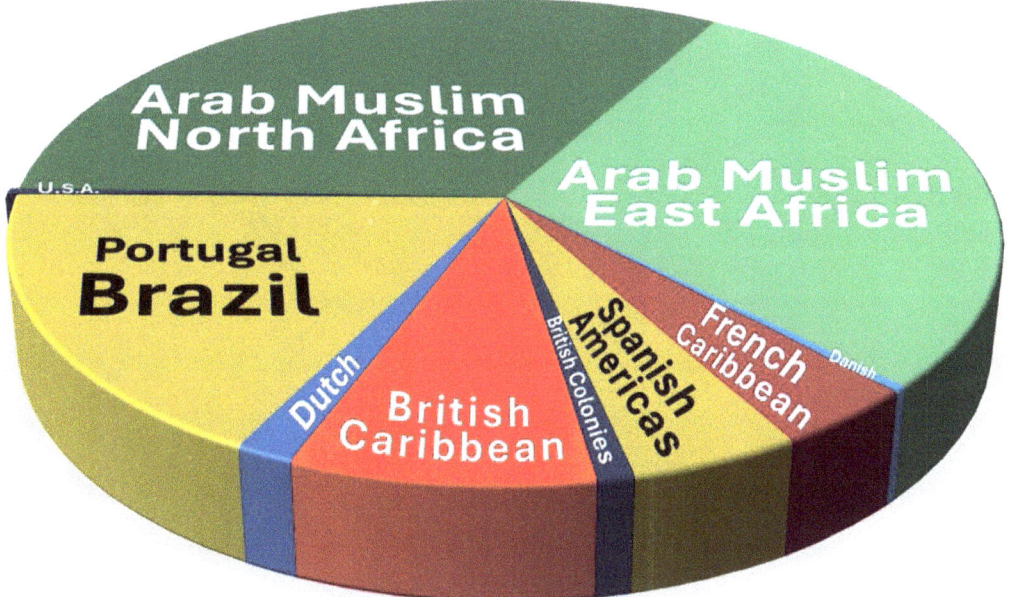

Above: Chart of African slave trade. Representation of the 1,300 year Arab Muslim slave trade is approximate.[121]

Below: The Congo Rubber Terror (1885-1909)

Below: At the Berlin Conference of 1885, Belgian King Leopold was given the Congo Free State in Africa as his personal kingdom. He was going to "civilize and uplift the Congolese population." But the pneumatic tire had been invented by John Dunlap of Scotland. This drove demand for rubber sky high and he enslaved nearly the entire population.[122]

Approximately **35 million were enslaved** and forced by terrible cruelty to meet rubber production quotas. The next decades came to be known as the **"Rubber Terror."** If a village did not produce enough rubber, members of the 18,000 man "Force Publique" cut off the hands of thousands of children to encourage compliance.[123] Slavery and death over that 25 year period exceeded that of the entire 364 years of the Trans-Atlantic Slave Trade and the Arab-Muslim Slave Trade. **Ten to fifteen million slaves died as Leopold became the richest man in the world**. He was worth up to $18 billion in today's dollars. Author Mark Twain's satire *King Leopold's Soliloquy* voiced outrage over the enslavement and massacre of the Congolese people. Leopold was forced to cede the Congo to Belgium in 1908. His funeral cortege was booed as it passed through Brussels.[124]

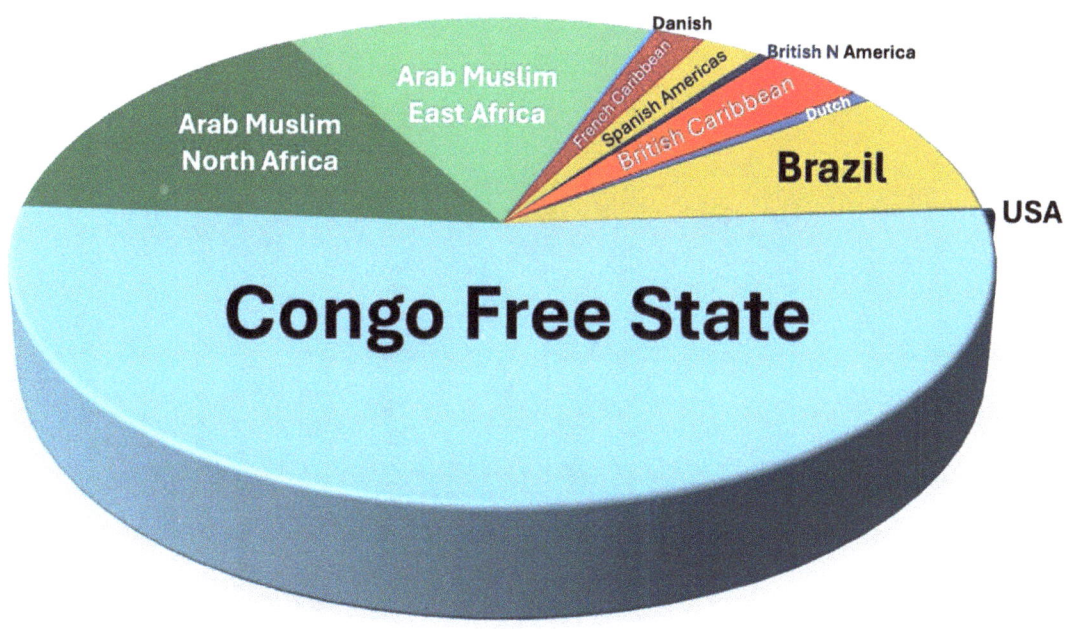

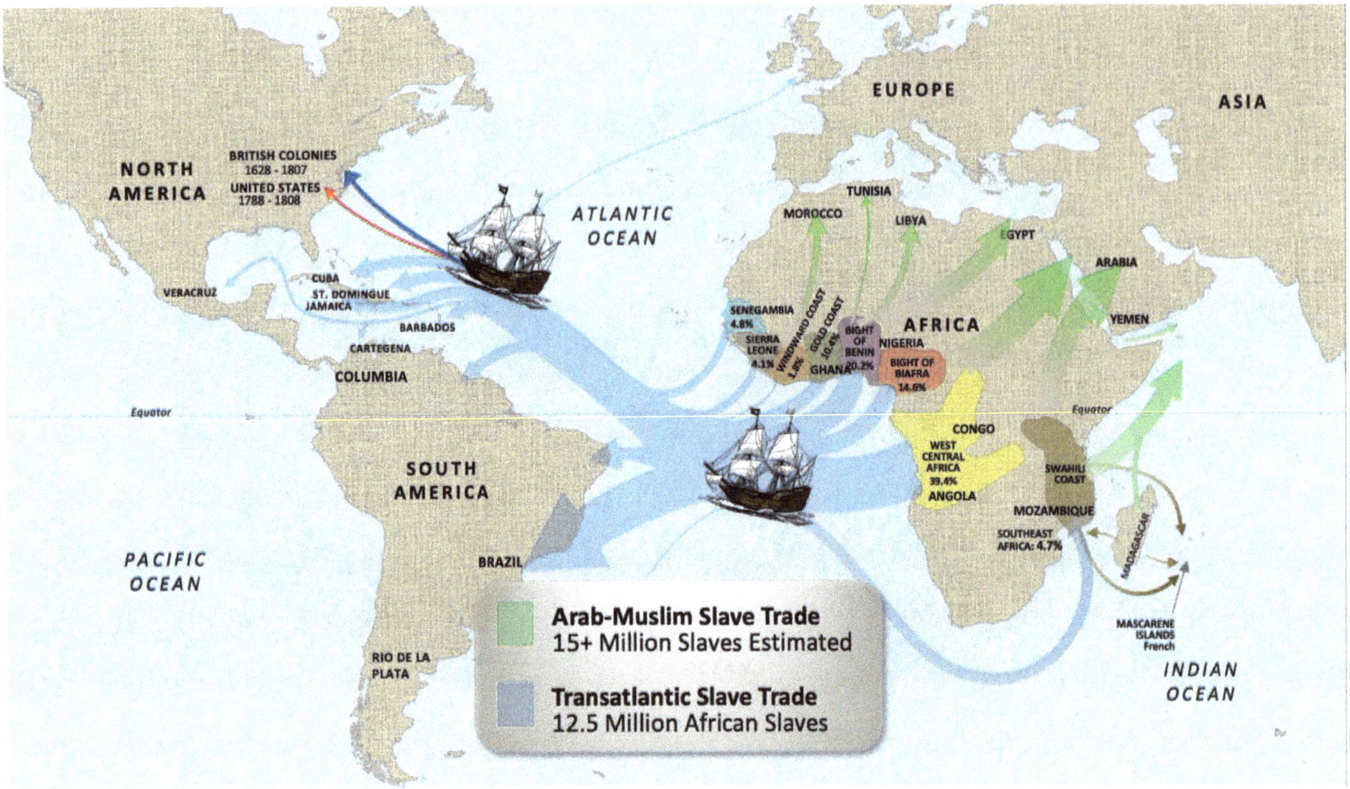

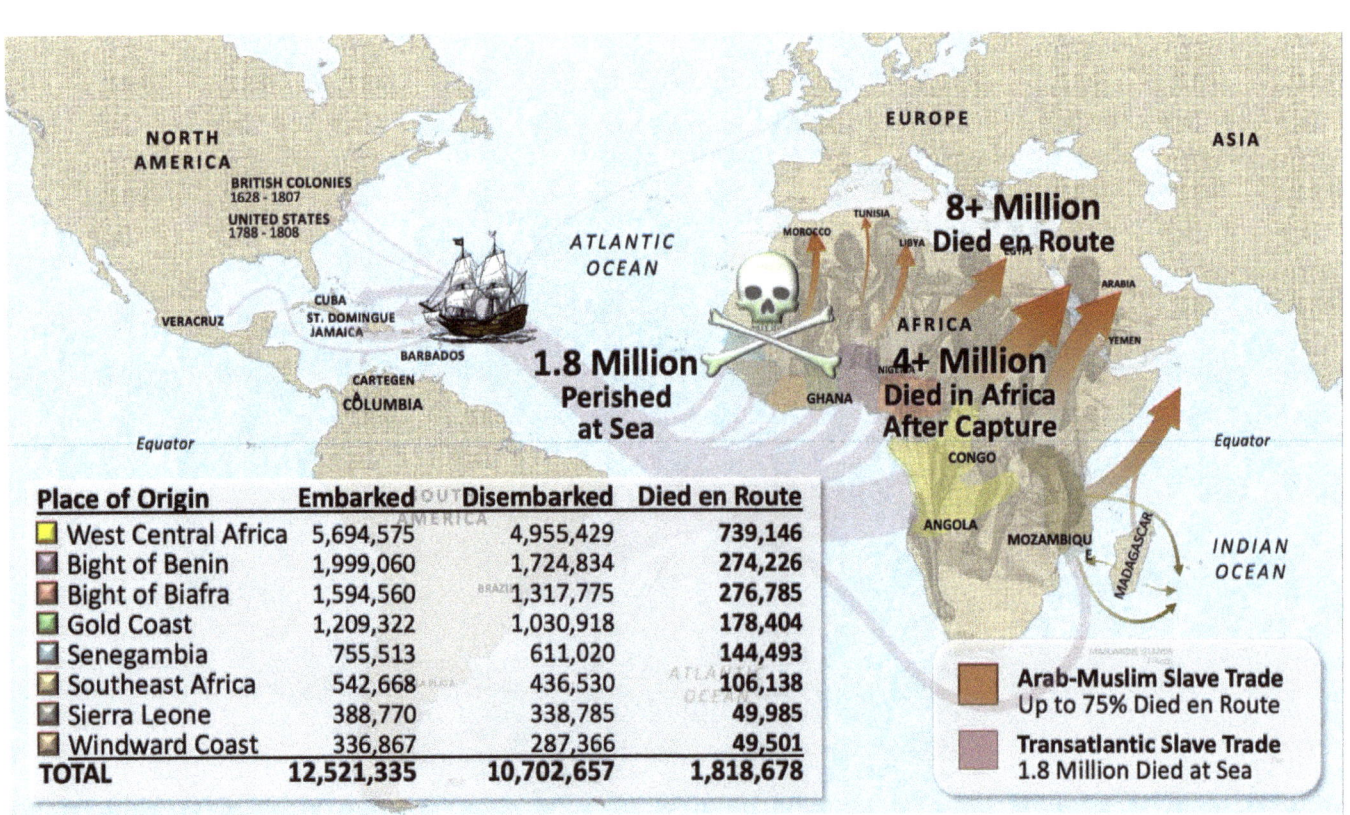

Representations of Trans-Atlantic Slave Trade Transport and Death[125]

Place of Origin	Embarked	Disembarked	Died en Route
West Central Africa	5,694,575	4,955,429	**739,146**
Bight of Benin	1,999,060	1,724,834	**274,226**
Bight of Biafra	1,594,560	1,317,775	**276,785**
Gold Coast	1,209,322	1,030,918	**178,404**
Senegambia	755,513	611,020	**144,493**
Southeast Africa	542,668	436,530	**106,138**
Sierra Leone	388,770	338,785	**49,985**
Windward Coast	336,867	287,366	**49,501**
TOTAL	**12,521,335**	**10,702,657**	**1,818,678**

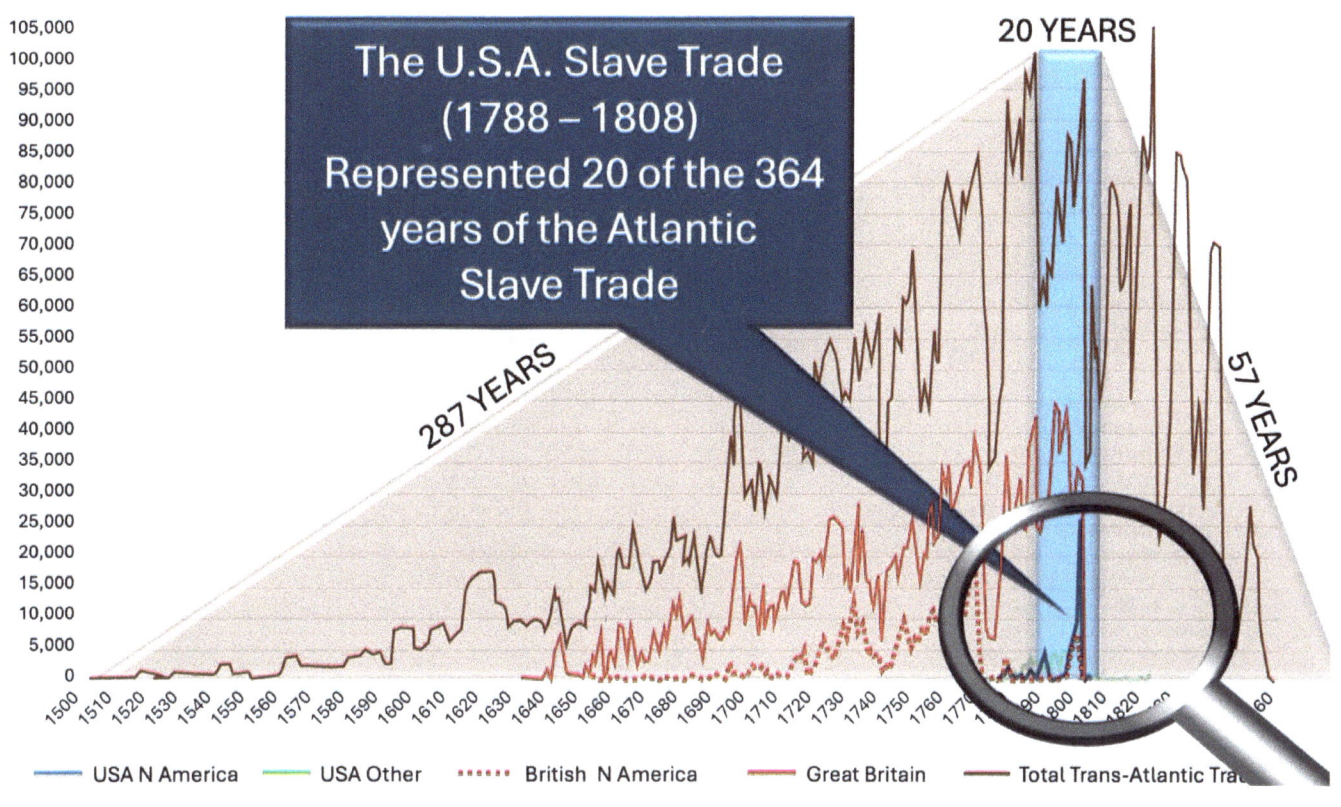

Above: U.S.A., British North America, all British, and total slave trade

Below: Transport and death by slave-trading nation

Country	Slaves Delivered	Died at Sea
United States	63,927	14,664
Danish West Indies	108,999	19,307
British North America	264,912	52,674
Dutch Americas	444,728	79,096
French Caribbean	1,120,214	216,436
Spanish Americas	1,292,913	176,501
British Caribbean	2,318,252	526,117
Brazil (Portugal)	4,864,373	748,450
Total	**10,702,654**	**Total 1,818,678**

12.5 million Africans were captured, mostly by other Africans, sold to traders, and marched to the sea. They were packed aboard slave ships in chains and shipped to the Americas as slaves.

1.8+ million perished at sea.

*Each standing figure represents **100,000 people** who arrived alive at their port of debarkation*
*Each prone figure represents **100,000 people** who died at sea*

Source: SlaveVoyages.org

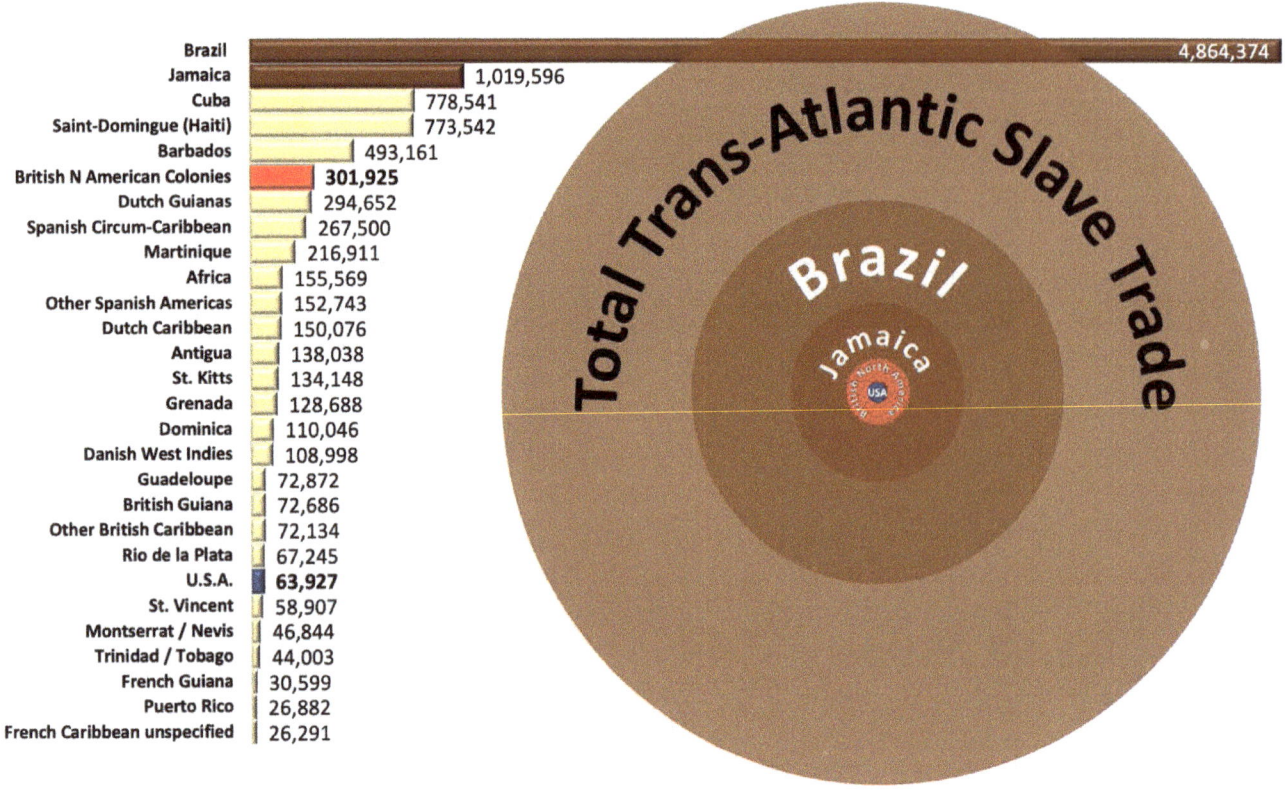

Above: Western hemisphere Trans-Atlantic slave trade destinations.

Below: This screenshot displays SlaveVoyages.org analysis of African Slaves transported under U.S. ships to the United States between 1788 and 1808. It also gives the number of slaves transported by New England slave merchants during that same period. The majority of their destinations outside of the United States were to the Caribbean and West Indies. The data on slides related to the slave trade were extracted from this database, the gold standard in slave trade research. The image below is used with permission from Slave.Voyages.org.

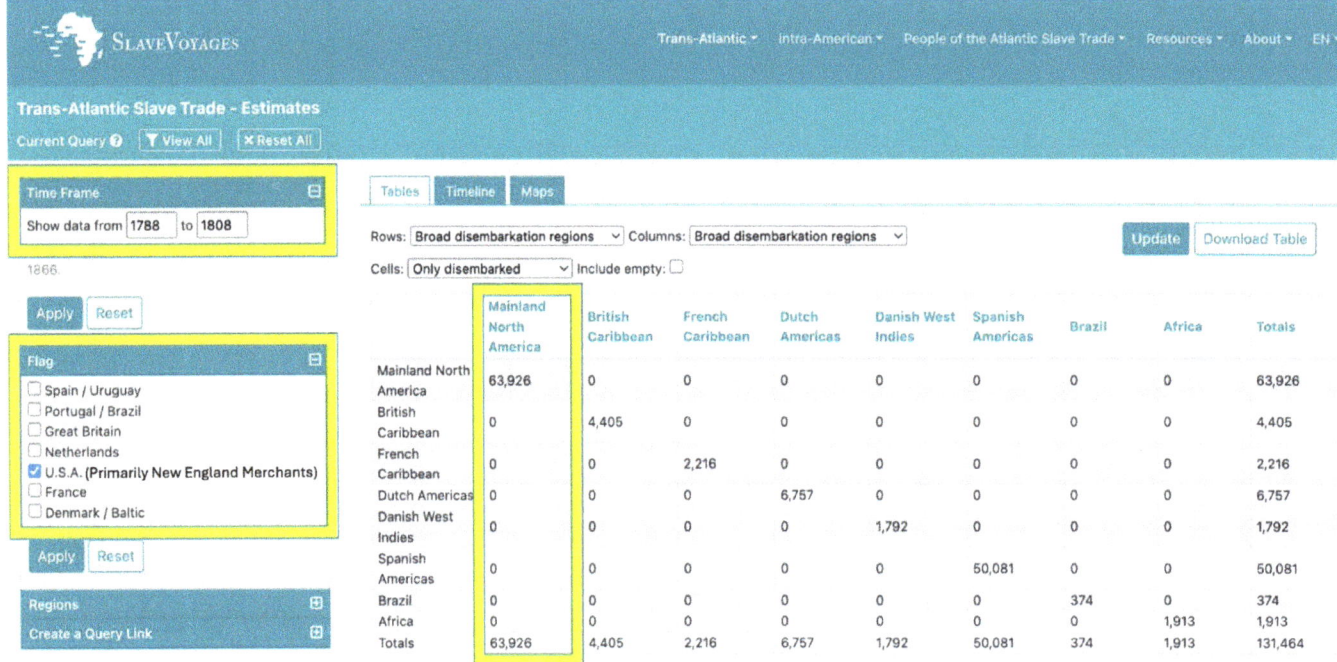

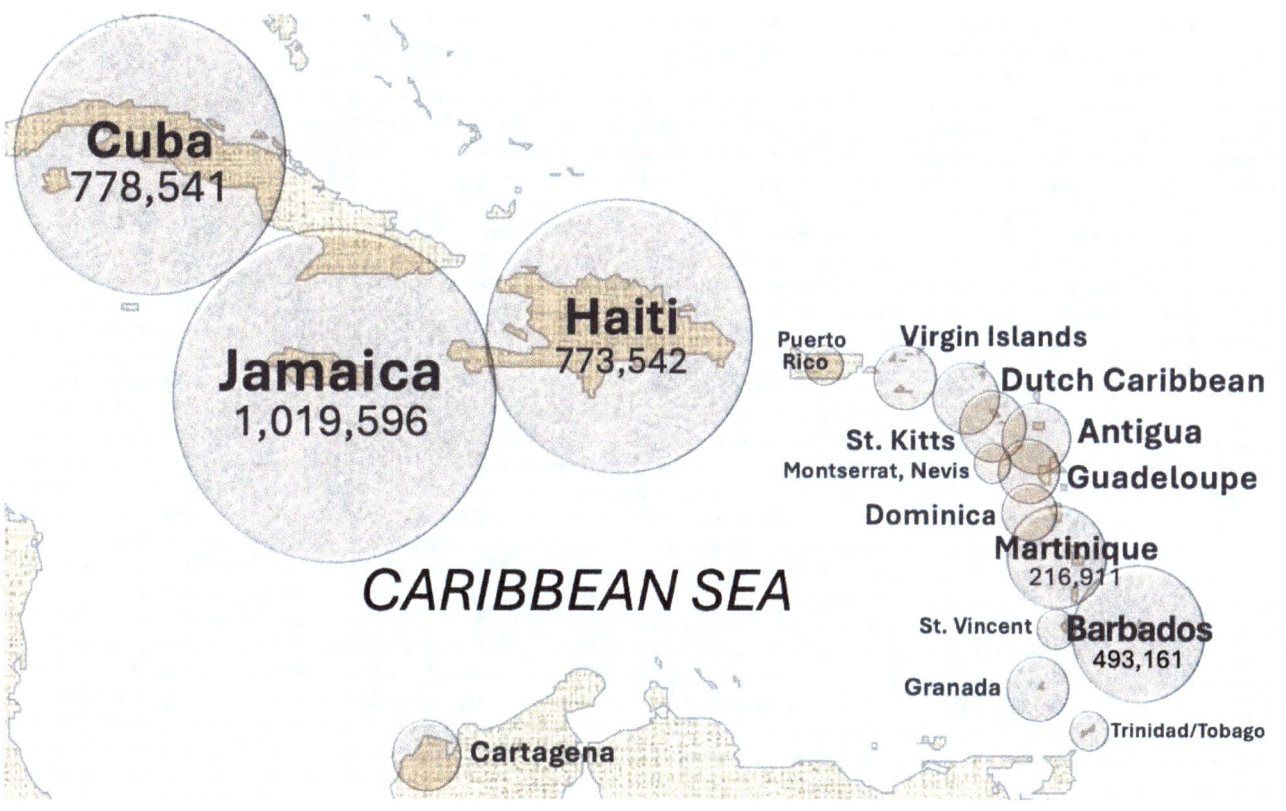

"Bubbles" in the maps above and below represent the relative number of imported slaves.

Above: Five million enslaved Africans arrived in South America, most taken to Brazil by Portuguese traders.

Below: Five million were taken to the Caribbean and West Indies, of which the British were responsible for nearly half.[126]

The Three-Fifths Compromise

The Three-Fifths Compromise: A Difficult Decision

The U.S. Constitution decided that each state's population would determine its number of representatives in Congress. But there was a problem—should enslaved people be counted as part of the population?

Some Southern states wanted to count all enslaved people to increase their representation and power in Congress—even though enslaved people had no rights and couldn't vote. But Northern states argued that if enslaved individuals weren't treated as citizens, they shouldn't be counted as part of the voting population.

This led to a fierce debate. If the South got its way, it would have 38 representatives to the North's 36, giving pro-slavery states control of Congress. If the North's plan won, Northern states would have a clear 36 to 25 majority, weakening the South's influence. The South said, "No." Neither side would agree to the other's plan.[127]

Finding a Middle Ground

James Wilson of Pennsylvania proposed a compromise—enslaved people would be counted as three-fifths (60 percent) of a person for both federal taxation and representation. While this 3/5 number seems strange today, it was not about measuring a person's worth. It was a way to manage the South's power in Congress while still keeping them in the Union.

By counting only three-fifths of enslaved people, the North held a slight majority in Congress—35 representatives to the South's 30. This meant pro-slavery states couldn't fully control federal laws. Without this compromise, Southern states might have refused to join the United States at all. Alexander Hamilton later said, "No union could have possibly been formed" without it.

What It Meant for America

The three-fifths compromise weakened the power of slaveholding states, preventing them from having control over national policies. It didn't end slavery, but it made it harder for the South to pass laws that expanded it.

Although the compromise wasn't perfect, it was an important step toward creating a government where all people could eventually be free. Later, after the Civil War, the 13th Amendment abolished slavery entirely, making sure no one could ever be counted as "three-fifths" of a person again.

A Step Toward Change

The three-fifths compromise was not a perfect solution, but it was part of a long struggle to limit the power of slavery in America. Over time, more and more people spoke out against slavery, and new laws were passed to challenge it. The fight for freedom didn't stop with the *Constitution*—it continued through the Civil War, the 13th Amendment, and beyond.

This debate also showed that compromise was essential in forming the United States. Without it, the Southern states might have refused to join the Union, leaving the country divided before it had even begun. By agreeing to the compromise, the Founders ensured that America could move forward, setting the stage for future generations to continue working toward true equality.

THE CONSTITUTION'S THREE-FIFTHS COMPROMISE & REPRESENTATION

North	Slaves	Total Population	Pct. Slave	Population Minus Slaves	3/5 of Slave Population	Effective for Representation	South Plan	North Plan	Actual 3/5's Plan
Pennsylvania	3,707	443,611	1%	439,904	2,224	442,128	9	9	8
Massachusetts	0	378,566	0%	378,566	0	378,566	7	7	8
New York	21,193	340,241	6%	319,048	12,716	331,764	7	6	6
Connecticut	2,648	237,655	1%	235,007	1,589	236,596	5	5	5
New Jersey	11,423	184,139	6%	172,716	6,854	179,570	4	3	4
New Hampshire	157	141,899	0%	141,742	94	141,836	3	3	3
Rhode Island	958	69,112	1%	68,154	575	68,729	1	1	1
Total	**40,086**	**1,880,564**	**2%**	**1,755,137**	**24,052**	**1,779,189**	**36**	**36**	**35**
South									
Virginia	292,627	747,550	39%	454,923	175,576	630,499	15	9	10
North Carolina	100,783	395,005	26%	294,222	60,470	354,692	8	6	5
Maryland	103,036	319,728	32%	216,692	61,822	278,514	6	4	6
South Carolina	107,094	249,073	43%	141,979	64,256	206,235	5	3	5
Georgia	29,264	82,548	36%	53,284	17,558	70,842	2	1	3
Delaware	8,887	59,096	15%	50,209	5,332	55,541	1	1	1
Total	**654,121**	**1,926,677**	**34%**	**1,211,309**	**385,015**	**1,596,324**	**38**	**25**	**30**

Source: 1790 U.S. Census © 2024 Charles A Castleberry

THREE-FIFTHS COMPROMISE BY REGION

U.S. House Representatives by State

North	South Plan	North Plan	Three Fifths Compromise
Pennsylvania	9	9	8
Massachusetts	7	7	8
New York	7	6	6
Connecticut	5	5	5
New Jersey	4	3	4
New Hampshire	3	3	3
Rhode Island	1	1	1
Total	**36**	**36**	**35**
South			
Virginia	15	9	10
North Carolina	8	6	5
Maryland	6	4	6
South Carolina	5	3	5
Georgia	2	1	3
Delaware	1	1	1
Total	**38**	**25**	**30**

Source: 1790 U.S. Census

NH 3/3/3
New York 7/6/6
MA 7/7/8
CT 5/5/5
Rhode Island 1/1/1
Pennsylvania 9/9/8
New Jersey 4/3/4
Delaware 1/1/1
Maryland 6/4/6
Virginia 15/9/10
North Carolina 8/6/5
South Carolina 5/3/5
Georgia 2/1/3

Key: Plan
Left — South Plan
Center — North Plan
Right — 3/5 Compromise

© 2024 Charles A Castleberry

The Three-Fifths and 20-Year Compromises

The Constitution: Racist or Not?
Many today believe that the U.S. Constitution declared Black Americans to be "three-fifths of a person." This misunderstanding has fueled claims that our founding documents were inherently racist. The reality, however, is quite different.

The Three-Fifths Compromise was not a statement of human worth—**it was a strategic constitutional measure to limit the power of slaveholding states**. Southern states wanted enslaved individuals fully counted in the population to gain more congressional representation and more influence in presidential elections. Northern delegates, many of whom opposed slavery, argued that if the South treated enslaved people as property, they should not be counted at all, but taxed as property. The compromise prevented the Southern states from gaining excessive political control and, in doing so, slowed the spread of slavery.

More importantly, **by limiting the political power of the Southern states, the compromise helped lead to enough will in Congress to pass legislation on March 2, 1807, banning U.S. involvement in the international slave trade**, to take effect on January 1, 1808. President Jefferson had encouraged this action in his December 2, 1806, "State of the Union" letter to Congress, where he praised them for being the body that would finally remove the nation from participating in such a barbaric trade.

A Delicate Balancing Act
This compromise also played a key role in shaping the balance of power between North and South, influencing future legislative battles over slavery. While the Southern states sought to maintain and expand slavery, the restriction on their representation prevented them from gaining unchecked influence in the federal government. Over time, as free states grew in population and influence, they were able to push back more effectively against the expansion of slavery. However, it took our nation's deadliest war and a constitutional amendment to end it.

Additionally, the idea that the Constitution was designed to protect slavery ignores the broader historical context. Many of the Founding Fathers were deeply troubled by the institution of slavery, and several took active steps to restrict or abolish it in their respective states. The Northwest Ordinance of 1787, passed under the Articles of Confederation and reaffirmed under the new Constitution, prohibited slavery in new territories north of the Ohio River. This demonstrated that even in the nation's infancy, leaders took steps to curtail the spread of slavery.

Our Founding Fathers were not perfect men, but they laid the foundation for a system that ultimately led to freedom for all. The Constitution, far from being a document that enshrined racism, became the very tool used to abolish slavery and expand liberty through its amendment process. The Three-Fifths Compromise is a reminder that even in difficult circumstances, strategic decisions can bend the arc of history toward justice.

The Twenty-Year Compromise
The Constitution included another important compromise regarding slavery: a twenty-year delay before Congress could ban the importation of enslaved people. This provision, found in Article 1, Section 9, Clause 1, prevented Congress from stopping the transatlantic slave trade until January 1, 1808.

Hamilton later explained to New York's ratifying convention that *"without this indulgence, no union could have possibly been formed."*[128]

Although this delay allowed the slave trade to continue for two more decades, it didn't stop individual states from taking action. Many Northern states outlawed slavery during this period, but some Southern states—especially South Carolina—ramped up their imports of enslaved people before the deadline.

When the twenty-year period was about to end, Congress acted quickly. **On March 2, 1807, Congress passed the law banning American participation in the transatlantic slave trade, with the ban taking effect on January 1, 1808.** Remarkably, this occurred three weeks before Britain's own abolition of the trade, underscoring America's early—if imperfect—step toward moral leadership. The law had a built-in "trigger" that made it go into effect automatically at the start of 1808. No further votes or legislative actions were required.

However, even after the ban, illegal smuggling continued. Historians estimate that about 5,000 enslaved people were secretly brought into the U.S. after 1808. Still, this number was small compared to the 2.9 million Africans were enslaved and transported to the Americas by Spain and Portugal during the same period.[129]

A Changing Nation

Before the *Constitution*, **under the Articles of Confederation, the federal government had no power to regulate trade**, meaning each state set its own policy on slavery. The new *Constitution* changed that, but only after the twenty-year waiting period. However, prior to 1808, every state except South Carolina had banned the importation of slaves from Africa.[130]

The compromise also reflected the Founders' attempt to balance immediate union with future justice. They knew that without agreement, the southern states would refuse to join the new Constitution—and the dream of a single republic would collapse before birth. The framers therefore accepted a flawed provision, not to enshrine slavery, but to create the framework through which it could one day be abolished by law rather than entrenched by disunion. In that sense, the Constitution was both a shield and a time-bomb—protecting unity while setting a fuse under the very institution it temporarily tolerated.

This compromise was one of many that held the young nation together. Northern states accepted the delay to keep the Southern states in the Union, and Southern states agreed to the future federal ban on the transatlantic slave trade. While this was not an immediate victory for abolition, it helped limit the expansion of slavery in America.

Jefferson may have lost thirty years earlier when Congress struck his antislavery clause from *The Declaration of Independence*—but he was given a second chance, and this time, it worked:

> "I congratulate you, fellow citizens, on the approach of the period at which you may interpose your authority constitutionally to withdraw the citizens of the United States from all further participation in those violations of human rights."   —Thomas Jefferson, State of the Union Message, Dec. 2, 1806

Summary

The charts on the following pages show how the transatlantic slave trade changed leading up to and after the 1808 ban. Notice how U.S. slave imports averaged just 1,026 per year after the *Constitution* was signed, but skyrocketed as the twenty-year deadline approached. In 1807 alone, imports surged past 25,000—mostly because South Carolina's slave owners feared Congress might vote to ban the trade as soon as they were allowed to.

At the time, there was no guarantee that Congress would take action—the *Constitution* only prevented them from banning the trade before 1808. Many feared Northern lawmakers would heed **Jefferson's plea to "withdraw the citizens of the United States from all further participation in those violations of human rights."** They were right. Congress acted at the first lawful opportunity—March 2, 1807—and the ban took effect on January 1, 1808, the earliest date the Constitution allowed.

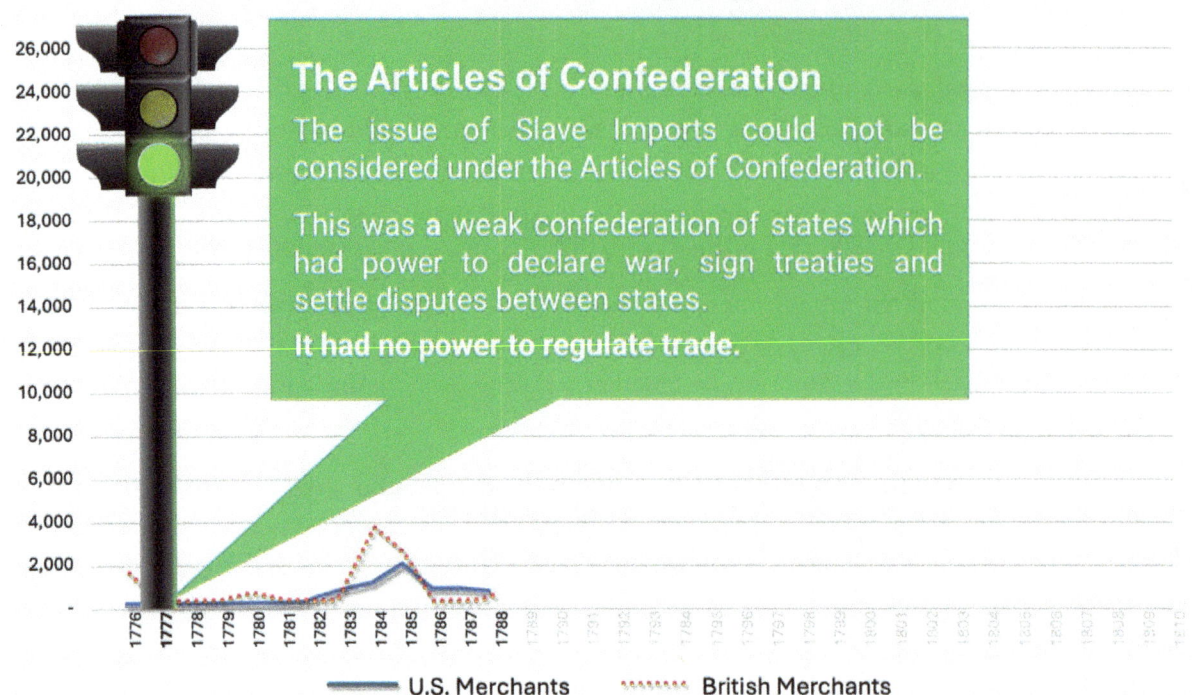

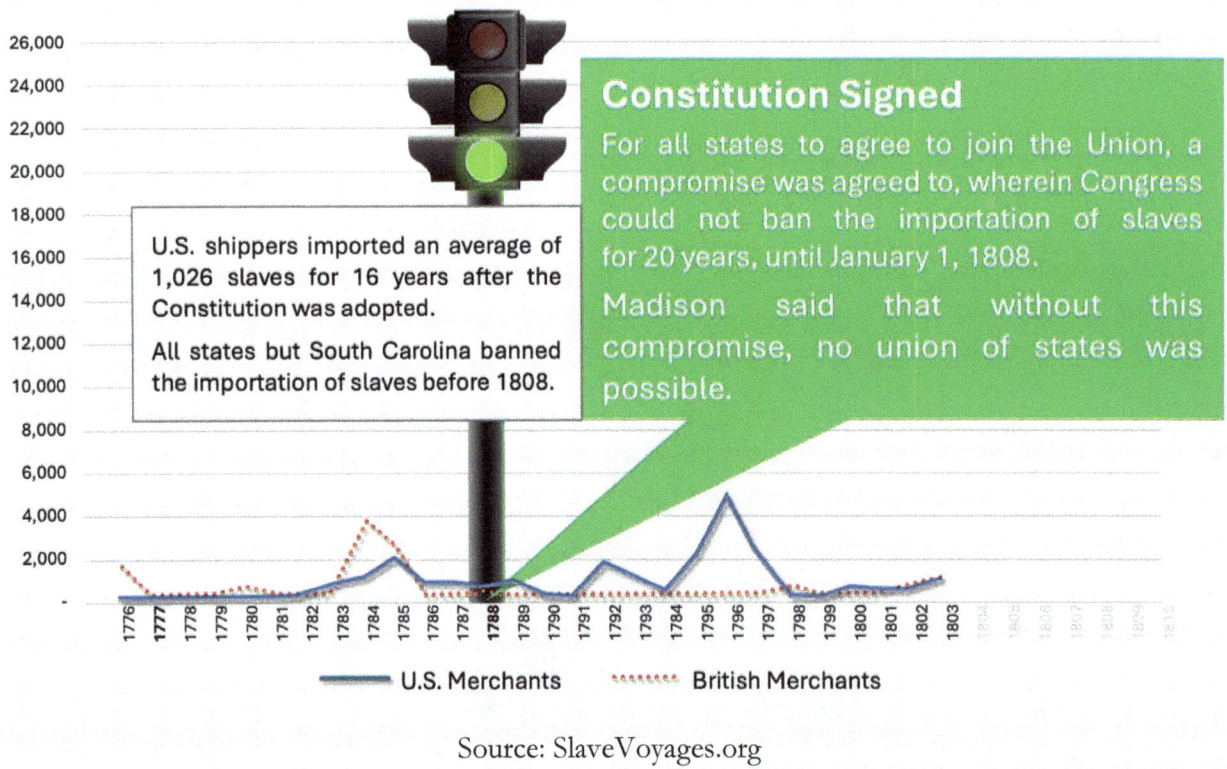

Source: SlaveVoyages.org

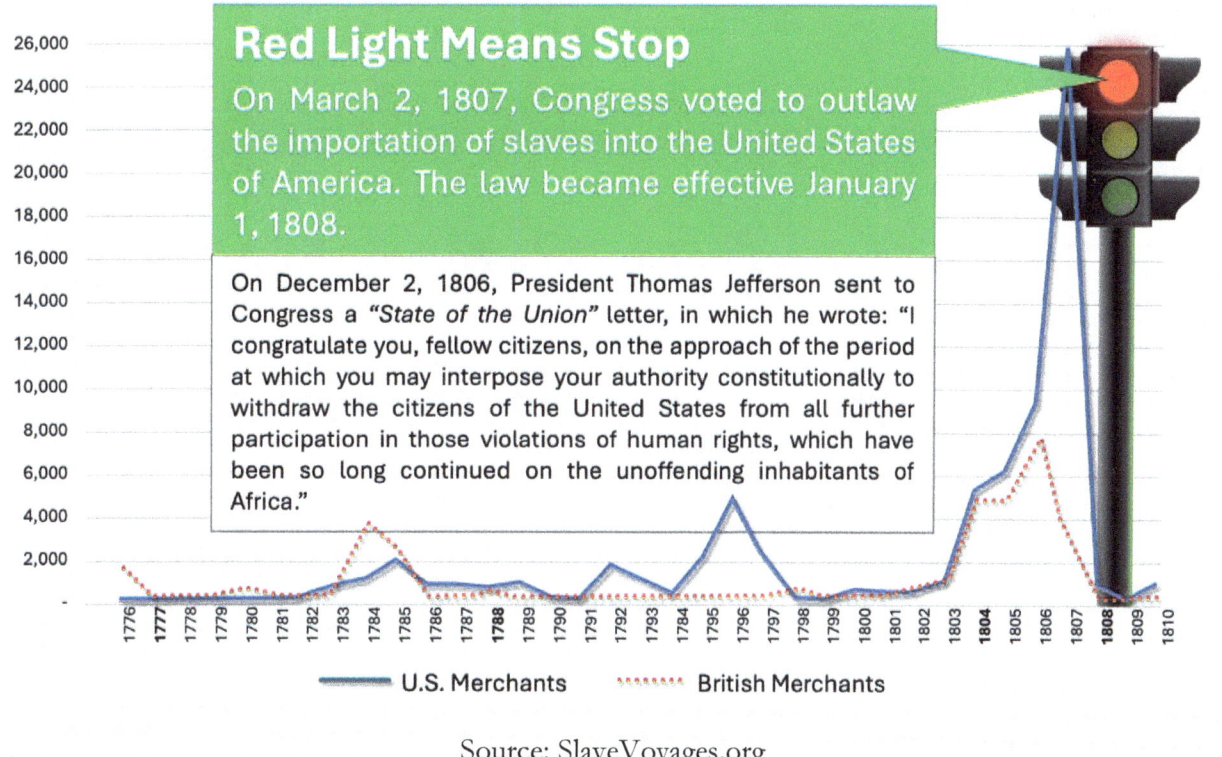

American Slave Merchants

New England Triangular Trade

Newport, Bristol, and Providence merchants engaged in commerce with West Africa, the West Indies, the Caribbean, and North American port cities:

PRIMARY EXPORTS
- Rum
- "African Iron"

PRIMARY IMPORTS
- African Slaves
- Sugar

OTHER EXPORTS
- Lumber
- Beef
- Pork
- Butter
- Cheese
- Onions
- Cider
- Candles
- Horses

OTHER IMPORTS
- Molasses
- Gold
- Pepper
- Cotton
- Ginger
- Indigo
- Linen
- Woolens
- Spanish iron

Above: Eleven million gallons of rum were exchanged by Rhode Island slave merchants for over 100,000 slaves in Africa between 1709 and 1809. Exchange was often; 130 gallons for a males, women for 110 gallons, 80 for a child. Major universities were founded on profits from this illicit trade, such as Yale and Brown (named for a major slave trading family).[131]

Below: An illustration of a sample Rhode Island slave trading voyage. This is what came to be called the New England Triangular Trade. It paled in comparison to the British Triangular Trade which resulted in the transport of more than 2.5 million slaves, primarily to the British Caribbean.

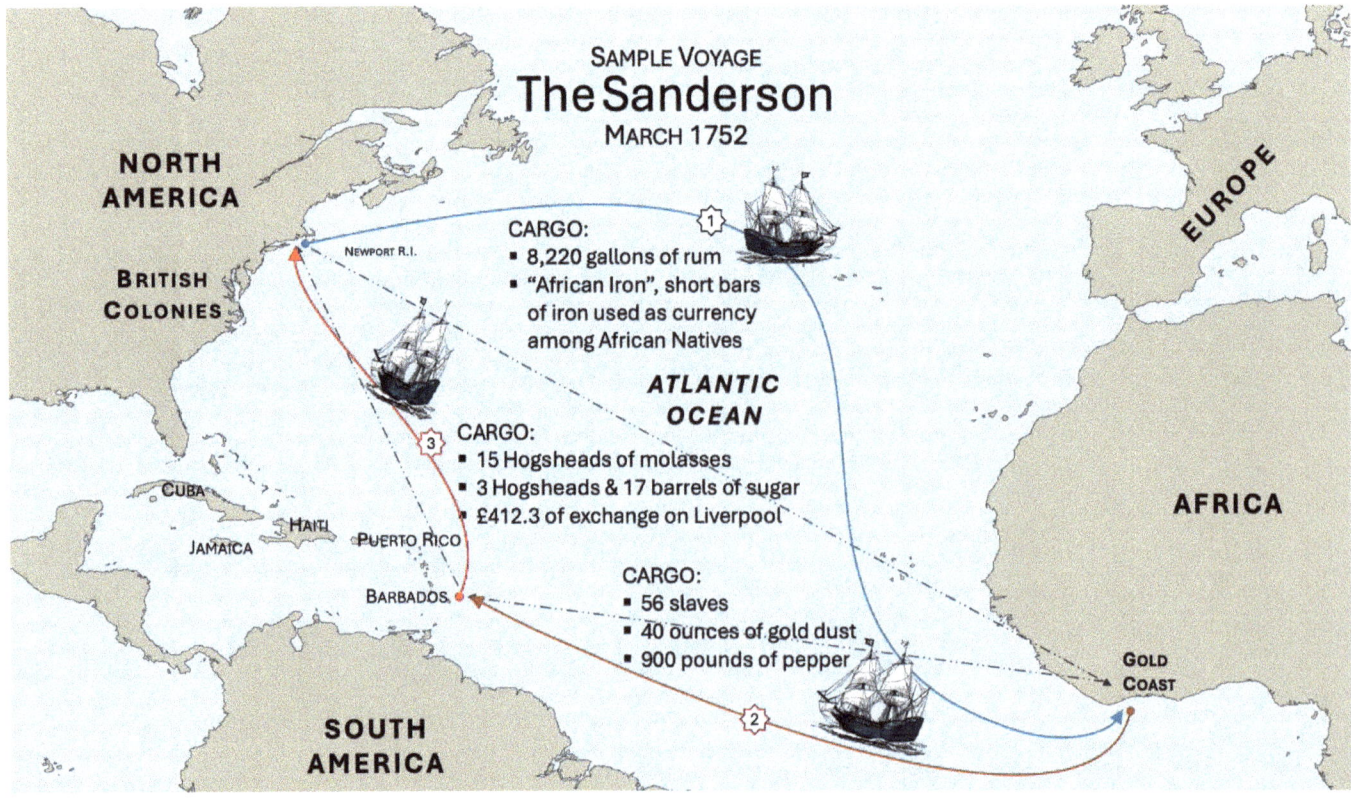

The Distorted Legacy of Jeremiah Dixon

In June of 1761, British astronomer, Charles Mason, and a surveyor, Jeremiah Dixon, were sent by the Royal Society of London to Sumatra to measure the transit of Venus across the sun. They never made it. They were attacked by French ships of war and sailed back to England with cannonballs in the ship's hull. Their trip resumed, but they only made it as far as Cape Town, South Africa, in time to take their measurements. Their findings were later triangulated with teams who had taken readings at distant locations to determine the size of the sun and its distance from the Earth, with similar results regarding Venus.

Amid these groundbreaking contributions to science, Mason and Dixon were called upon to settle a colonial dispute that would ultimately define their legacy.

A Royal Dispute

King Charles I awarded Maryland's charter in 1632, setting its northern boundary at the 40th parallel. Problems soon arose because the king's mapmakers did not know America very well and didn't know where the 40th parallel actually was. Later, in 1681, King Charles II paid off debts he had owed to William Penn's father with a grant of the Province of Pennsylvania. Conflicting interpretations of the boundaries fueled disputes that lasted for 80 years, even leading to Cresap's War in the mid-1730s.[132]

The Mason-Dixon Line

By 1763, after decades of disputes, Mason and Dixon were contracted to establish the boundary once and for all.

Mason and Dixon began their work by confirming the line between the Lower Counties of Pennsylvania (now Delaware) and Maryland. They then started the east-west boundary between Maryland and Pennsylvania, which began at a point 15 miles south of the southernmost house in Philadelphia and extended west from the Delaware River. First, they had to survey a 12-mile radius around New Castle, Delaware. Then, they moved westward into the wilderness, taking bearings from the sun and stars as they traversed the rugged terrain.

Within about 20 miles of their intended endpoint, Mason and Dixon's Native guides refused to go further. Some historians speculate that they had crossed into lands reserved for Native nations under the 1763 Proclamation Line, reinforcing the reality that British surveyors had little control over these contested territories. With no way to proceed safely, Mason and Dixon turned back, completing their portion of the line in 1767.

A Tainted Legacy

When Mason and Dixon completed their survey in 1767, slavery existed in every colony, North and South. Yet in 1820, during the debate over Missouri's admission as a slave state, the term "Mason-Dixon Line" was invoked for the first time as a symbolic dividing line between free and slave states. Over time, Jeremiah Dixon's name—"Dixie"—became tangled in the rhetoric of division. Rather than being honored for their precision and problem-solving which healed division, Mason and Dixon's legacy has been distorted into a symbol of division and strife.

The First Slavery Protest
The 1688 Germantown Petition Against Slavery

When most people think about the fight against slavery, they picture events from the 1800s—like the Underground Railroad or the Civil War. But nearly a century before America became a country, a small group of settlers near Philadelphia took a stand against slavery.

In 1683, a group of German immigrants arrived in Pennsylvania searching for religious freedom. They settled in an area that became Germantown, just outside of Philadelphia. Their first winter was brutal—many had to live in caves along the Delaware River to survive. But through hardship, they held onto their strong belief in justice and equality.

One of their leaders, Francis Daniel Pastorius, saw something happening in the colony that deeply troubled him—people were being bought and sold as slaves. The Quakers, the religious group these settlers belonged to, believed in peace and equality—but surprisingly, more than half of British Quakers owned slaves.

Pastorius and three other settlers refused to stay silent. In 1688, they wrote a bold protest called the 1688 Germantown Petition Against Slavery—the first formal document against slavery in American history.[133]

A Bold Stand for Freedom
The petition was simple but powerful. It asked an important question:

> **"How can we say we believe in equality while keeping others in chains?"**

The petition argued that slavery was wrong because it violated basic human rights. The men presented their petition to their local Quaker Meeting—the group that made decisions for their religious community.

But instead of taking action, Quaker leaders hesitated. They agreed slavery was a serious issue, but they weren't ready to take a stand. The petition was passed from one Quaker meeting to another, eventually reaching Philadelphia and then the Yearly Meeting in Burlington, New Jersey. The official response? "It is too weighty a matter."

Hoping for more support, the men sent their petition to England, believing that Quaker leaders—or even the king—might take notice. But it arrived at a terrible time. England was in the middle of the Glorious Revolution, a major political crisis. The petition was likely lost in the chaos.[134]

For years, the petition was forgotten. But its words did not disappear. Over time, more and more Quakers came to believe that slavery was wrong. By 1776—the year of *The Declaration of Independence*—the Quakers had officially banned slavery in their communities, becoming the first religious group in America to take such a stand.

What Did the Petition Say?

Even though the petition was written in 1688, its ideas still make sense today. If we put its arguments into modern words, it might sound like this:

- **Would you want to be enslaved?** (If not, how can we do it to others?)
- **Pennsylvania was built on freedom,** but slavery **took away people's freedom.**
- **People in Europe wouldn't want to move to a place where people were treated like animals.**
- **Just because someone has darker skin doesn't mean they should be enslaved.**
- **Slaveholders broke families apart, forcing men and women into adultery against their will.**
- **Slavery was stealing**—if Quakers believed stealing was wrong, how could they allow people to be stolen from Africa? And if they purchased slaves they were buying stolen goods!
- **If enslaved people fought back for their freedom, wouldn't they have the right to do so?**

The 1688 Germantown Petition was rejected at first, but its ideas were ahead of their time. It was **the first religious protest in American history to demand the end of slavery**, and it **helped lay the foundation for the abolitionist movement**—the people who fought to end slavery.[135]

Why This Matters

It took almost 90 more years before Pennsylvania officially abolished slavery. It was another 177 years before slavery ended nationwide. But the petition shows that from the very beginning, **there were people in America who believed in freedom for all**.

This document reminds us that standing up for what's right isn't always easy—but it can change history. Today, the petition is recognized as an incredible first step toward ending slavery in America.

The original document is carefully stored in a safe in Lutnick Library at Haverford College near Philadelphia. The author of this book had the rare opportunity to hold that historic petition in his hands—and his immigrant great-grandmother, Catherine, was among those who attended that first protest.

A House Divided Against Itself Cannot Stand
The Fight to End Slavery

On June 16, 1858, Abraham Lincoln gave a speech in Springfield Illinois. This speech was given to over 1,000 delegates at the Illinois State Republican Convention, when he and Stephen A. Douglas were candidates for the U.S. Senate. Many believe the Civil War was not about ending slavery and freeing four million enslaved persons. They claim it was about "States Rights." Sure, the right to own slaves!

This speech led to Lincoln's defeat in his 1858 bid for the Senate but set him up for the 1860 Presidential Election.

> We are now far into the fifth year, since a policy was initiated (The Kansas-Nebraska Act), with the avowed object, and confident promise, of putting an end to slavery agitation. Under the operation of that policy, that agitation has not only, not ceased, but has constantly augmented.
>
> In my opinion, it will not cease, until a crisis shall have been reached, and passed. **"A house divided against itself cannot stand."** I believe **this government cannot endure, permanently half slave and half free**.
>
> I do not expect the Union to be dissolved – **I do not expect the house to fall – but I do expect it will cease to be divided. It will become all one thing or all the other**.
>
> **Either the opponents of slavery, will arrest the further spread of it,** and place it where the public mind shall rest in the belief that it is in the course of ultimate extinction; **or its advocates will push it forward, till it shall become alike lawful in all the States, old as well as new – North as well as South**.
>
> … The new year of 1854 found slavery excluded from more than half the States by State Constitutions, and from most of the national territory by congressional prohibition. Four days later, commenced the struggle, which ended in **repealing that congressional prohibition (The Missouri Compromise). This opened all the national territory to slavery, and was the first point gained**.
>
> Speaking of the 1856 election, Lincoln continued… Two years ago the **Republicans of the nation** mustered over thirteen hundred thousand strong… we gathered from the four winds, and formed and **fought a battle though, under the constant hot fire of a disciplined, proud, and pampered enemy**.
>
> **Did we brave all then to falter now?** – now – when **that same enemy is wavering**, dissevered and belligerent? The result is not doubtful. We shall not fail – if we stand firm, we shall not fail. **Wise councils may accelerate or mistakes delay it, but sooner or later the victory is sure to come**.[136]

Abraham Lincoln was not the first Republican candidate for president. That honor belonged to **John C. Fremont** who led the new party of **former Whigs and anti-slavery Democrats**. In opposition to the Kansas-Nebraska Act, **the Republican Party was formed to defeat the party of slavery—the Democratic Party**.[137] **The 1856 Democratic National Platform threatened disunion if Congress tampered with "domestic slavery."**[138] Fremont lost that 1856 election, but set the stage for Lincoln's victory in 1860.

To the right is a political map prepared in 1856 for John C. Fremont and William L. Dayton, the first candidates for president and vice president on the first Republican Party ticket. It was all about slavery.[139]

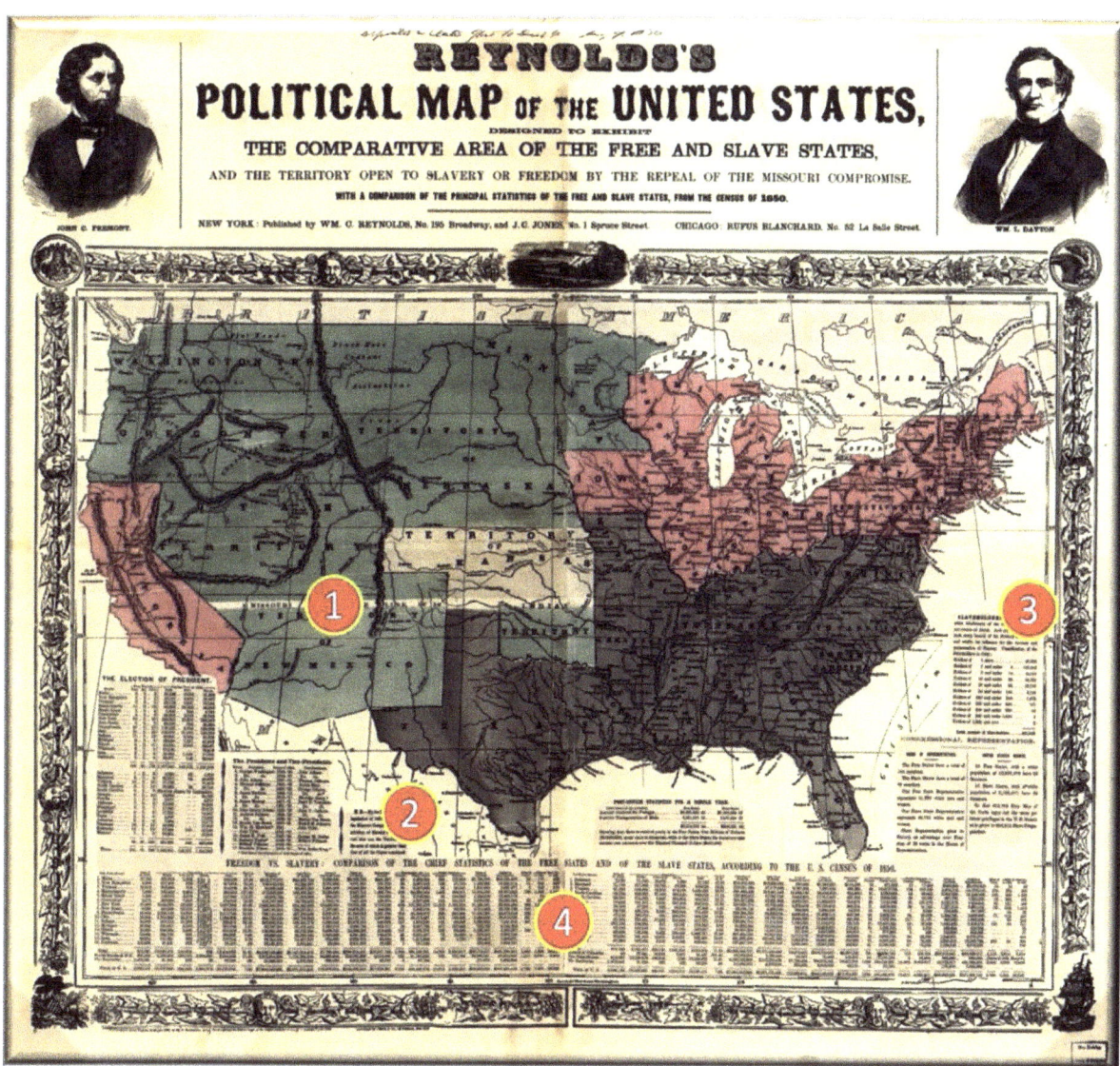

Key Points the Republican Party Stressed on Their 1856 Political Map

1. **36° 30' Slavery Line Erased:**
   The Missouri Compromise Slavery Demarcation Line was erased by the 1854 Democratic Party's Kansas/Nebraska Act. This allowed ALL Territories to vote whether to become Free States or Slave States.

2. **The Democratic legislation of 1854:**
   Repealed the Missouri Compromise, which banned slavery in new states above the southern boundary of Missouri. The institution of Slavery may be carried to all the Territories—the area of which is greater than that of all the States combined.

3. **Large Slaveholders Control Every Branch of the Federal Government:**
   Of the 6,222,418 white inhabitants of the South, only 347,525 are owners of slaves. And yet this faction controls every branch of the Federal Government, and wields its influence for the increase and perpetuation of Slavery.

Southern Slaveholders by the Numbers:

Own 1 slave........68, 820	Own 50 – 99 6,196
2 -4.....................105,683	100 – 199 1,479
5 – 9 80,765	200 – 299 187
10 – 19.................54,595	300 – 499 56
20 – 49.................29,744	500 – 999 9
	1,000 and over 2

During the Civil War, the Twenty-Slave Law was passed by the Confederate Congress October 11, 1862. It created an exemption from military conscription for the owners of 20 or more slaves. This law was controversial in that it enflamed social divisions and led to claims by drafted soldiers that they were fighting a "rich man's war."

4. **Industry, Agriculture, Transportation, Social Advancement:**
   The table at the bottom compares the overall prosperity and advancement between the North and South. The differences illustrate how slavery curses, rather than benefits the people—both slave and free.

Blood and Treasure: The Civil War

"**Once let the Black man get upon his person the brass letter, U.S.,** let him get an eagle on his button, and a musket on his shoulder and bullets in his pocket, **there is no power on earth that can deny that he has earned the right to citizenship.**"[140]
Frederick Douglas

Northern, Southern, and Union Black Casualties

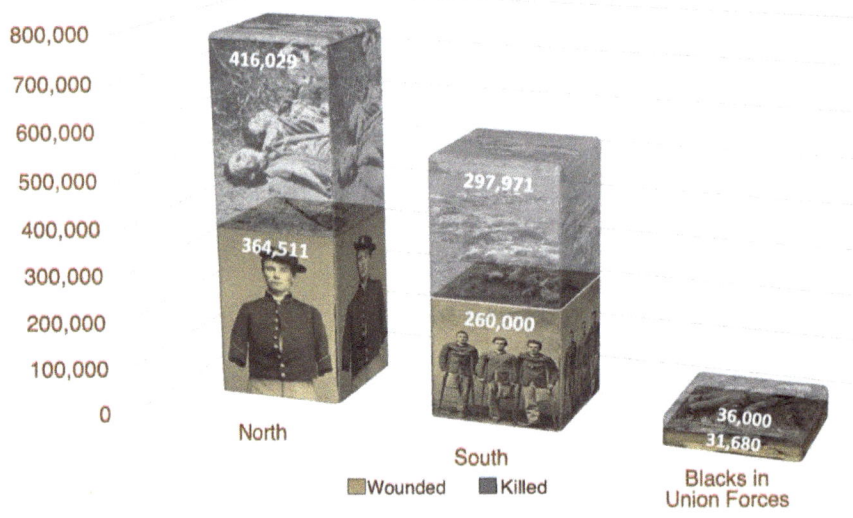

One-point-five million casualties represent the blood of soldiers to free four million slaves during the American Civil War…and they were not all White. 210,000 Black soldiers fought to free their brothers and sisters in chains. Altogether, **186,000 black soldiers served in the Union Army, while another 29,000 served in the Navy,**[141] accounting for nearly **10 percent of all Union forces and 68,178 of the Union dead or missing. Twenty-six African Americans received the Congressional Medal of Honor** for extraordinary bravery in battle.[142]

More Lives Were Lost in the Civil War than All Other Wars Combined

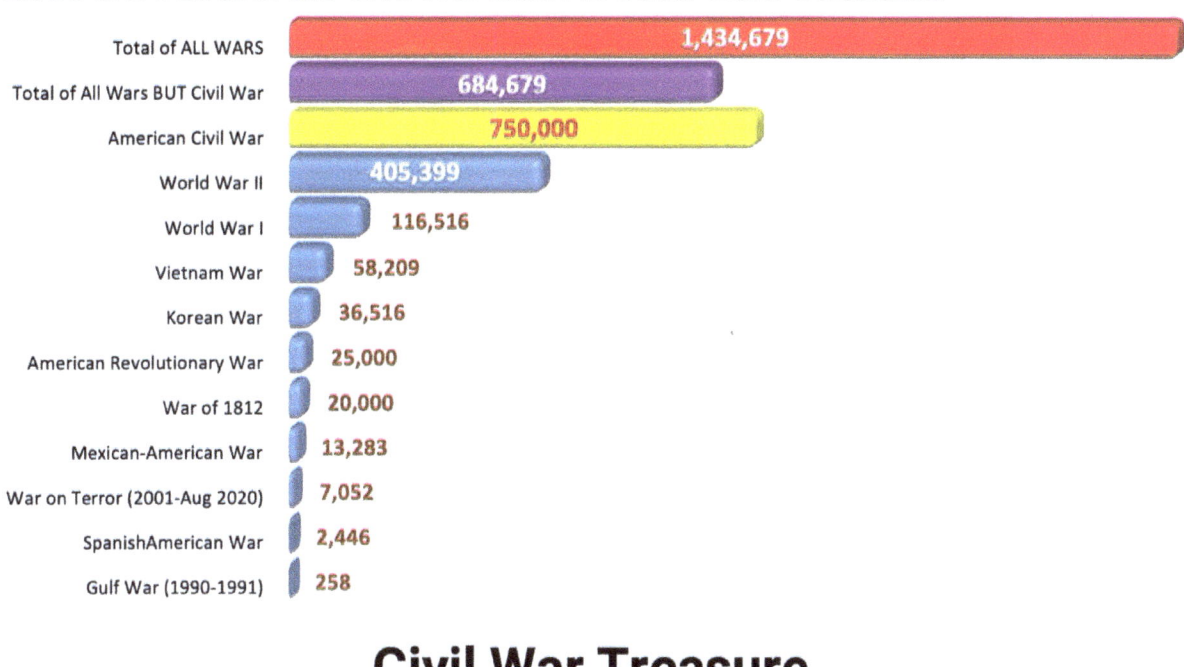

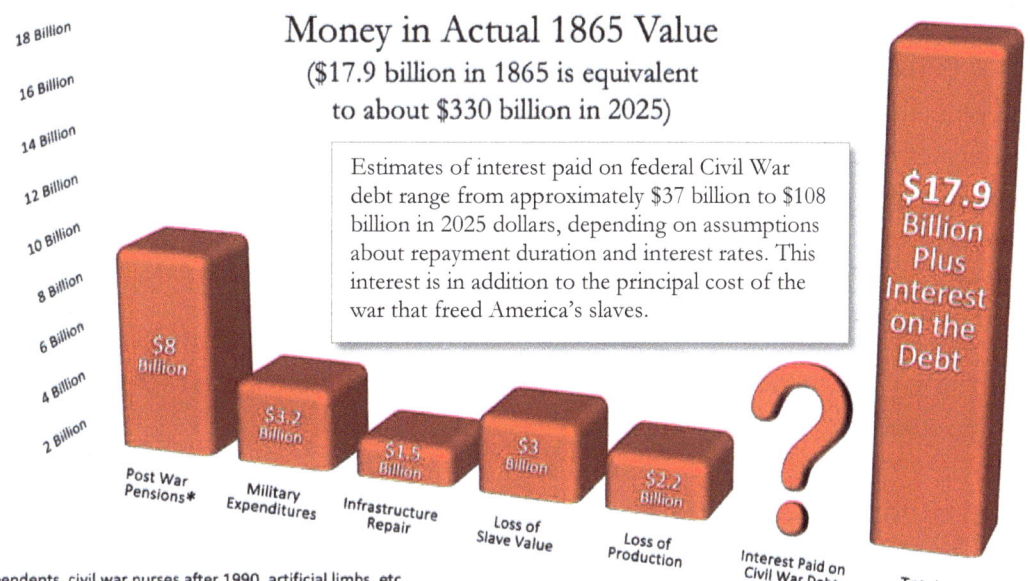

* Vets, dependents, civil war nurses after 1990, artificial limbs, etc.
These figures do not include pension payments made to Southern Vets by Southern states.
The last Civil War Pension payment was made in May 2020 to Irene Triplett, the aged daughter of a Civil War Veteran who had a child late in life.

The blood and treasure spent on the Civil War was immense. More lives were lost in the Civil War than all other conflicts combined. New research estimates Civil War loss of life at 750,000[143] and casualties to have been 1.5 million. These sacrifices resulted in the freeing of over 4 million slaves at a cost of $330 billion in today's money.[144] The patriotism exhibited by Black soldiers who fought and died for the cause of freedom was inspiring.

Most Black soldiers enlisted after the **Emancipation Proclamation** of January 1863. The **Emancipation Proclamation freed few slaves**, but **held the promise of freedom for all slaves**. Slaves in states that did not secede (Missouri, Kentucky, West Virginia, Maryland, and Delaware) and areas in the South controlled by the Union were not affected. Nor did it free slaves controlled by states in rebellion. Fulfillment of **that promise was dependent upon winning the war and the Thirteenth Amendment, which passed in December 1865**.[145]

Forgotten Heroes
Black and Native Americans in Our Nation's Military

Throughout American history, Black and Native American soldiers have shown incredible courage, loyalty, and sacrifice—even when they were denied the very freedoms they fought to protect. Their contributions, though often overlooked, have been vital in shaping the history of our nation.

Fighting for a Nation That Didn't Always Fight for Them

During the Revolutionary War, about 5,000 Black men fought for independence, even though many of them were still enslaved. Some were promised freedom in exchange for their service, while others believed in the cause of liberty despite being denied its full benefits. Heroes like Crispus Attucks, Colonel George Middleton, and Salem Poor risked their lives in battles like Bunker Hill and Boston, proving that Black men were willing to fight for America's freedom—even when their own was not guaranteed. [146]

Native Americans also played a major role in the fight for independence, even though they were often caught between the British and the American colonists. Some tribes, like the Stockbridge-Mohican, fought alongside the Patriots, hoping it would protect their land and rights. Others sided with the British, believing they had a better chance of stopping American expansion into their territories. Regardless of their choice, Native warriors fought bravely, but their sacrifices were often met with broken promises after the war.

Unsung Heroes: The Buffalo Soldiers and Immune Troops

When people think of the Spanish-American War, they often picture Teddy Roosevelt and his Rough Riders charging up San Juan Hill. But the real heroes of the battle were the Buffalo Soldiers, the all-Black regiments of the U.S. Army, and the Immune Troops, Black soldiers believed to have resistance to tropical diseases.

At Las Guásimas and San Juan Hill, the Buffalo Soldiers saved Roosevelt and his men—twice. Fighting through intense enemy fire, they cleared paths, took key positions, and held the line against Spanish forces. Without them, the Rough Riders might have been wiped out. Yet their contributions are barely mentioned in many history books.

The bravery of Black soldiers had already been proven time and again. During the Civil War, at least 26 Black soldiers received the Medal of Honor, the nation's highest award for valor. From Fort Wagner to the Battle of Chaffin's Farm, they fought with unmatched courage, risking everything for a country that still denied them full citizenship.

World War I: The Harlem Hellfighters and Code Talkers

During World War I, more than 350,000 Black men served in the U.S. military. Many were assigned to labor and support roles rather than combat, but some fought on the front lines. The 369th Infantry Regiment, known as the Harlem Hellfighters, spent more time in battle than any other American unit and became legendary for their bravery. They fought under the French army, which treated them as equals, and many earned France's highest military honor, the Croix de Guerre.

Native Americans also served in high numbers, with over 12,000 enlisting despite not even being considered U.S. citizens at the time. While Choctaw Soldiers are the most documented group of World War I Code Talkers, the Army used nine tribal languages during the war. Cheyenne, Cherokee, Comanche, Ho-Chunk, Osage, and Yankton Sioux were used as "code talkers," using their Native languages to send secret military messages—an idea that would later become crucial in World War II.[147]

World War II: Breaking Barriers on the Battlefield

In World War II, Black and Native American soldiers once again answered the call to defend freedom. The Tuskegee Airmen, a group of elite Black fighter pilots, shattered stereotypes with their incredible skill and courage in the skies over Europe. Flying more than 15,000 missions, they proved that race had nothing to do with ability—and helped push for the eventual desegregation of the U.S. military.

Meanwhile, 44,000 Native Americans fought in World War II, including the famous Navajo Code Talkers. Their unbreakable code, based on the Navajo language, played a key role in the Pacific battles, including the victory at Iwo Jima. Messages that had taken more than 20 minutes to go through channels took less than 30 seconds for Code Talkers to send and receive. Their secret communication system saved thousands of lives, and decades later, they were finally honored as some of the war's greatest heroes.[148]

Korea, Vietnam, and Beyond: The Fight Continues

By the time of the Korean and Vietnam Wars, the U.S. military had officially ended segregation, allowing Black and Native American soldiers to serve alongside their White counterparts. However, challenges remained. Native Americans volunteered for service at five times the national average, showing their deep commitment to protecting their homeland—even as the U.S. government continued breaking treaties with their tribes.

Black soldiers also faced discrimination, despite making up nearly one-third of front-line troops in Vietnam. They fought bravely but often returned home to racial inequality and unrest. Still, their sacrifices helped push forward the Civil Rights Movement and led to greater opportunities in the military and beyond.[149]

Their Stories Still Matter

The bravery of these soldiers—many of whom never received the recognition they deserved—reminds us that the fight for freedom was never just for all groups of people. The same ideals that inspired *The Declaration of Independence* and the U.S. Constitution apply to everyone. From Crispus Attucks, the first man to die for American liberty, to the unsung heroes who broke barriers in every major war, their legacy is one of courage in the face of injustice. They fought, not just for themselves, but for the future of a country that did not always respect them. Their stories challenge us to ask: What does it really mean to be an American? It means standing up for what's right, even when it is difficult. It means recognizing the contributions of those who were overlooked. And it means continuing to build a country that truly honors the sacrifices made by all who serve.

Colonel George Middleton
Patriot, Protector, and Pioneer

George Middleton, born around 1735, was one of 5,000 African Americans who fought for American independence during the Revolutionary War. He wasn't just a soldier—he was a leader. Skilled in music and an expert horse trainer, Middleton was known and respected among Black and White communities in Boston. But we remember him today because he fought for liberty during the Revolution and long after it ended.[150]

The Bucks of America

During the Revolutionary War, Middleton helped form and lead a Black militia called the Bucks of America. At the time, the Continental Army did not allow all-Black units, so many Black soldiers fought in integrated regiments or worked as laborers. But Middleton's militia was different—it was one of the few all-Black units in the war.

While history hasn't recorded all their battles, the Bucks played a key role in defending Boston. They helped keep order, protect supply routes, and maintain security in the city as "The Protectors." They showed that Black Patriots had just as much at stake in America's future as anyone else. Their service was so valued that after the war, Governor John Hancock personally honored them with a special flag featuring a leaping buck and a pine tree, symbols of strength and freedom in New England. Today, that flag is carefully preserved by the Massachusetts Historical Society, one of the few surviving artifacts that prove the contributions of Black soldiers during the war.[151]

During the Battle of Bunker Hill, 103 Blacks and Native Americans fought with the colonial forces. Among these soldiers were George Middleton, Prince Hall, Salem Poor, Peter Salem, Caesar Brown, and Grant Cooper. Brown and Estabrook were killed in the battle. Peter Salem was credited with shooting British commander, Major Pitcairn, and forcing the British troops to regroup. This gave the smaller colonial force time to retreat rather than surrender. The efforts of these brave soldiers helped avoid a catastrophe.[152]

Fighting for Freedom—Even After the War

Middleton didn't stop fighting for his community once the war ended. He believed that freedom meant more than just independence from Britain—it also meant helping Black Americans build better lives. In 1796, he helped found the African Benevolent Society, one of the first Black-led organizations dedicated to helping those in need.

The society helped freed Black men and women find jobs, provided food and housing for those struggling, and supported widows and orphans. At the time, there weren't many safety nets for people of color, so Middleton and others stepped up to take care of their own. His work helped set an example for future Black mutual aid societies that would form across the country in the years to come.

Standing His Ground

Middleton was also known for his courage. One of the most famous stories about him happened later in his life, when a group of African Americans gathered in a Boston park to celebrate their freedom. Suddenly, a White mob showed up, trying to break up the gathering.

Though Middleton was older at this point, he refused to back down. He grabbed his musket, stood in front of the crowd, and warned the attackers that if they wanted a fight, he was ready. The mob, seeing Middleton's fearless stance, turned and ran. His bravery made him a legend among Boston's Black community.[153]

The Grand Master

Middleton wasn't just a military hero—he was also a leader in the world of Freemasonry, an important social and charitable organization. He worked closely with Prince Hall, one of the most famous Black leaders of the time, and helped run African Lodge No. 459, the first Black Masonic lodge in America.

By 1809, Middleton became the Grand Master of the lodge, helping it grow into a place where Black men could unite, educate themselves, and support one another. The lodge helped provide education, leadership, and community programs, proving that Middleton's dedication to service never ended.[154]

A Lasting Legacy

Middleton's home, located at 5 Pinckney Street in Boston, still stands today as part of the Boston Black Heritage Trail. His leadership—both on and off the battlefield—helped shape the future for Black Americans in Boston and beyond.

Middleton's efforts to defend freedom didn't end in 1783. He, and others like him, continued to push for equality, justice, and opportunity long after the war was won. His courage, leadership, and determination made him a true American hero—one whose name deserves to be honored.

John Howland
The Boy Who Fell Off the Mayflower

John Howland's story is one of survival, leadership, and legacy. At just 21 years of age, he nearly lost his life before the Pilgrims even reached land—falling overboard during a storm on the Mayflower and clinging to a trailing rope until he was rescued. Yet, this young, indentured servant would go on to sign the Mayflower Compact, help secure the colony's financial future, and become a patriarch whose descendants now number over two million people worldwide—including American presidents, world leaders, and cultural icons.

A Hand in Writing the Mayflower Compact

As the clerk and scribe for Governor John Carver, Howland was responsible for recording official documents. Some historians believe he may have actually penned the Mayflower Compact, and he signed it as an indentured servant, not yet a free man. This document laid the foundation for self-governance in America, ensuring that the new colony would be ruled by the consent of the people rather than by a single ruler.

Fur Trade, Diplomacy, and a Risky Encounter on the Kennebec River

After gaining his freedom, Howland became one of Plymouth's key leaders in trade and diplomacy with the Native nations. For 25 years, he traveled annually up the Kennebec River in present-day Maine, where he traded with the Abenaki and other tribes for valuable beaver pelts—essential to paying off the London merchants who financed the Pilgrims' journey.

One of his most harrowing moments came in 1634, when a rival English trader, John Hocking, defied an agreement and anchored his boat in Plymouth's trading territory. Howland sent men in a canoe to cut his boat loose, but Hocking drew his gun, threatening to shoot Howland's men. With tensions running high, Howland yelled at Hocking to aim the gun at him because the men were acting on his orders. Hocking shot a man in the canoe point blank, and his mates returned fire, killing Hocking.

Aiding a Native Leader and Navigating Political Upheaval

Howland also played a key role in keeping peace with the Wampanoag and Abenaki tribes. When a powerful Native chief fell gravely ill, Howland personally helped him recover—solidifying goodwill between Plymouth and its Indigenous neighbors. However, as the English Crown tightened its grip on colonial trade, events like the Hocking incident fueled growing resentment among the colonies. Some historians believe that these early struggles over trade and self-rule foreshadowed the very conflicts that led to the American Revolution.

The Last Standing Mayflower Pilgrim Home

In his later years, Howland and his wife, Elizabeth, moved into their son's home, which still stands today as the only surviving home of a Mayflower Pilgrim. This historic site, part of the Plymouth Antiquarian Society, preserves Howland's story for future generations—giving visitors a direct connection to one of America's earliest settlers and leaders.

A Legacy That Shaped America...and the World

John Howland wasn't just a survivor—he was an early builder of the American Republic. He signed one of the first self-governing documents in the New World, helped finance the survival of Plymouth Colony, and played a role in the diplomatic struggles that shaped early American politics.

Howland lived into his 80s, passing away in 1672 as one of Plymouth's most respected elders. His descendants include some of the most influential figures in history, among them:

- Franklin D. Roosevelt
- Winston Churchill
- Richard Nixon
- George H.W. Bush and George W. Bush
- Ralph Waldo Emerson
- Henry Wadsworth Longfellow
- Joseph Smith
- Laura Ingalls Wilder
- Astronaut John Glenn
- Humphrey Bogart
- Elvis Presley
- Jane Austin
- Dr. Benjamin Spock
- Henry Cabot Lodge, Jr.

Howland's legacy isn't just about famous names—it's about the millions of people who carry his story forward today. His descendants now number over two million worldwide—proof that one person's resilience can echo through generations.

I know this well—John Howland is my 10th great-grandfather. His story isn't just history to me—it's family history. But what makes history so exciting is that it belongs to all of us. Whether or not you're one of Howland's descendants, his journey helped shape the nation we live in today.

His story reminds us all that even those who fall overboard can rise to shape a nation. And maybe, just maybe, his adventurous spirit lives on in you.

Benjamin Lay
The "Quaker Comet"

Benjamin Lay was a dwarf—only 4½ feet tall—but his determination to end slavery made him a giant in the fight for justice. A Quaker with bold ideas and even bolder actions, Lay was never afraid to challenge people—even when it made him unpopular.

A Man Ahead of His Time

Born in 1682 in England, Lay grew up on a farm before becoming a glove maker, and then a sailor. His travels took him to Barbados, where he married and ran a store. He witnessed the horrifying brutality of slavery. The way enslaved people were treated shocked him to his core. He knew he could never be silent about it.

Lay and his wife, Sarah, moved to Philadelphia, expecting to find a more just society. But to their dismay, they discovered that Quakers—who preached peace and equality—were involved in slavery. More than half of Quakers in Pennsylvania owned enslaved people, including the colony's founder, William Penn.[155]

Lay, no hypocrite, refused to look the other way. He boycotted all goods produced by slave labor, including:
- Sugar
- Tobacco
- Coffee
- Cotton
- Rum
- Chocolate

He even made his own clothes out of flax so he wouldn't wear anything made from enslaved labor. Lay believed that if you truly opposed slavery, you had to live your values—not just talk about them.

Benjamin Lay's Big Protest

Lay wasn't just against slavery—he was willing to call people out for supporting it. And he didn't do it quietly.

One of his most famous protests happened in 1738 at a Quaker Yearly Meeting in New Jersey. Lay knew that many of the wealthy Quakers in the audience owned slaves. He stood before the assembly, holding a hollowed-out book filled with red pokeberry juice—a symbol of blood.

With fire in his eyes, Lay shouted, "God respects all people equally, be they rich or poor, man or woman, White or Black!" Then, he pulled out a dagger and stabbed the book—causing the "blood" to pour down his arm. He splattered the "blood" over the heads of slaveholders, warning that those who enslave others would face judgment—"of body and soul!" People gasped. Women fainted. But Lay didn't care. He had made his point.[156]

An Outcast, But a Legend

Lay's protests made him an outcast among the Quakers, but they also made people think. He lived in a cave outside Philadelphia, choosing a simple life over one that depended on enslaved labor. Even though he was disowned by the Quakers, he never stopped speaking out.

His 1738 book, All Slave-keepers that Keep the Innocent in Bondage, Apostates Pretending to Lay Claim to the Pure & Holy Christian Religion…, was published by Benjamin Franklin, who, at the time, was still involved in slavery himself and advertised for the capture of runaway slaves in his newspaper. But Lay's words were powerful, and Franklin eventually changed his views—becoming an abolitionist later in life.[157]

By the time Lay died in 1759, the Quakers had finally started turning against slavery. In 1776—the same year America declared independence—Quakers officially banned their members from owning slaves. It was a victory Lay didn't live to see, but one that happened because of his fearless fight for justice.

Benjamin Lay Anecdotes

The Snowy Protest – One winter morning, Benjamin Lay stood barefoot in the snow outside a Friends Meetinghouse, refusing to move. His pant-legs were pulled up and he looked like he was about to freeze to death. When concerned Quakers urged him to come inside, he rebuked them: "You pity me, but you do not pity the poor slaves who suffer far worse every day!" His dramatic protests left a lasting impression.

Calling Out Slaveholders – Lay had no patience for hypocrisy. If a Quaker slaveholder dared to speak in a meeting, he would leap to his feet and shout, "There's a man with the blood of slaves on his hands!" His fearless voice made slaveholders squirm—and made abolition impossible to ignore.

Why Benjamin Lay Still Matters

Lay wasn't just against slavery—he lived his beliefs every single day. Unlike Thomas Jefferson, who spoke against slavery but still owned enslaved people, Lay refused to compromise.

His story reminds us that one person can make a difference, even if they stand alone. Change doesn't happen overnight, and it is not always easy. But Lay's life proves that doing what's right is always worth it—even if it means shaking people up.

His nickname, **"The Quaker Comet,"** wasn't just because of his energy—it was because he lit up the sky and left a trail of change burning behind him. Today, he is remembered as one of the boldest voices against slavery in early America—**a man with the spirit of a giant** who refused to remain silent in the face of injustice.

Sarah Bradlee Fulton
"Mother of the Boston Tea Party" and Daughter of Liberty

Sarah Bradlee Fulton wasn't just a witness to history—she was a bold participant who helped shape the American Revolution. Known as the Mother of the Boston Tea Party, she played a critical role in one of the most famous acts of protest against British rule. But her courage didn't stop there. Fulton took action throughout the war, proving that women were just as vital to the Patriot cause as the men who took up arms.

A Patriot from the Beginning
Born in 1740 near Boston, Sarah Bradlee grew up surrounded by discussions of liberty and resistance to British rule. She married John Fulton in 1762, and together, they joined a growing movement of colonists determined to fight for their rights. Sarah became an active member of the **Daughters of Liberty**, a group of women who found creative ways to resist British oppression.

The Daughters of Liberty weren't soldiers, but they used their daily lives as acts of rebellion. They refused to buy British goods, organized spinning bees to make their own cloth, and encouraged colonial businesses to stop relying on imports from England. Their message was clear: America could stand on its own.

The Boston Tea Party: Her Defining Moment
By 1773, tensions between the colonies and Britain had reached a boiling point—especially over unfair taxes. When the British government imposed the Tea Act, colonists in Boston decided to send a clear message: **No taxation without representation!**

On the night of December 16, 1773, Sarah Bradlee Fulton played a key role in the event that would become known as the Boston Tea Party. She disguised the Sons of Liberty as Mohawk Indians, so they wouldn't be recognized when they boarded British ships and dumped 342 chests of tea into Boston Harbor. She also provided shelter for the men afterward, helping them remove their disguises and hide any evidence of their involvement.

Without her quick thinking, many of these Patriots might have been caught and punished by British authorities. Her bravery that night earned her the title **Mother of the Boston Tea Party**, a name that would follow her for the rest of her life.

Serving the Cause in Wartime

When war broke out in 1775, Sarah didn't hesitate to take action. After the Battle of Bunker Hill, she turned her home into a makeshift hospital for wounded soldiers, organizing local women to provide bandages and medical supplies.

She also took on one of the most dangerous missions of the war—delivering a secret message to General George Washington. The journey required her to travel through enemy-controlled territory, where she could have been captured at any moment. But Sarah succeeded, and when she handed the message to Washington, he personally thanked her for her bravery.

Another time, when British forces tried to steal firewood meant for the Continental Army, Sarah physically grabbed the oxen pulling the supply cart and turned them away from the Redcoats. Her defiant act left the British stunned, and she successfully delivered the much-needed firewood to the troops.

The Fight Didn't End in 1776

Sarah Bradlee Fulton's courage didn't just help win the Revolution—it also inspired future generations of women to take action for their country. The Daughters of Liberty set the stage for women's involvement in politics, protest, and community leadership. They proved that patriotism wasn't just about fighting on the battlefield—it was also about making sacrifices, organizing resistance, and standing up for what is right.

Even though she lived in a time when women had few legal rights, Sarah's bravery and leadership were undeniable. She didn't wait for permission to act—she saw what needed to be done and did it. Whether it was disguising the Sons of Liberty, nursing wounded soldiers, or standing up to the British, she proved that women were a force to be reckoned with in the fight for independence.

Her story reminds us that history isn't just made by famous generals or politicians. It's shaped by ordinary people who take extraordinary risks for freedom.

A Lasting Legacy

After the Revolution, Sarah Bradlee Fulton continued to support her country and community. She lived to be 95 years old, passing away in 1835. Sarah's story shows that not all Revolutionary War heroes carried muskets. There were many other patriots, men and women, who dared to take extraordinary risks for the promise of liberty.[158]

Mercy Otis Warren
The Revolutionary Woman Who Wielded a Mighty Pen

Most people involved in the American Revolution fought with muskets, but **Mercy Otis Warren fought with words**. At a time when women weren't supposed to be involved in politics, she used her writing to challenge British rule, inspire Patriots, and later, hold the new government accountable.

A Woman with a Powerful Voice

Born in Massachusetts in 1728, Mercy grew up in a family that believed in education—even for girls, which was unusual at the time. She loved to read and write, and when she married James Warren, a fellow Patriot, she became part of Boston's most important political circles. **The Sons of Liberty**, including leaders like Samuel Adams and John Hancock, **often met in her home to discuss how to resist British rule**.[159]

But Mercy didn't just listen—she took action. She wrote plays and poems that made fun of the Royal Governor and other leaders to expose unfair policies. Her first play, *The Adulator,* was published anonymously in 1772, mocking Massachusetts' governor, Thomas Hutchinson. Another play, *The Defeat,* was just as bold. These writings helped stir up support for the Patriot cause. People who read them began to see how British rule was limiting their freedoms.[160]

Mercy's influence extended beyond the political elite—her work reached ordinary men and women, encouraging them to question authority and fight for their rights. Unlike many political pamphlets of the time, her plays and satirical works were easy to understand, making them effective tools for rallying public opinion. Her ability to blend humor with sharp political critique made her a formidable force, proving that ridicule and wit could be just as powerful as muskets and cannons. At a time when women were expected to remain silent on public affairs, Mercy defied convention, showing that intellect and patriotism knew no gender.

Mercy's talent for writing earned her a place in Revolutionary circles. She exchanged letters with some of the most powerful men of her time, including George Washington, Thomas Jefferson, and John Adams. Many of them respected her sharp mind and political insights, even though it was rare for women to be part of these discussions.[161]

Writing Through the Revolution

During the war, Mercy continued to use her pen as a weapon. She and her husband worked closely with the **Committees of Correspondence**—groups of Patriots who spread news between the colonies. Mercy also helped manage important letters and messages while her husband served as paymaster in the Continental Army.

She was not afraid to speak her mind, even when it meant standing up to friends. After the war, when the U.S. Constitution was being debated, Mercy had serious concerns. She feared the new government might become too powerful—just like the British had been. **She argued that a Bill of Rights was needed** to protect individual freedoms. Her writings encouraged many people to push for these protections, which were finally added in 1791.

Historian of the Revolution

In 1805, **Mercy Otis Warren published** *History of the Rise, Progress, and Termination of the American Revolution*—a massive three-volume account of the war. It was one of the first books written about the Revolution from an American perspective, and the first by a woman.

Unlike other histories of the time, Mercy didn't just celebrate the victories. **She also pointed out mistakes and injustices, including the mistreatment of Native Americans**. She wrote about the Gnadenhutten Massacre of 1782, where nearly 100 peaceful Christian Native Americans were killed by American soldiers. She believed that history should tell the whole truth, even the uncomfortable parts.

Not everyone agreed with her views. John Adams, once one of her closest friends, dismissed her concerns about government power, saying history was "not the province of the ladies." But that didn't stop her. She kept writing, speaking, and fighting for the ideals of liberty, justice, and equality.

A Revolutionary Legacy

Mercy Otis Warren was more than a writer—**she was a voice for freedom when women's voices were often ignored**. She proved that words could change history, and her work continues to remind us that **freedom must be protected, not just won**.

Even today, her book remains an important record of the Revolutionary War, showing what life was like from a perspective that many history books leave out. Mercy's work also set an example for future generations of women who wanted to be involved in shaping their country's future.

More than just a chronicler of history, Mercy Otis Warren was a force in shaping it. As one of the most influential female voices of the Revolutionary era, **she defied expectations, wielding her pen as skillfully as any statesman wielded a sword**. Her sharp political satire exposed British tyranny, while her keen historical analysis ensured that the Revolution's ideals would not be forgotten. Warren understood that **liberty was not won on the battlefield alone—it had to be imprinted and defended in the hearts and minds of the people**. Through her writings, she preserved the Revolution's principles for future generations, proving that true patriotism is measured not just in action, but in **the courage to speak truth to power**.[162]

Benjamin Banneker
A Genius Who Read the Stars, and Saved Washington, D.C.

Benjamin Banneker was born in 1731 near Ellicott's Mills, Maryland. He grew up on a self-sufficient tobacco farm, where he developed a love for nature, science, and learning. Unlike most Black children of the time, Banneker had access to education—a rare privilege. A Quaker schoolteacher, Peter Heinrich, from Bucks County, Pennsylvania, briefly taught Benjamin and shared his books, igniting a passion for mathematics and astronomy. His incredible skill in math, paired with a photographic memory soon set Benjamin apart as a very special child.

Banneker's superior intellect was matched with an insatiable curiosity. He constantly experimented, questioned, and observed the world around him—qualities that would one day make him one of the most remarkable scientific minds in America.

The Boy Who Built a Clock

One of the most famous stories of Banneker's childhood involves a simple pocket watch. A neighbor lent it to him, and instead of just admiring the timepiece, Banneker carefully took it apart piece by piece, studying every tiny gear, wheel, and spring. Then, using only wood and his remarkable memory, he built a fully functional wooden clock—the first of its kind in America.

Even more astonishing? It kept perfect time until the day he died!

At a time when few people even owned watches, Banneker's handmade wooden clock amazed all who saw it. This was a clear sign that his mind was built for invention, precision, and discovery.

A Self-Taught Astronomer Who Corrected the Experts

Banneker wasn't just good with gears and wood—he was also fascinated by the stars. With no formal education in astronomy, he taught himself how to track celestial movements, predict eclipses, and calculate planetary orbits. Using homemade instruments and simple math tables, he charted the heavens with astonishing accuracy.

At a time when only the most elite scholars in Europe understood celestial mechanics, Banneker rivaled the greatest minds in the world. It has been said that his ancestors in Africa could read the stars and chart their courses. Some of this knowledge may have been passed to Benjamin by his father.

His skills were so advanced that he once discovered a major mathematical error in a highly respected British astronomy book. When Banneker corrected the mistake, scholars were stunned. His ability to predict eclipses and track the movements of planets years in advance proved that his brilliance was undeniable.

Saving Washington D.C.

In 1791, the newly formed United States needed a capital city, Banneker worked as an assistant to French engineer Pierre L'Enfant, who was hired to design Washington, D.C. But when L'Enfant had a falling-out with the government, he quit in frustration—taking all the city's plans with him!

It is said, that with the entire project at risk, Banneker was asked to help. Using his remarkable memory, he redrew the entire city layout from scratch, including the locations of its streets, squares, and major buildings. His incredible ability to recall every detail saved the capital's design.[163]

But that wasn't his only contribution. As an astronomer and surveyor, Banneker knew how to use the stars to set precise geographic locations. He is believed to have used the same star-based navigation techniques that Mason and Dixon used to lay out the Mason-Dixon Line a few years earlier. With only the night sky as his guide, Banneker set the cornerstone of Washington, D.C., marking the foundation of the nation's capital.

Challenging Jefferson

Banneker wasn't just a scientist—he was also a man of deep moral conviction. In 1791, he wrote a powerful letter to Thomas Jefferson, the author of *The Declaration of Independence*, challenging him on the hypocrisy of slavery. Jefferson had written that "all men are created equal," yet he enslaved people.

In his letter, Banneker reminded Jefferson that Black Americans were just as intelligent and capable as White Americans. He urged Jefferson to live up to the ideals of *The Declaration of Independence* and take action to end slavery.

> "Sir," he wrote, "how pitiable it is to reflect that although you were so fully convinced of the benevolence of the Father of mankind, you should at the same time counteract His mercies by detaining thousands of my brethren under groaning captivity and cruel oppression."

Surprisingly, Jefferson wrote back, expressing admiration for Banneker's talents and promising to forward a copy of Banneker's almanac to scientists in France. Though Jefferson did not take action by freeing his own slaves, Banneker's courage in speaking out set an example for generations to come.

The Man Who Measured the Stars

By the 1790s, almanacs were among the most widely read books in America. They contained vital information about:

- Solar and lunar eclipses
- Tide tables to help sailors navigate safely
- Weather forecasts for farmers to plant their crops
- Mathematical puzzles and proverbs for education and entertainment
- Anti-slavery essays, where Banneker boldly spoke out against injustice

The Struggle to Publish

Even though Banneker's almanacs were highly accurate and respected, he faced immense challenges in getting them published. Many White printers refused to work with a Black author. Some even doubted that Banneker could have written them himself.

Despite these obstacles, Banneker continued publishing almanacs from 1792 to 1797, distributing them in Pennsylvania, Maryland, Delaware, and Virginia. Thanks to Jefferson, copies even made it across the Atlantic to scientists in France, giving Banneker international recognition.

A Lasting Legacy—And a Tragic Fire

Benjamin Banneker never sought fame or fortune. He simply followed his curiosity, using his mind to better understand the world and help others.

- His wooden clock amazed all who saw it.
- His work in Washington, D.C. helped shape the capital of the United States.
- His letter to Jefferson challenged one of the most powerful men in America to reconsider his views on race and equality.
- His almanacs changed how people viewed African American intellect and ability.

But tragedy struck just hours after Banneker's death on October 19, 1806. His farmhouse, where he had spent years carefully studying the stars and recording his scientific discoveries, burned to the ground. The fire destroyed nearly all of his papers, books, and even the wooden clock he had built as a boy—the one that had kept perfect time for over 40 years.

Everything he had worked so hard to create—his lifetime of research, calculations, and observations—was lost forever. Some believe the fire was accidental, but others suspect it may have been set deliberately to erase his legacy. Despite this terrible loss, Banneker's story could not be erased. His ideas, his writings, and his influence had already spread far beyond his farm. He had changed minds, shattered barriers, and proven that intelligence, creativity, and brilliance know no race or background. Though we will never recover the pages that were lost in the flames, the impact of Benjamin Banneker's life still burns brightly in the history of America.

His almanacs, city maps, and fearless letters all remind us that true greatness comes not from where you are born—but from the fire inside you to learn, explore, and never give up. And so, every time you look up at the night sky, remember Benjamin Banneker—the boy who read the stars and helped shape a nation.

Big Ma-Ma and Prince Banneka

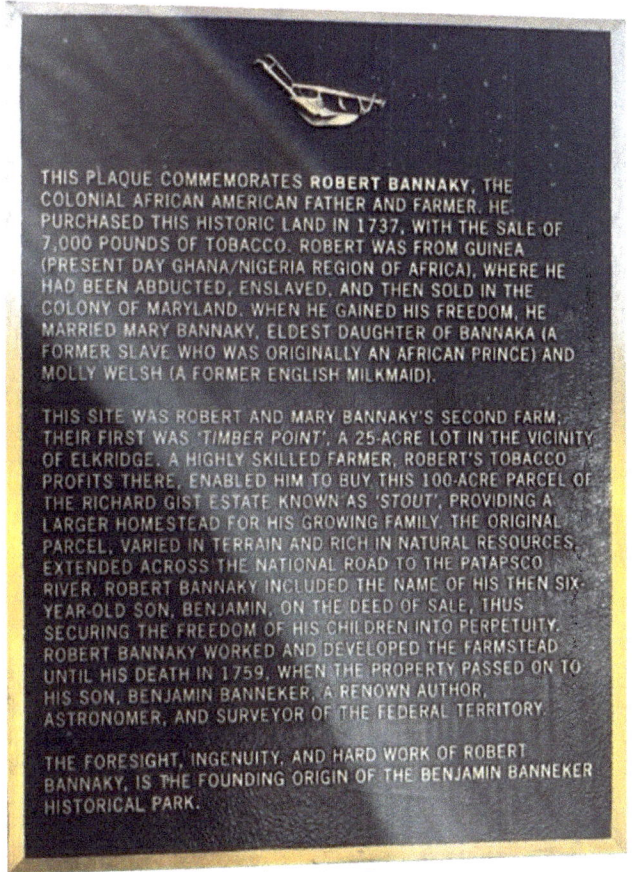

Photo taken by author Feb. 16, 2024
Benjamin Banneker Historical Park, Catonsville, MD

The story of Benjamin Banneker begins long before he was born, in an unlikely pairing that defied all odds—an African prince married an English convict.

His grandparents, Banneka, the son of a West African king, and Molly Welsh, a former indentured servant from England, built a life together in Maryland that would lay the foundation for their grandson's extraordinary mind.

Molly Welsh's journey to America began under cruel circumstances. As a young woman in England, she was falsely accused of theft after spilling a pail of milk and sentenced to seven years of indentured servitude in Maryland instead of execution (because she could read). Unlike many servants who never escaped their bonds, Molly not only survived but thrived, eventually securing land of her own. But she needed help to make it work.

That help came in an unusual form. At an auction of enslaved men, Molly purchased two African laborers fresh off the boat—one strong and muscular, the other lean and regal in demeanor. She soon discovered that the second man was Banneka, the son of an African king, captured in a raid and sold into slavery. Though many viewed him as ill-suited for labor, Molly recognized something different—a sharp mind and a quiet strength.

Over time, respect turned to love. Molly freed Banneka and married him, an astonishing act in colonial Maryland. Maryland law did not yet prohibit interracial marriage, but that would soon change. She called him "The Prince," and the family referred to her as "Big Ma-Ma"—a woman whose sheer willpower had built a life from nothing. Together, they raised four daughters, including Mary Banneky, Benjamin's mother.

The Prince, though weakened by the horrors of the Middle Passage, possessed remarkable skills that set him apart from other farmers. He was an expert hunter, ensuring the family always had food, but his most astonishing gift was his ability to predict the weather with uncanny accuracy. Long before scientific meteorology, he could sense shifts in the wind and patterns in the sky, allowing his crops to thrive while others struggled.

It's easy to see how young Benjamin inherited his grandfather's talents. Banneka's knowledge of the stars, seasons, and tides—passed down from the Dogon people of West Africa, acclaimed for their mastery of astronomy—seemed to take root in Benjamin's mind, preparing him for his own discoveries.

But it wasn't just nature that shaped Banneker—it was nurture, too. Big Ma-Ma saw something special in her grandson and poured every ounce of wisdom she had into him. She taught him to read using the same Bible that had saved her life in England and told him stories of survival, courage, and resilience.

This unusual heritage—a prince's knowledge, a convict's determination, and a family's belief in the power of education—shaped Benjamin Banneker into the genius he became—that and his photographic memory!

His destiny was written not just in the stars he studied, but in the courage of those who came before him.

Frances Ellen Watkins Harper
Activist, Poet, and Prophet of an American Dream

Plaque marking the Philadelphia home of Frances Ellen Watkins Harper, placed by the Pennsylvania Historical and Museum Commission, 1991. Used by permission. This home, where she lived here from 1870 until her death in 1911 was designated a National Historic Landmark in 1976. Her 1872 image is at the Library of Congress.

In the annals of American history, certain voices resonate across the centuries, echoing wisdom, resilience, and a profound call for justice. Among these voices, Frances Ellen Watkins Harper stands out as a poet, writer, educator, and activist whose life and work defined the struggle for equality in nineteenth-century America.

Known as the **"Dean of African American Writers"** of her time, Harper used her gifts with language to champion the causes of abolition, suffrage, temperance, and education, becoming a guiding light for her people in a deeply divided nation.

A Voice for Justice

Born free in Baltimore, Maryland, in 1825, Frances Ellen Watkins was raised by her uncle, a minister, after being orphaned at a young age. Her uncle operated a school for Black children, where Harper received an education that was rare for African Americans in the pre–Civil War era. From an early age, she displayed a keen intellect and a passion for learning, characteristics that would shape her life's work. By the age of twenty, she had published her first collection of poetry, *Forest Leaves*, which showcased her burgeoning literary talent and laid the foundation for a prolific career that spanned nearly seven decades.

Abolition and Women's Rights

Harper's path soon took her beyond the world of poetry and into the public sphere. In the 1850s, she became actively involved in abolitionist causes, writing and lecturing to for the end of slavery. She traveled extensively, speaking on behalf of the Pennsylvania Anti-Slavery Society and other organizations. These travels often placed her in hostile environments and physical hardships, yet she remained undeterred. One of her most compelling public addresses, *"We Are All Bound Up Together,"* delivered at the National Women's Rights Convention in 1866, captivated audiences with its moral force and impassioned plea for freedom and justice. She reflected on these experiences in writings that paint a vivid picture of the challenges faced in the fight against slavery.

Service and Sacrifice

The end of the Civil War marked a new chapter for Harper. With the abolition of slavery came the task of rebuilding the nation and ensuring the full participation of African Americans in society. Harper dedicated herself to this work, journeying into the heart of the post-war South to educate and support newly emancipated African Americans. Her accounts of these travels reveal the privations she endured: the long, uncomfortable journeys, the hostile environments, and the daily struggles of those she sought to help. Yet, her spirit remained unbroken. Harper viewed this work as both a duty and a calling, feeling a deep connection to the people she served.

Speaking Her Mind

Harper expressed deep disgust with President Lincoln's proposal to colonize the formerly enslaved outside of the United States. She saw the plan as both a betrayal of the very principles of freedom and a misguided notion that four million people could simply be removed from American society. Harper criticized this idea as an attempt to erase the contributions and future potential of freed Blacks, pointing out the absurdity of replacing such a vital part of the nation's workforce. The following selection, written in the midst of the Civil War in 1862, is from "Mrs. Frances E. Watkins Harper on the War and the President's Colonization Scheme:"

> Heavy is the guilt that hangs upon the neck of this nation, and where is the first sign of national repentance? The least signs of contrition for the wrongs of the Indian and the negro? As this nation has had glorious opportunities for standing as an example to the nations leading the van of the world's progress, and inviting the groaning millions to a higher destiny; but instead of that she has dwarfed herself to slavery's base and ignoble ends, and now, smitten of God and conquered by her crimes, she has become a mournful warning, a sad exemplification of the close connexion between national crimes and national judgments.

Harper's opinion was in response to a colonization movement which had never gained popularity among African Americans or abolitionists. Frederick Douglass condemned it in 1849, declaring, "We live here—have lived here—have a right to live here, and mean to live here." Yet, in 1862, President Lincoln met with Black leaders at the White House, advocating for their emigration as he argued, "It is better for us both…to be separated."[164]

In addition to her educational efforts, Harper's advocacy extended to the realms of women's suffrage and temperance. She recognized that the struggle for African American freedom was intrinsically linked to the rights of women, arguing eloquently for universal suffrage. Her speeches and writings on the topic showcased her ability to weave the threads of race, gender, and social justice into a coherent and compelling argument for equality. As she stated in her 1866 address: "We are all bound up together in one great bundle of humanity, and society cannot trample on the weakest and feeblest of its members without receiving the curse in its own soul." Her words exhibited prophetic clarity, insisting that the promise of the American republic could only be realized when all its citizens, regardless of race or gender, were granted their full rights.

The Dean of African American Writers

Her poetry often reflected a call for newly freed men to rise to the demands of newfound freedom and citizenship. In works *like "Aunt Chloe's Politics,"* Harper urged Black men not to squander their hard-won rights for fleeting pleasures, cautioning against selling their votes for a drink of liquor. Harper contrasted this with the steadfastness of women, whom she saw as more grounded and unwavering in their commitment to building a just society.

One of Harper's most poignant contributions was her novel, Iola Leroy, published in 1892. Through its narrative, Harper explored themes of race, identity, and the complexities of life for African Americans in the Reconstruction era. The novel not only offered readers a rare glimpse into the Black experience of the time but also served as a form of resistance, countering the prevailing stereotypes and assumptions about African Americans. *Iola Leroy* stands today as one of the earliest novels published by an African American woman and remains a testament to Harper's literary genius and her commitment to social justice.

Her poetry, often imbued with a prophetic tone, struck at the moral conscience of the nation. In works like *"Bury Me in a Free Land,"* she lamented the horrors of slavery and invoked a powerful vision of liberty and human dignity. Her words transcended the page, becoming a rallying cry for generations of activists who followed. Harper's pen was her sword, and she wielded it with unmatched skill, challenging her readers to confront the injustices of their time. **In** *"Bury Me in a Free Land,"* she wrote, **"I ask no monument, proud and high, to arrest the gaze of the passers-by; All that my yearning spirit craves, is bury me not in a land of slaves."**

A Life Among Legends

During her life, Harper enjoyed close associations with prominent figures of the abolitionist and suffrage movements, yet she carved out a unique space for herself as an independent thinker and leader. She corresponded with Frederick Douglass, admired Harriet Tubman for her courage and tenacity, and engaged with W. E. B. Du Bois, who at one time lived just down the street from her in Philadelphia. These connections placed her at the heart of the intellectual and social movements that shaped the course of African American history.

It was in Philadelphia that she spent the final years of her life, continuing her activism and writing until her death in 1911. Harper's presence in Philadelphia's vibrant community of African American leaders imbued her work with an unyielding sense of hope. Her house, now marked as a National Historic Site, was a gathering place for like-minded individuals who believed in the possibility of a better future. The city itself, home to so many luminaries like Tubman and Du Bois, became a symbol of the potential for progress and the perseverance of the African American spirit. Standing in front of Harper's former residence, one can almost hear the echoes of her words, urging us forward: *"We can do this."*

Note from the Author

In my journey through American history, I came across the works of Benson J. Lossing and felt compelled to order three volumes of his 1879 series, *Our Country*. When the books arrived, I noticed a beautifully inscribed signature on an otherwise blank page near the front of each volume. It was *"F. E. Watkins,"* the first owner of these three rare books. The significance of these signatures did not strike me until I compared them with an online sample. They were the same! **Imagine my astonishment when I realized these incredible books had once belonged to one of the most powerful voices for abolition and the dean of nineteenth-century African American literature!**

Polly Cooper, Oneida Angel of Valley Forge

Winter was bitter at Valley Forge. Rivers froze in silence beneath sheets of ice, trees stood skeletal and still, and snow fell heavy and unrelenting across the hills—as hungry soldiers froze.

"Allies in War, Partners in Peace," Smithsonian National Museum of the American Indian, Courtesy of Edward Hlavka, Rapid City, SD

But help was coming—from deep within the Northern forests, where tall pines whispered to the sky. General Lafayette had been sent from Valley Forge to Albany, New York, to lead an attack on Canada. The promised force did not materialize, and he learned the folly of the venture. Lafayette turned instead to the Oneida, heroes of the Battles of Oriskany and Saratoga, inviting 47 warriors to join him at Valley Forge.[165]

When old Chief Shenandoah heard of the suffering at Valley Forge, he was determined to help. Towering at six feet five and full of quiet strength, he was a man respected for both wisdom and courage. He had pledged his support to the rebels and was ready to help.

Shenandoah sent the warriors, including one of his two sons. Oneida legend says they brought with them six hundred baskets of dried white corn. This corn, used by the People of the Longhouse for generations, could nourish—but only if properly prepared. Its kernels were tough, its husks thick, and if eaten raw, would swell painfully in the stomach and sicken the starving men it was meant to save. And so, just as spring began to break winter's grip, the Oneida began their journey.

Walking beside the braves on the last part of the journey was Polly Cooper, a half-Oneida woman known for her strong heart and deep wisdom. She was neither warrior nor chief, but she carried something just as vital: the ancestral knowledge to turn that corn into life-saving food. When they arrived at Valley Forge, the weak and desperate soldiers began to reach for the corn, ready to eat it raw. But Polly stopped them. She told them plainly that doing so would make them sick.

Then she showed them the old ways—soaking and boiling the corn, stirring it into mush and soup, using the care her People had passed down through generations. She sometimes added dried berries, crushed nuts, or even husks, transforming simple food into something not just filling, but nourishing. She tended the pots, feeding the soldiers one bowl at a time. Slowly, strength returned to their bodies, and the light returned to their eyes.

For her kindness, the soldiers were deeply grateful. The wives of General Washington and his officers offered Polly money in thanks, but she gently refused. She had not come for pay. Instead, they gave her a gift: a finely woven black shawl and bonnet, offered with respect. Polly accepted the gifts. "I came because it was right," she told them. "Helping others is the way of the People."[166]

On May 20th, Lafayette led 2,200 soldiers who were about to be annihilated by a far superior British force at Barren Hill. Brave Oneida warriors protected the retreat, allowing the Continentals to escape across the river and return to Valley Forge. Six Oneida gave their lives that day, and may have saved not just an army, but a nation.

The Fight Goes On

Enslaved People Today:

- Nearly 25 million are in forced labor
- 15 million are in forced marriages
- Nearly three-quarters are female
- One in four is a child

Human trafficking generates an estimated $150 billion each year in illicit profits for traffickers and slave masters.

TOP 10 NATIONS WITH SLAVES TODAY

1. India — 8 million
2. China — 3.86 million
3. Pakistan — 3.19 million
4. North Korea — 2.64 million
5. Nigeria — 1.39 million
6. Iran — 1.29 million
7. Indonesia — 1.22 million
8. Dem. Republic of the Congo — 1 million
9. Russia — 794,000
10. Philippines — 784,000

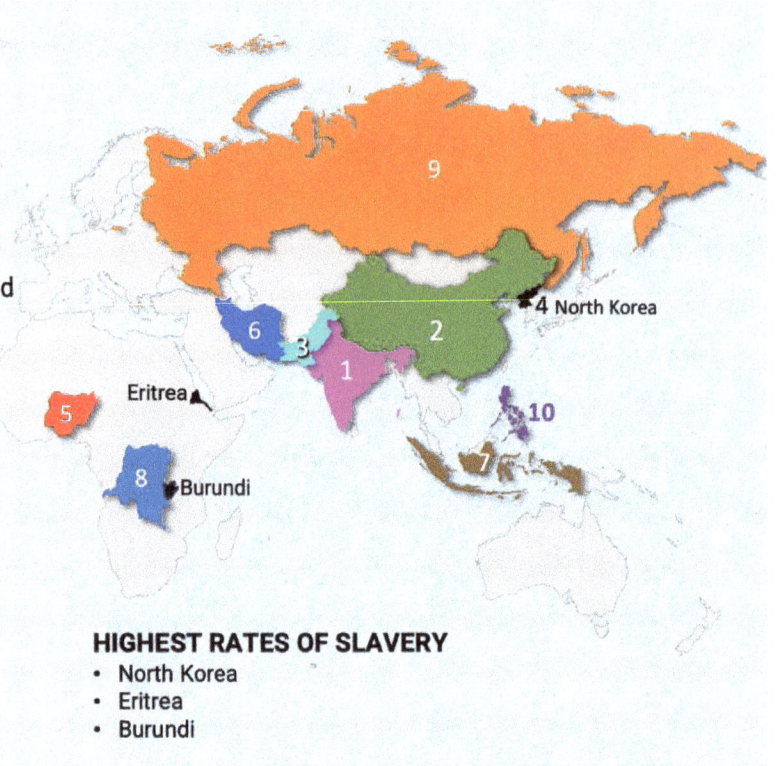

HIGHEST RATES OF SLAVERY
- North Korea
- Eritrea
- Burundi

Today, over 150 products available to us are made with slave labor, generating $150 billion in profits annually for slave owners. The map above shows the top ten countries utilizing slave labor and the staggering numbers in each. Alongside, we see the nations with the highest rates of enslavement. In addition to the fifteen million forced into child marriages and sex slavery, twenty-five million are in forced labor today—many times the number enslaved during the Civil War. One-fourth of these enslaved individuals are children. Shockingly, we may be unwittingly supporting this modern slavery by purchasing goods tainted by forced labor.[167]

Products Made with Slave Labor

Alcoholic Beverages	Amber	Artificial Flowers	Baked Goods
Bamboo	Bananas	Beans	Beans (green beans)
Beans (green, soy, yellow)	Beef	Bidis (hand-rolled cigarettes)	Blueberries
Bovines	Brassware	Brazil Nuts/Chestnuts	Bricks
Broccoli	Cabbages	Carpets	Carrots
Cashews	Cattle	Cement	Ceramics
Cereal Grains	Charcoal	Chile Peppers	Christmas Decorations
Citrus Fruits	Cloves	Coal	Cobalt ore
Coca (stimulant plant)	Cocoa	Coconuts	Coffee
Copper	Corn	Cotton	Cottonseed (hybrid)
Cucumbers	Cumin	Diamonds	Dried Fish
Eggplants	Electronics	Embellished Textiles	Emeralds
Fashion Accessories	Fireworks	Fish	Flowers
Fluorspar (mineral)	Footwear	Footwear (sandals)	Fruits (Pome and Stone)
Furniture	Furniture (steel)	Garlic	Garments
Gems	Glass	Glass Bangles	Gloves
Goats	Granite	Granite (crushed)	Grapes
Gravel (crushed stones)	Gypsum (mineral)	Hair Products	Hazelnuts
Hogs	Incense (agarbatti)	Iron	Jade
Khat	Khat/Miraa (stimulant plant)	Leather	Leather Goods

Lettuce	Lobsters	Locks	Manioc/Cassava
Matches	Meat	Melons	Mica
Nails	Nile Perch (fish)	Oil (palm)	Olives
Onions	Palm Thatch	Peanuts	Pepper
Peppers	Pineapples	Poppies	Pornography
Potatoes	Poultry	Pulses (legumes)	Pyrotechnics
Rice	Rubber	Rubber Gloves	Rubies
Salt	Sand	Sandstone	Sapphires
Sesame	Sheep	Shellfish	Shrimp
Silk Cocoons	Silk Fabric	Silk Thread	Silver
Sisal	Soap	Soccer Balls	Stones (limestone)
Stones (pumice)	Strawberries	Sugar Beets	Sugarcane
Sunflowers	Surgical Instruments	Sweet Potatoes	Tantalum ore (coltan)
Tanzanite (gems)	Tea	Textiles	Textiles (hand-woven)
Textiles (jute)	Thread/Yarn	Tilapia (fish)	Timber
Tin	Tin ore (cassiterite)	Tobacco	Tomato Products
Tomatoes	Toys	Trona (mineral)	Tungsten ore (wolframite)
Vanilla	Wheat	Yerba Mate (stimulant plant)	Zinc[168]

A Call to Action

It is not easy to discern which products are made with slave labor. It will require a concerted effort from governments, industries, and consumers to eliminate these products from global supply chains. Sadly, some would rather focus solely on our nation's past sins while ignoring these current injustices that continue to plague society. Real change demands a unified and determined effort.

When I brought this issue to one of my congressional representatives, he responded that federal laws implemented in the 1930s are sufficient to regulate the production, import, and sale of items made by slave labor. But these laws, quite simply, are not adequate.

What Can WE Do?

By purchasing products made with slave labor, we become complicit in the cycle of exploitation. We can look to Benjamin Lay as an example, but in today's interconnected world, it is nearly impossible to produce everything ourselves as he once did. Nevertheless, we can demand transparency and ethical practices from government, industry, and merchants. Are we buying products made with slave labor? How can we encourage businesses to ensure no slave labor is involved in their supply chains?

How Could We Do Without Sugar and Rum?

I OWN I am shock'd at the purchase of slaves,
And fear those who buy them and sell them are knaves;
What I hear of their hardships, their tortures, and groans,
Is almost enough to draw pity from stones.
I pity them greatly, but I must be mum,
For how could we do without sugar and rum?

(William Cowper, Pity for Poor Africans, 1788)

A Final Reflection

America did not win the right to govern itself as a free nation just by declaring its independence. It took winning a war for self-determination and enshrining their new-found liberty in law, in the form of the Constitution of the United States and the Bill of Rights.

About three generations later, the pattern repeated itself. Abraham Lincoln, who abhorred slavery, issued the Emancipation Proclamation on January 1, 1863. Yet, this proclamation did not immediately free any enslaved people—it was only a promise of freedom, dependent on the Union's victory in the Civil War. It applied only to states still in rebellion, leaving slavery untouched in border states that had not seceded and in southern counties already under Union control. Even so, the proclamation inspired 210,000 African American men to don the Union blue and fight for the cause of liberty. Their sacrifices were immense—approximately 67,680 became casualties of battle or disease, with 36,000 making the ultimate sacrifice to help free four million of their brothers and sisters. For extraordinary bravery in combat, **twenty-six African Americans were awarded the Congressional Medal of Honor. They were heroes!**

The proclamation freed no slaves in the border states that had not seceded. Neither had it freed the slaves in many counties in the South that were firmly under the control of the Union. Enslaved persons in these areas were spelled out in the proclamation as if no proclamation had been issued. It only "freed" slaves in states still in rebellion as of January 1, 1863, but that was freedom in name only. They were still under the control of Confederate forces and needed to escape to become free. Even so, many were kept in Union encampments and were classified as "contraband," a derogatory term for "illicit goods," or property relieved from their masters.

It took winning the war and the rebellious states returning to the Union with the promise that their citizens would support the Emancipation Proclamation. Our founding documents worked just as before, following that inspired pattern of Liberty Enshrined in Law, culminating in the Thirteenth Amendment. The fight for freedom did not end there, however, as Jim Crow, the Klan, and lynchings left ugly stains upon our nation.

As we reflect on the legacies of Jefferson and Lincoln's, we are reminded of the enduring struggle for freedom and equality that defines the American experience. This journey is marked by progress and setbacks, triumphs and tragedies, yet the timeless principles of liberty, justice, and equality also fuel this journey.

Learning how each Grievance lent teeth to the arguments surrounding the king's *"long train of abuses"* helps us realize that these *Charters of Freedom* were not merely flowery prose and lofty ideals but each had history behind it. Those men of a bygone era looked forward to our time with dreams and hope that we would understand their difficulties, appreciate the enormity of their tasks, and improve upon their efforts.

In navigating the complexities of our present moment, let us draw inspiration from the courage and conviction of those who came before. Let us reaffirm our commitment to the principles that have guided our nation through its darkest hours. We can build a future worthy of the sacrifices made by those who dared to dream of a *More Perfect Union*. This was said quite well in a poem by Francis Daniel Pastorius, leader of the 1688 Germantown Protest Against Slavery. During that very year, Pastorius wrote a poem entitled ***"Greeting to Posterity"*** in the first official document of Germantown. Translated from Latin by John Greenleaf Whittier, it reads in part:

HAIL to posterity! …

Remember, and wherein we have done well

Follow our footsteps, men of coming years!

Where we have failed to do aright, or wisely live,

Be warned by us, the better way pursue,

And, knowing we were human, even as you,

Pity us and forgive!

Farewell, Posterity! …

…Forevermore farewell.

Francis Daniel Pastorius
German-born educator, lawyer, poet, and public official
Founder of Germantown, Pennsylvania
September 26, 1651—c. 1720

Pastorius' poem serves as a timeless challenge to future generations, urging us to learn from the past, build upon its successes, and correct the failures. His words remind us that history is not just a record of what was, but a guide for what may be. We are the posterity Pastorius was speaking to, entrusted with the responsibility to advance the cause of liberty, justice, and human dignity. If we truly honor those who laid the foundation of liberty, we must ensure their sacrifices were not in vain by standing against injustice in our own time.

The Choice is Ours

It is easy to view the distant past and harshly judge former generations and men like Thomas Jefferson for their failures in ending slavery. We blame them for tolerating and supporting slave labor. Their legacies are dimmed by the evils and darkness of slavery. Yet, we ignorantly support slavery today with our purchases and allow it to continue through our complacency.

The reality of slavery today, including the sex slave trade, should shake our souls and stir our hearts. It presents an urgent call to rally together and extend the inalienable rights of life and liberty to every individual. This is not just a problem of the past—it is our problem.

Will we rise to the challenge and take a stand for liberty, as many of our ancestors fearlessly did? The choice is ours. OUR legacy rests upon it.

This is OUR Jefferson moment.

Bibliography

Books

Barton, David. *American History in Black & White*. Aledo, TX: WallBuilder Press, 2004. ISBN: 978-1-932225-27-3.

Banneker, Benjamin. Banneker's Almanack, 1795. Facsimile reprint. Delhi, India: Facsimile Publisher, 2018.

Beck, Derek W. *Igniting the American Revolution 1773-1775*. ISBN: 978-1-4926-3132-3.

Bedini, Silvio A. The Life of Benjamin Banneker: The First African-American Man of Science. New York: Scribner, 1972.

Boyd, Julian P., ed. *The Papers of Thomas Jefferson, Volume 1: 1760-1776*. Princeton, NJ: Princeton University Press, 1950.

Braght, Thieleman J. van. *Martyrs Mirror: The Story of Seventeen Centuries of Christian Martyrdom from the Time of Christ to A.D. 1660*. Scottdale, PA: Herald Press, 1950. ISBN: 978-0-8361-1390-7.

Cappon, Lester J., ed. *The Adams-Jefferson Letters: The Complete Correspondence Between Thomas Jefferson and Abigail and John Adams*. Chapel Hill, NC: University of North Carolina Press, 1988. ISBN: 978-0-8078-4230-0.

Captivating History. *History of Colonial America*. ISBN: 9781637165546.

Channing, Edward. *A History of the United States. Vol. 3*. New York: Macmillan, 1907–1929.

Chernow, Ron. *Alexander Hamilton*. New York: Penguin Press, 2004. ISBN: 978-1-59420-009-0.

Cook, Jane Hampton. *Stories of Faith and Courage from the Revolutionary War*. ISBN: 9780899570426.

Davis, Burke. *Black Heroes of the American Revolution*. New York: Harcourt, Inc., 1976. ISBN: 0-15-238739-8.

Ellis, Joseph J. *Friends Divided: John Adams and Thomas Jefferson*. New York: Penguin Press, 2017. ISBN: 978-0-7352-2471-1.

Fried, Stephen. *Rush: Revolution, Madness, and the Visionary Doctor Who Became a Founding Father*. New York: Crown, 2018. ISBN: 978-0-8041-4006-5.

Glubok, Shirley. *Home and Child Life in Colonial Days*. New York: Macmillan, 1969.

Goodrich, Charles Augustus, and Thomas W. Lewis. *Lives of the Signers to The Declaration of Independence*. WallBuilders Press, 1995. ISBN: 978-1-946100-10-8.

Herrick, Cheesman A. *White Servitude in Pennsylvania: Indentured and Redemption Labor in Colony and Commonwealth*. Philadelphia: John Joseph McVey, 1926.

Hull, William I. *William Penn and the Dutch Quaker Migration to Pennsylvania*. ISBN: 9781163453209.

Jennings, Francis. *Benjamin Franklin, Politician: The Mask and the Man*. ISBN: 0-393-03983-8.

Jordan, Don, and Michael Walsh. *White Cargo: The Forgotten History of Britain's White Slaves in America*. New York: New York University Press, 2008. ISBN: 978-0-8147-4296-9.

Lay, Benjamin. *All Slave-Keepers That Keep the Innocent in Bondage, Apostates Pretending to Lay Claim to the Pure & Holy Christian Religion; Of What Congregation So Ever; But Especially in Their Ministers*. Philadelphia: Printed by Benjamin Franklin, 1737.

Lewis, Claude. *Benjamin Banneker: The Man Who Saved Washington*. New York: McGraw-Hill, 1970.

Lynch, John Roy. *Reminiscences of an Active Life: The Autobiography of John Roy Lynch*. Edited by John Hope Franklin. Chicago: University of Chicago Press, 1970. ISBN: 0-226-49818-2.

Lynch, P.J. The Boy Who Fell Off the Mayflower, or John Howland's Good Fortune. Candlewick Press, 2015.

Maier, Pauline. *American Scripture: Making The Declaration of Independence*. ISBN: 0-679-45492-6.

McCullough, David. *1776*. New York: Simon & Schuster, 2005. ISBN: 978-0-7432-2672-1.

Memoirs of the Private and Public Life of William Penn. ISBN: 9781162949710.

Miller, John Chester. *The Wolf by the Ears: Thomas Jefferson and Slavery*. The Free Press, a Division of Macmillan Publishing Co., Inc., New York, 1977. ISBN: 0-02-921500-5.

Nell, William Cooper. *The Colored Patriots of the American Revolution*. Boston: Robert F. Wallcut, 1855. ISBN: 978-1-9733-7947-8.

Oakley, Violet. *The Holy Experiment: Our Heritage from William Penn 1644-1944*. Philadelphia: Cogslea Studio Publications, 1950.

Pennypacker, Samuel W. *The Autobiography of a Pennsylvanian*. ISBN: 9781345867589.

Petersen, Eric S., ed. *Light and Liberty: Reflections on the Pursuit of Happiness*. New York: Modern Library, 2004. ISBN: 978-0-8129-7432-4.

Ragosta, John A. *For the People, for the Country: Patrick Henry's Final Political Battle*. ISBN: 978-0-8139-5022-8.

Raphael, Ray. *Founding Myths: Stories That Hide Our Patriotic Past*. New York: The New Press, 2004. ISBN: 978-1-56584-921-1.

Rankin, Hugh F. *Francis Marion: The Swamp Fox*. New York: Thomas Y. Crowell Company, 1973. ISBN: 0-690-00097-9.

Schiapp, Stacy. *The Revolutionary: Samuel Adams*. New York: Little, Brown and Company, 2020. ISBN: 978-0-316-44111-7.

Souter, Gerry, and Janet Souter. *The Constitution: The Story of the Creation and Adaptation of the Most Important Document in the History of the United States of America*. London: Arcturus Publishing, 2019. ISBN: 978-1-83861-007-4.

The Complete Frances Harper. ISBN: 978-1-5131-3348-5.

Warren, Mercy Otis. *History of the Rise, Progress and Termination of the American Revolution*. ISBN: 9781015707108.

Webb, Simon. *Jeremiah Dixon: Surveyor of the Mason-Dixon Line*. CreateSpace Independent Publishing Platform, 2015. ISBN: 978-1-5229-4825-4.

Wood, Gordon S. *Revolutionary Characters: What Made the Founders Different*. New York: Penguin Press, 2006. ISBN: 1-59420-093-9.

Anthologies and Compilations

The Constitution of the United States of America and Selected Writings of the Founding Fathers. New York: Barnes & Noble, 2012. ISBN: 978-1-4351-3930-5.

The Essential Debate on the Constitution: Federalist and Anti-Federalist Speeches, Articles, and Letters During the Struggle Over Ratification. Edited by Bernard Bailyn. New York: Library of America, 2018. ISBN: 978-1-59853-583-9.

Lives of the Signers to The Declaration of Independence. Edited by B. J. Lossing. WallBuilders Press, 1995. ISBN: 978-1-932225-10-5.

The Founding Fathers: The Essential Guide to the Men Who Made America. Hoboken, NJ: Wiley, 2007. ISBN: 978-0-470-11792-7.

The Signers: The 56 Stories Behind The Declaration of Independence. Edited by Dennis Brindell Fradin. New York: Scholastic, 2002. ISBN: 0-439-49560-1.

End Notes

1. St. James Episcopal Church, "Our History," last accessed January 16, 2025, https://stjames-episcopal.org/our-history/.

2. "May 27, 1776: Six Nations Meet with Continental Congress," *Nations & Cannons*, accessed February 20, 2025, https://www.nationsandcannons.com/blog/may-27-1776-six-nations-meet-with-continental.

3. "Fast Facts: Democracy and the Haudenosaunee," Oneida Indian Nation, accessed February 20, 2025, https://www.oneidaindiannation.com/fast-facts-democracy-and-the-haudenosaunee/.

4. Oneida Indian Nation, "There Is Strength in Unity," last accessed January 16, 2025, https://www.oneidaindiannation.com/there-is-strength-in-unity/.

5. Oneida Indian Nation, "There Is Strength in Unity," last accessed January 16, 2025, https://www.oneidaindiannation.com/there-is-strength-in-unity/.

6. Great Law of Peace, *Haudenosaunee (Iroquois) Confederacy*, Portland State University, accessed February 24, 2025, https://web.pdx.edu/~caskeym/iroquois_web/html/greatlaw.html.

7. "The Great Tree of Peace (Skaehetsi'kona)," Indigenous Values Initiative, accessed February 20, 2025, https://indigenousvalues.org/haudenosaunee-values/great-tree-peace-skaehetsi%CB%80kona/.

8. Library of Congress, "Broadside Collection: Rare Book and Special Collections Division," last accessed January 16, 2025, https://www.loc.gov/resource/rbpe.1900040a/?sp=1&st=text.

9. Akhil Reed Amar, *America's Constitution: A Biography* (New York: Random House, 2005), 15–20.

10. Akhil Reed Amar, *The Bill of Rights: Creation and Reconstruction* (New Haven: Yale University Press, 1998), 245–252.

11. "Abraham Lincoln, Collected Works of Abraham Lincoln: Volume 4, Mar. 5, 1860–Oct. 24, 1861," last accessed January 16, 2025, https://constitutingamerica.org/90day-dcin-apple-gold-picture-silver-declaration-of-independence-influence-on-united-states-constitution-guest-essayist-tony-williams/#:~:text=the%20American%20Founding.-,Using%20a%20biblical%20metaphor%2C%20he%20thought%20.

12. Abraham Lincoln, *Fragment on the Constitution and the Union*, ca. January 1861, in Roy P. Basler, ed., *The Collected Works of Abraham Lincoln, Vol. 4* (New Brunswick: Rutgers University Press, 1953), 168.

13. Pauline Maier, *Ratification: The People Debate the Constitution, 1787–1788* (New York: Simon & Schuster, 2010), 50–57.

14. *History Today*, "Waves of Revolution," last accessed January 16, 2025, https://www.historytoday.com/archive/waves-revolution#:~:text=They%20sparked%20the%20Haitian%20Revolution,the%20barricades%20to%20confront%20absolutism.

15. Project Gutenberg, "The Project Gutenberg eBook of Second Treatise of Government," by John Locke, last accessed January 16, 2025, https://www.gutenberg.org/files/7370/7370-h/7370-h.htm?ref=americanpurpose.com.

16. Lawrence A. Harper, *The English Navigation Laws: A Seventeenth-Century Experiment in Social Engineering* (New York: Columbia University Press, 1939), 112–118.

17. Thomas C. Barrow, *Trade and Empire: The British Customs Service in Colonial America, 1660–1775* (Cambridge, MA: Harvard University Press, 1967), 145–150.

18. Joseph Albert Ernst, *Money and Politics in America, 1755–1775: A Study in the Currency Act of 1764 and the Political Economy of Revolution* (Chapel Hill: University of North Carolina Press, 1973), 45–50.

19. Peter J. Kastor, *The Nation's Crucible: The Louisiana Purchase and the Creation of America* (New Haven: Yale University Press, 2004), 28–33.

20. Colin G. Calloway, *The Scratch of a Pen: 1763 and the Transformation of North America* (Oxford: Oxford University Press, 2006), 78–84.

21. Edmund S. Morgan and Helen M. Morgan, *The Stamp Act Crisis: Prologue to Revolution* (Chapel Hill: University of North Carolina Press, 1953), 48–53.

22. Joseph Albert Ernst, *Money and Politics in America, 1755–1775: A Study in the Currency Act of 1764 and the Political Economy of Revolution* (Chapel Hill: University of North Carolina Press, 1973), 85–90.

23. Edmund S. Morgan and Helen M. Morgan, *The Stamp Act Crisis: Prologue to Revolution* (Chapel Hill: University of North Carolina Press, 1953), 85–92.

24. David Ammerman, *In the Common Cause: American Response to the Coercive Acts of 1774* (Charlottesville: University Press of Virginia, 1974), 75–79.

25 Benjamin L. Carp, *Defiance of the Patriots: The Boston Tea Party and the Making of America* (New Haven: Yale University Press, 2010), 45–50.

26 Hiller B. Zobel, *The Boston Massacre* (New York: W.W. Norton, 1970), 145–150.

27 Benjamin L. Carp, *Defiance of the Patriots: The Boston Tea Party and the Making of America* (New Haven: Yale University Press, 2010), 60–65.

28 Benjamin L. Carp, *Defiance of the Patriots: The Boston Tea Party and the Making of America* (New Haven: Yale University Press, 2010), 75–82.

29 David Ammerman, *In the Common Cause: American Response to the Coercive Acts of 1774* (Charlottesville: University Press of Virginia, 1974), 80–85.

30 David Ammerman, *In the Common Cause: American Response to the Coercive Acts of 1774* (Charlottesville: University Press of Virginia, 1974), 85–90.

31 David Ammerman, *In the Common Cause: American Response to the Coercive Acts of 1774* (Charlottesville: University Press of Virginia, 1974), 90–95.

32 John Phillip Reid, *Constitutional History of the American Revolution: The Authority of Law* (Madison: University of Wisconsin Press, 1993), 175–180.

33 David Ammerman, *In the Common Cause: American Response to the Coercive Acts of 1774* (Charlottesville: University Press of Virginia, 1974), 95–100.

34 Pauline Maier, *American Scripture: Making The Declaration of Independence* (New York: Knopf, 1997), 120–126.

35 Thomas Jefferson, *A Summary View of the Rights of British America* (Williamsburg, VA: Clementina Rind, 1774), in *The Papers of Thomas Jefferson*, vol. 1, ed. Julian P. Boyd (Princeton: Princeton University Press, 1950), 121–126; Jack N. Rakove, *Original Meanings: Politics and Ideas in the Making of the Constitution* (New York: Alfred A. Knopf, 1996), 183–189; Gordon S. Wood, *The Creation of the American Republic, 1776–1787* (Chapel Hill: University of North Carolina Press, 1969), 143–148.

36 Thomas Jefferson, *A Summary View of the Rights of British America* (Williamsburg, VA: Clementina Rind, 1774), in *The Papers of Thomas Jefferson*, vol. 1, ed. Julian P. Boyd (Princeton: Princeton University Press, 1950), 121–126; Bernard Bailyn, *The Ideological Origins of the American Revolution* (Cambridge, MA: Harvard University Press, 1992), 198–203; Gordon S. Wood, *The American Revolution: A History* (New York: Modern Library, 2002), 64–67.

37 Thomas Jefferson, *A Summary View of the Rights of British America* (Williamsburg, VA: Clementina Rind, 1774), in *The Papers of Thomas Jefferson*, vol. 1, ed. Julian P. Boyd (Princeton: Princeton University Press, 1950), 121–126; Gordon S. Wood, *The Radicalism of the American Revolution* (New York: Alfred A. Knopf, 1992), 174–178; Jack P. Greene, *The Constitutional Origins of the American Revolution* (Cambridge: Cambridge University Press, 2011), 92–97.

38 Journals of the House of Burgesses of Virginia, 1773–1776, ed. H. R. McIlwaine (Richmond: The Colonial Press, 1905), 154–155.

See also: Paul Leicester Ford, The Writings of Thomas Jefferson, vol. 1 (New York: G. P. Putnam's Sons, 1892), 426–427.

39 David Ammerman, *In the Common Cause: American Response to the Coercive Acts of 1774* (Charlottesville: University Press of Virginia, 1974), 45–49; Jack P. Greene, *The Constitutional Origins of the American Revolution* (Cambridge: Cambridge University Press, 2011), 102–107; Bernard Bailyn, *The Ideological Origins of the American Revolution* (Cambridge, MA: Harvard University Press, 1992), 210–214.

40 *Jack P. Greene, The Constitutional Origins of the American Revolution* (Cambridge: Cambridge University Press, 2010), 146–149

41 J.R. Jones, *The Revolution of 1688 in England* (New York: W.W. Norton, 1972), 189–192; Mark Kishlansky, *A Monarchy Transformed: Britain 1603–1714* (London: Penguin Books, 1997), 311–315; David L. Smith, *A History of the British Bill of Rights* (Cambridge: Cambridge University Press, 2019), 78–81.

42 J.R. Jones, *The Revolution of 1688 in England* (New York: W.W. Norton, 1972), 189–192; Mark Kishlansky, *A Monarchy Transformed: Britain 1603–1714* (London: Penguin Books, 1997), 311–315; Jack P. Greene, *The Constitutional Origins of the American Revolution* (Cambridge: Cambridge University Press, 2011), 92–97; Pauline Maier, *From Resistance to Revolution: Colonial Radicals and the Development of American Opposition to Britain, 1765-1776* (New York: W.W. Norton, 1991), 154–159.

43 Thomas Jefferson, *A Summary View of the Rights of British America* (Williamsburg, VA: Clementina Rind, 1774), in *The Papers of Thomas Jefferson*, vol. 1, ed. Julian P. Boyd (Princeton: Princeton University Press, 1950), 121–126; Jack P. Greene, *The Constitutional Origins of the American Revolution* (Cambridge: Cambridge University Press, 2011), 97–102; David Ammerman, *In the Common Cause: American Response to the Coercive Acts of 1774* (Charlottesville: University Press of Virginia, 1974), 53–57; Pauline Maier, *From Resistance to Revolution: Colonial Radicals and the Development of American Opposition to Britain, 1765-1776* (New York: W.W. Norton, 1991), 162–167.

44 Jack P. Greene, The Constitutional Origins of the American Revolution (Cambridge: Cambridge University Press, 2010), 93–98.

45 *Charter of Maryland (1632)*, in *Archives of Maryland Online*, vol. 3, ed. William Hand Browne (Baltimore: Maryland Historical Society, 1885), 7–17.

46 Francis Parkman, La Salle and the Discovery of the Great West (Boston: Little, Brown, 1869), 225–232.

47 Royal Proclamation of 1763, in The Avalon Project: Documents in Law, History and Diplomacy (Yale Law School), accessed October 2025, https://avalon.law.yale.edu/18th_century/proc1763.asp

48 Thomas Jefferson, Albemarle County Resolves (July 26, 1774), in The Papers of Thomas Jefferson, vol. 1, 1760–1776, ed. Julian P. Boyd (Princeton, NJ: Princeton University Press, 1950), 127–128.

49 Robert M. Calhoon, Timothy M. Barnes, and Robert S. Davis, eds., *The Loyalist Perception and Other Essays* (Columbia: University of South Carolina Press, 1989), 45–47; John Phillip Reid, *Constitutional History of the American Revolution: The Authority of Law* (Madison: University of Wisconsin Press, 1993), 106–109; James M. Volo and Dorothy Denneen Volo, *Daily Life During the American Revolution* (Westport, CT: Greenwood Press, 2003), 224–226.

50 David Ammerman, In the Common Cause: American Response to the Coercive Acts of 1774 (Charlottesville: University Press of Virginia, 1974), 45–49; Jack P. Greene, The Constitutional Origins of the American Revolution (Cambridge: Cambridge University Press, 2011), 102–107; John Phillip Reid, Constitutional History of the American Revolution: The Authority of Law (Madison: University of Wisconsin Press, 1993), 106–109; Pauline Maier, From Resistance to Revolution: Colonial Radicals and the Development of American Opposition to Britain, 1765-1776 (New York: W.W. Norton, 1991), 154–159.

51 Jack P. Greene, *The Constitutional Origins of the American Revolution* (Cambridge: Cambridge University Press, 2011), 109–113; John Phillip Reid, *Constitutional History of the American Revolution: The Authority of Law* (Madison: University of Wisconsin Press, 1993), 119–123; Mary Sarah Bilder, *The Transatlantic Constitution: Colonial Legal Culture and the Empire* (Cambridge, MA: Harvard University Press, 2004), 152–157; Gordon S. Wood, *The Creation of the American Republic, 1776-1787* (Chapel Hill: University of North Carolina Press, 1969), 296–301.

52 The Townshend Acts (1767), in The Avalon Project: Documents in Law, History and Diplomacy (Yale Law School), accessed October 2025, https://avalon.law.yale.edu/18th_century/townshend.asp

53 John Phillip Reid, *Constitutional History of the American Revolution: The Authority of Law* (Madison: University of Wisconsin Press, 1993), 132–136; Jack P. Greene, *The Constitutional Origins of the American Revolution* (Cambridge: Cambridge University Press, 2011), 118–122; William R. Leslie, *The Enforcement of the American Revolution: A Study of the British Customs Service in Colonial America* (New York: Octagon Books, 1980), 64–69; Pauline Maier, *From Resistance to Revolution: Colonial Radicals and the Development of American Opposition to Britain, 1765-1776* (New York: W.W. Norton, 1991), 171–175.

54 John Shy, *A People Numerous and Armed: Reflections on the Military Struggle for American Independence* (Ann Arbor: University of Michigan Press, 1990), 83–88; David Ammerman, *In the Common Cause: American Response to the Coercive Acts of 1774* (Charlottesville: University Press of Virginia, 1974), 58–62; Fred Anderson, *Crucible of War: The Seven Years' War and the Fate of Empire in British North America, 1754-1766* (New York: Vintage, 2000), 634–639; Pauline Maier, *From Resistance to Revolution: Colonial Radicals and the Development of American Opposition to Britain, 1765-1776* (New York: W.W. Norton, 1991), 183–187.

55 David Hackett Fischer, *Paul Revere's Ride* (New York: Oxford University Press, 1994), 195–201; David Ammerman, *In the Common Cause: American Response to the Coercive Acts of 1774* (Charlottesville: University Press of Virginia, 1974), 64–68; John Phillip Reid, *Constitutional History of the American Revolution: The Authority of Law* (Madison: University of Wisconsin Press, 1993), 140–145; Jack P. Greene, *The Constitutional Origins of the American Revolution* (Cambridge: Cambridge University Press, 2011), 125–130.

56 John Phillip Reid, *Constitutional History of the American Revolution: The Authority of Law* (Madison: University of Wisconsin Press, 1993), 148–152; *Jack P. Greene, The Constitutional Origins of the American Revolution* (Cambridge: Cambridge University Press, 2011), 135–140; Mary Sarah Bilder, *The Transatlantic Constitution: Colonial Legal Culture and the Empire* (Cambridge, MA: Harvard University Press, 2004), 162–167; David Ammerman, *In the Common Cause: American Response to the Coercive Acts of 1774* (Charlottesville: University Press of Virginia, 1974), 70–74.

57 John Phillip Reid, Constitutional History of the American Revolution: The Authority of Law (Madison: University of Wisconsin Press, 1993), 148–152; Jack P. Greene, The Constitutional Origins of the American Revolution (Cambridge: Cambridge University Press, 2011), 135–140; Mary Sarah Bilder, The Transatlantic Constitution: Colonial Legal Culture and the Empire (Cambridge, MA: Harvard University Press, 2004), 162–167; William R. Leslie, The Enforcement of the American Revolution: A Study of the British Customs Service in Colonial America (New York: Octagon Books, 1980), 74–79.

58 Stephen Conway, *Britain's War of American Independence: A New History* (New York: Cambridge University Press, 2000), 54–58; Benjamin L. Carp, *Rebels Rising: Cities and the American Revolution* (Oxford: Oxford University Press, 2007), 133–137; H.T. Dickinson, *A Companion to Eighteenth-Century Britain* (Malden, MA: Blackwell, 2002), 426–429; Peter D. G. Thomas, *Tea Party to Independence: The Third Phase of the American Revolution, 1773-1776* (Oxford: Clarendon Press, 1991), 94–99.

59 Hiller B. Zobel, The Boston Massacre (New York: W.W. Norton, 1970), 245–250; John Phillip Reid, Constitutional History of the American Revolution: The Authority of Law (Madison: University of Wisconsin Press, 1993), 160–164; David Ammerman, In the Common Cause: American Response to the Coercive Acts of 1774 (Charlottesville: University Press of Virginia, 1974), 80–84;

Pauline Maier, From Resistance to Revolution: Colonial Radicals and the Development of American Opposition to Britain, 1765–1776 (New York: W.W. Norton, 1991), 190–195.

[60] Lawrence A. Harper, The English Navigation Laws: A Seventeenth-Century Experiment in Social Engineering (New York: Columbia University Press, 1939), 139–41; Thomas C. Barrow, Trade and Empire: The British Customs Service in Colonial America, 1660–1775 (Cambridge, MA: Harvard University Press, 1967), 88–90; Oliver M. Dickerson, The Navigation Acts and the American Revolution (Philadelphia: University of Pennsylvania Press, 1951), 47–50.

[61] Bernard Bailyn, *The Ideological Origins of the American Revolution* (Cambridge, MA: Harvard University Press, 1992), 229–235; Jack P. Greene, *The Constitutional Origins of the American Revolution* (Cambridge: Cambridge University Press, 2011), 145–150; David Ammerman, *In the Common Cause: American Response to the Coercive Acts of 1774* (Charlottesville: University Press of Virginia, 1974), 85–89; Thomas Jefferson, *A Summary View of the Rights of British America* (Williamsburg, VA: Clementina Rind, 1774), in *The Papers of Thomas Jefferson*, vol. 1, ed. Julian P. Boyd (Princeton: Princeton University Press, 1950), 121–126.

[62] John Phillip Reid, *Constitutional History of the American Revolution: The Authority of Law* (Madison: University of Wisconsin Press, 1993), 165–170; *Jack P. Greene, The Constitutional Origins of the American Revolution* (Cambridge: Cambridge University Press, 2011), 150–155; David Ammerman, *In the Common Cause: American Response to the Coercive Acts of 1774* (Charlottesville: University Press of Virginia, 1974), 90–94; William E. Nelson, The Common Law in Colonial America, Vol. 2: The Middle Colonies and the Carolinas, 1660–1730 (Oxford: Oxford University Press, 2013), 201–206.

[63] John Phillip Reid, *Constitutional History of the American Revolution: The Authority of Law* (Madison: University of Wisconsin Press, 1993), 172–176; Jack P. Greene, *The Constitutional Origins of the American Revolution* (Cambridge: Cambridge University Press, 2011), 157–162; David Ammerman, *In the Common Cause: American Response to the Coercive Acts of 1774* (Charlottesville: University Press of Virginia, 1974), 95–99; Thomas Jefferson, *A Summary View of the Rights of British America* (Williamsburg, VA: Clementina Rind, 1774), in *The Papers of Thomas Jefferson*, vol. 1, ed. Julian P. Boyd (Princeton: Princeton University Press, 1950), 121–126.

[64] The Papers of Thomas Jefferson, vol. 1, 1760–1776, ed. Julian P. Boyd [Princeton: Princeton University Press, 1950], 187–192.

[65] Jack P. Greene, The Constitutional Origins of the American Revolution (Cambridge: Cambridge University Press, 2010), 98–102.

[66] Fred Anderson, *Crucible of War: The Seven Years' War and the Fate of Empire in British North America, 1754–1766* (New York: Vintage, 2000), 562–568; Colin G. Calloway, *The Scratch of a Pen: 1763 and the Transformation of North America* (Oxford: Oxford University Press, 2006), 94–101; Jack P. Greene, *The Constitutional Origins of the American Revolution* (Cambridge: Cambridge University Press, 2011), 165–170; H.T. Dickinson, *The British Empire and the American Revolution* (London: Pickering & Chatto, 2014), 210–215.

[67] Samuel Flagg Bemis, *Diplomacy of the American Revolution* (Bloomington: Indiana University Press, 1957), 225–230; Richard B. Morris, *The Peacemakers: The Great Powers and American Independence* (New York: Harper & Row, 1965), 318–324; Jonathan R. Dull, *A Diplomatic History of the American Revolution* (New Haven: Yale University Press, 1985), 152–157; George C. Herring, *From Colony to Superpower: U.S. Foreign Relations Since 1776* (New York: Oxford University Press, 2008), 24–29.

[68] Massachusetts Historical Society, "Signed, Sealed, and Delivered: The Treaty that Ended the Revolutionary War," last accessed January 16, 2025, https://www.masshist.org/beehiveblog/2014/09/signed-sealed-and-delivered-the-treaty-that-ended-the-revolutionary-war/.

[69] Fred Anderson, *Crucible of War: The Seven Years' War and the Fate of Empire in British North America, 1754–1766* (New York: Vintage, 2000), 562–568; Colin G. Calloway, *The Scratch of a Pen: 1763 and the Transformation of North America* (Oxford: Oxford University Press, 2006), 94–101; Jack P. Greene, *The Constitutional Origins of the American Revolution* (Cambridge: Cambridge University Press, 2011), 165–170; H.T. Dickinson, *The British Empire and the American Revolution* (London: Pickering & Chatto, 2014), 210–215; Francis D. Cogliano, *Revolutionary America, 1763–1815: A Political History* (New York: Routledge, 2000), 38–42.

[70] Jack P. Greene, *The Constitutional Origins of the American Revolution* (Cambridge: Cambridge University Press, 2011), 85–89; Bernard Bailyn, *The Ideological Origins of the American Revolution* (Cambridge, MA: Harvard University Press, 1992), 203–207; Mary Sarah Bilder, *The Transatlantic Constitution: Colonial Legal Culture and the Empire* (Cambridge, MA: Harvard University Press, 2004), 145–149.

[71] See *Journals of the Continental Congress*, Vol. 1 (Washington: Government Printing Office, 1904), pp. 67–69; "Declaration and Resolves of the First Continental Congress" (October 14, 1774), which condemned Parliamentary acts that "abolish the free system of English laws in a neighboring province, establishing therein an arbitrary government." Also see Bernard Bailyn, *The Ideological Origins of the American Revolution* (Cambridge: Harvard University Press, 1967), 107–112; Jack P. Greene, *The Constitutional Origins of the American Revolution* (Cambridge: Cambridge University Press, 2011), 87–94; and Merrill Jensen, *The Founding of a Nation: A History of the American Revolution, 1763–1776* (New York: Oxford University Press, 1968), 406–410.

[72] David Ammerman, *In the Common Cause: American Response to the Coercive Acts of 1774* (Charlottesville: University Press of Virginia, 1974), 72–77; John Phillip Reid, *Constitutional History of the American Revolution: The Authority of Law* (Madison: University of Wisconsin Press, 1993), 150–155; Jack P. Greene, *The Constitutional Origins of the American Revolution* (Cambridge: Cambridge

University Press, 2011), 135–140; H.T. Dickinson, *The British Empire and the American Revolution* (London: Pickering & Chatto, 2014), 225–230.

73 David Ammerman, *In the Common Cause: American Response to the Coercive Acts of 1774* (Charlottesville: University Press of Virginia, 1974), 80–85; John Phillip Reid, *Constitutional History of the American Revolution: The Authority of Law* (Madison: University of Wisconsin Press, 1993), 175–180; Jack P. Greene, *The Constitutional Origins of the American Revolution* (Cambridge: Cambridge University Press, 2011), 145–150; H.T. Dickinson, *The British Empire and the American Revolution* (London: Pickering & Chatto, 2014), 235–240; James H. Merrell, *Into the American Woods: Negotiators on the Pennsylvania Frontier* (New York: W.W. Norton, 1999), 312–318.

74 David Hackett Fischer, *Paul Revere's Ride* (New York: Oxford University Press, 1994), 256–261; John Ferling, *A Leap in the Dark: The Struggle to Create the American Republic* (New York: Oxford University Press, 2003), 211–215; Mary Beth Norton, *1774: The Long Year of Revolution* (New York: Alfred A. Knopf, 2020), 305–311.

75 Rodney Atwood, *The Hessians: Mercenaries from Hessen-Kassel in the American Revolution* (Cambridge: Cambridge University Press, 1980), 95–102; Stephen Conway, *Britain's War of American Independence: A New History* (New York: Cambridge University Press, 2000), 215–221; David Hackett Fischer, *Washington's Crossing* (New York: Oxford University Press, 2004), 150–155; Richard M. Ketchum, *Saratoga: Turning Point of America's Revolutionary War* (New York: Henry Holt, 1997), 276–282.

76 Isaac Land, "Anti-Impressment Riots and the Origins of the Age of Revolution," International Review of Social History 58, no. 2 (August 2013): 177–202

77 David Brion Davis, *The Problem of Slavery in the Age of Revolution, 1770–1823* (Ithaca, NY: Cornell University Press, 1975), 124–130; Pauline Maier, *American Scripture: Making the Declaration of Independence* (New York: Knopf, 1997), 150–156; Garry Wills, *Inventing America: Jefferson's Declaration of Independence* (Boston: Houghton Mifflin, 1978), 78–83; Merrill D. Peterson, *Thomas Jefferson and the New Nation: A Biography* (New York: Oxford University Press, 1970), 105–110.

78 Thomas Jefferson, *Draft Constitution for Virginia*, 1760-1776, in *The Papers of Thomas Jefferson*, vol. 1, ed. Julian P. Boyd (Princeton: Princeton University Press, 1950). 337-365.

79 George Washington, "Fairfax County Resolves, 18 July 1774," *Founders Online*, National Archives, last accessed January 16, 2025, https://founders.archives.gov/documents/Washington/02-10-02-0080.

80 Monticello, "George Wythe," last accessed January 16, 2025, https://www.monticello.org/research-education/thomas-jefferson-encyclopedia/george-wythe/.

81 Benjamin Franklin, "A Conversation between an Englishman, a Scotchman, and an American, on the Subject of Slavery," The Papers of Benjamin Franklin, vol. 17, January 1 through December 31, 1770, last accessed January 20, 2025, https://founders.archives.gov/documents/Franklin/01-17-02-0019.

82 Lossing, Benson J. *Our Country: A Household History for All Readers.* Vol. 1. New York: Johnson & Miles, 1878, 409–410.

83 Pauline Maier, *American Scripture: Making The Declaration of Independence* (New York: Knopf, 1997), 143–148.

84 Connecticut Society of the Sons of the American Revolution, *The Price They Paid*, last accessed February 15, 2025, https://www.sarconnecticut.org/the-price-they-paid/.

85 Walter Isaacson, "Benjamin Franklin Joins the Revolution," Smithsonian Magazine, July 31, 2003, https://www.smithsonianmag.com/history/benjamin-franklin-joins-the-revolution-87199988/.

86 Daniel Webster, Adams and Jefferson, American Literature, last accessed February 15, 2025, https://americanliterature.com/history/daniel-webster/speech/adams-and-jefferson.

87 National Archives, Founding Fathers: Signers of The Declaration of Independence Fact Sheet, last accessed February 15, 2025, https://www.archives.gov/founding-docs/signers-factsheet.

88 Paul H. Smith, *Letters of Delegates to Congress*, 1774-1789, Vol. 4: July 17, 1776 - October 15, 1776 (Washington, D.C.: Library of Congress, 1979), 265–270.

89 Benson Bobrick, Angel in the Whirlwind: The Triumph of the American Revolution (New York: Simon & Schuster, 1997), 298–305.

90 Jefferson, Thomas. *The Writings of Thomas Jefferson*, edited by Paul Leicester Ford, vol. 4. New York: G.P. Putnam's Sons, 1893, 66.

91 Thomas Jefferson, *Extract from Thomas Jefferson's Notes of Proceedings in the Continental Congress*, July 2, 1776, in *Jefferson Quotes & Family Letters*, Monticello, accessed May 9, 2025, https://tjrs.monticello.org/letter/54.

92 Thomas Jefferson, *Draft Constitution for Virginia*, 1760-1776, in *The Papers of Thomas Jefferson*, vol. 1, ed. Julian P. Boyd (Princeton: Princeton University Press, 1950). 340.

93 Thomas Jefferson, *Draft Constitution for Virginia*, 1760-1776, in *The Papers of Thomas Jefferson*, vol. 1, ed. Julian P. Boyd (Princeton: Princeton University Press, 1950). 337.

94 Gregg, Edward. *Queen Anne*. New Haven: Yale University Press, 2001.

95 "Give Me Liberty or Give Me Death!" Currier & Ives, 1876. The Metropolitan Museum of Art.

96 John Adams, Thoughts on Government: Applicable to the Present State of the American Colonies (Philadelphia: John Dunlap, 1776).

97 Source: Jefferson, *Itinerary and Chronology, May 7–14, 1776, The Works of Thomas Jefferson*, vol. 2 (1904–1905), pp. xxv–xxvi (Liberty Fund Online Edition).

98 Thomas Jefferson, Autobiography (1821), in The Papers of Thomas Jefferson: Retirement Series, vol. 1 (Princeton University Press).

99 "*Resolutions of the Freeholders of Albemarle County, Virginia, July 26, 1774,*" Founders Online, National Archives.

100 Hastings, Patrick. "Jefferson's Revisions to *Summary View*." *Bibliomania: The Library of Congress Blog*, February 11, 2026. https://blogs.loc.gov/bibliomania/2026/02/11/jeffersons-revisions-to-summary-view/

101 Jefferson, Thomas. *Draft Constitution for Virginia (Proposed Constitution for Virginia)*, June 1776. Manuscript Division, The New York Public Library, New York. [Also printed in Paul L. Ford (ed.), *The Writings of Thomas Jefferson*, Federal Edition, Vol. 2 (New York & London: G.P. Putnam's Sons, 1904–05), p. 7.]

102 John Adams, Autobiography of John Adams, in *The Works of John Adams*, ed. Charles Francis Adams, vol. 3 (Boston: Little, Brown and Company, 1851), 293.

103 Library of Congress, "Creating the Declaration of Independence."

104 Library of Congress, *Mary Katharine Goddard Broadside* (1777).

105 John F. Kennedy, remarks at a White House dinner honoring Nobel Prize winners, April 29, 1962, Public Papers of the Presidents of the United States: John F. Kennedy, 1962 (Washington, D.C.: U.S. Government Printing Office, 1963), 347.

106 Thomas Jefferson to John Holmes, April 22, 1820, *Founders Online*, National Archives.

107 Reuters, "Chronology – Who Banned Slavery When?" last accessed February 16, 2025, https://www.reuters.com/article/economy/chronology-who-banned-slavery-when-idUSL15614649/.

108 Seymour Drescher, *Abolition: A History of Slavery and Antislavery* (Cambridge: Cambridge University Press, 2009), 223-225; David Eltis, *Economic Growth and the Ending of the Transatlantic Slave Trade* (New York: Oxford University Press, 1987), 100-102; and Michael Craton, *Testing the Chains: Resistance to Slavery in the British West Indies* (Ithaca, NY: Cornell University Press, 1982), 276-280.

109 Wikipedia, s.v. "Indentured Servitude," last accessed January 16, 2025, https://en.wikipedia.org/wiki/Indentured_servitude#:~:text=Colonial%20Indian%20indenture%20system,-Main%20article%3A%20Indian&text=It%20started%20from%20the%20end,1833%20and%20continued%20until%201920.

110 David W. Galenson, *White Servitude in Colonial America: An Economic Analysis* (Cambridge: Cambridge University Press, 1981), 14-18; Richard S. Dunn, *Sugar and Slaves: The Rise of the Planter Class in the English West Indies, 1624-1713* (Chapel Hill: University of North Carolina Press, 1972), 243-247; and Don Jordan and Michael Walsh, *White Cargo: The Forgotten History of Britain's White Slaves in America* (New York: NYU Press, 2008), 65-70.

111 Don Jordan and Michael Walsh, White Cargo: The Forgotten History of Britain's White Slaves in America (New York: New York University Press, 2008), 76–86.

112 Learning for Justice, Indentured Servitude (PDF file), accessed February 15, 2025, https://www.learningforjustice.org/sites/default/files/general/tt_indentured_servitude_09_h2.pdf.

113 Stephen Winick, "Beyond 1619: Slavery and the American Folklife Center," Folklife Today (blog), Library of Congress, August 27, 2019, https://blogs.loc.gov/folklife/2019/08/beyond-1619/.

114 "European Migrations Before the American Revolution," U.S. Immigration History (Pressbooks, City University of New York), accessed February 16, 2025, https://pressbooks.cuny.edu/immigrationhistory/chapter/chapter-1-european-migrations-before-the-american-revolution/.

115 Encyclopedia Virginia, s.v. "Convict Labor during the Colonial Period," accessed February 16, 2025, https://encyclopediavirginia.org/entries/convict-labor-during-the-colonial-period/.

116 South Carolina Encyclopedia, s.v. "Lucas Vasquez de Ayllón," last accessed January 16, 2025, https://www.scencyclopedia.org/sce/entries/ayllon-lucas-vasquez-de/.

117 "Negro Women's Children to Serve According to the Condition of the Mother, 1662," Encyclopedia Virginia, accessed February 16, 2025, https://encyclopediavirginia.org/primary-documents/negro-womens-children-to-serve-according-to-the-condition-of-the-mother-1662/.

118 *The Brookes Slave Ship, 1807 Commemorated, Institute of Historical Research,* accessed February 15, 2025, https://archives.history.ac.uk/1807commemorated/exhibitions/museums/brookes.html.

119 *Model of the Brookes Slave Ship, Understanding Slavery Initiative,* accessed February 15, 2025, https://understandingslavery.com/artefact/model-of-the-brookes-slave-ship/.

120 Slave Voyages: The Trans-Atlantic Slave Trade Database, last accessed February 11, 2025, https://www.slavevoyages.org/voyage/database.

121 "H.M. King Leopold II of the Belgians," Henry Poole & Co., accessed February 15, 2025, https://henrypoole.com/individual/hm-king-leopold-ii-belgians/.

122 Mac Mckinney, "Congo: The Horror Crescendos," LA Progressive, March 1, 2012, accessed February 15, 2025, https://www.laprogressive.com/foreign-policy/congo-horror-crescendos.

123 "King Leopold's Ghost: A Story of Greed, Terror, and Heroism in Colonial Africa," Harvard Kennedy School Library & Research Services, accessed February 15, 2025, https://www.hks.harvard.edu/faculty-research/library-research-services/collections/diversity-inclusion-belonging/king-leopolds.

124 "H.M. King Leopold II of the Belgians," Henry Poole & Co., accessed February 15, 2025, https://henrypoole.com/individual/hm-king-leopold-ii-belgians/.

125 Marcus Rediker, *The Slave Ship: A Human History* (New York: Viking, 2007), 98–105.

126 SlaveVoyages, *Trans-Atlantic Slave Trade Database,* accessed February 19, 2025, https://www.slavevoyages.org.

127 Paul Finkelman, *Slavery and the Founders: Race and Liberty in the Age of Jefferson* (Armonk, NY: M.E. Sharpe, 1996), 45–50.

128 Christopher Klein, "Alexander Hamilton's Complicated Relationship to Slavery," HISTORY, last modified October 16, 2020, https://www.history.com/news/alexander-hamilton-slavery-facts.

129 Paul Finkelman, *Slavery and the Founders: Race and Liberty in the Age of Jefferson* (Armonk, NY: M.E. Sharpe, 1996), 60–65; David Brion Davis, *Inhuman Bondage: The Rise and Fall of Slavery in the New World* (New York: Oxford University Press, 2006), 189–194.

130 Politico, "Congress Votes to Ban Slave Importation, March 2, 1807," Politico, March 2, 2018, accessed February 12, 2025, https://www.politico.com/story/2018/03/02/congress-votes-to-ban-slave-importation-march-2-1807-430820.

131 Sheila Scarborough Fitzgerald, "Newport Rum and Slavery History," Perceptive Travel Blog, July 5, 2011, accessed February 12, 2025, https://perceptivetravel.com/blog/2011/07/05/newport-rum-slavery-history/.

132 *Thomas Cresap and the Border War,* The Historical Marker Database, last modified [date if available], https://www.hmdb.org/m.asp?m=242835.

133 Francis Daniel Pastorius et al., *1688 Germantown Petition Against Slavery,* Haverford College Quaker & Special Collections, Haverford, PA.

134 National Park Service, "1688 Germantown Quaker Petition Against Slavery," U.S. National Park Service, accessed February 12, 2025, https://www.nps.gov/articles/quakerpetition.htm.

135 Library of Congress, "Memorial Against Slavery, Germantown, Pennsylvania, 1688," Library of Congress, accessed February 12, 2025, https://www.loc.gov/resource/rbpe.14000200/?st=text.

136 National Park Service, "A House Divided," Lincoln Home National Historic Site, U.S. Department of the Interior, accessed February 12, 2025, https://www.nps.gov/liho/learn/historyculture/housedivided.htm.

137 Institute, "The Free Soil Party," Bill of Rights Institute, accessed February 12, 2025, https://billofrightsinstitute.org/essays/the-free-soil-party.

138 Democratic Party, "1856 Democratic Party Platform," The American Presidency Project, University of California, Santa Barbara, accessed February 12, 2025, https://www.presidency.ucsb.edu/documents/1856-democratic-party-platform.

139 Harvard University, "1852 Bill of Sale for an Enslaved Woman and Child," HIST 1952: Harvard & Slavery, accessed February 12, 2025, https://hist1952.omeka.fas.harvard.edu/items/show/104.

140 National Archives, "Black Soldiers in the U.S. Military During the Civil War," last reviewed August 23, 2021, https://www.archives.gov/education/lessons/blacks-civil-war.

141 Gilder Lehrman Institute of American History, "Historical Context: Black Soldiers in the Civil War," Gilder Lehrman Institute of American History, accessed February 12, 2025, https://www.gilderlehrman.org/history-resources/teacher-resources/historical-context-black-soldiers-civil-war.

142 U.S. Army, "Meet Sgt. William Carney: The First African American Medal of Honor Recipient," Army.mil, accessed February 12, 2025, https://www.army.mil/article/181896/meet_sgt_william_carney_the_first_african_american_medal_of_honor_recipient.

143 J. David Hacker, "New Estimate Raises Civil War Death Toll," The New York Times, April 2, 2012, accessed February 12, 2025, https://www.nytimes.com/2012/04/03/science/civil-war-toll-up-by-20-percent-in-new-estimate.html.

144 Roger L. Ransom, "The Economics of the Civil War," EH.net, Economic History Association, accessed February 12, 2025, https://eh.net/encyclopedia/the-economics-of-the-civil-war/.

145 National Archives, "Emancipation Proclamation," Milestone Documents, accessed February 12, 2025, https://www.archives.gov/milestone-documents/emancipation-proclamation.

146 Museum of the American Revolution, "Black Founders Big Idea 2: Black Soldiers and Sailors in the Revolutionary War," last accessed January 20, 2025,

147 National Park Service, "The Iconic 369th Infantry Regiment," last accessed January 20, 2025, https://www.nps.gov/articles/000/iconic369thphoto.htm#:~:text=The%20369th%20Infantry%2C%20whose%20members,Guerre%20medals%20for%20their%20valor.

148 Partnership With Native Americans, "Code Talkers," last accessed January 20, 2025.

149 National Indian Council on Aging (NICOA), "American Indian Veterans Have Highest Record of Military Service," last accessed January 20, 2025, https://www.nicoa.org/american-indian-veterans-have-highest-record-of-military-service/.

150 Wikipedia, s.v. "George Middleton (Activist)," last accessed January 16, 2025, https://en.wikipedia.org/wiki/George_Middleton_(activist).

151 Wikipedia, s.v. "Bucks of America," last accessed January 16, 2025, https://en.wikipedia.org/wiki/Bucks_of_America#:~:text=Governor%20John%20Hancock%20and%20his,benefactor%2C%20John%20George%20Washington%20Hancock.

152 https://thewestendmuseum.org/history/era/west-boston/colonel-george-middleton/

153 Burke Davis, *Black Heroes of the American Revolution* (New York: Harcourt, Inc., 1976), 64–66.

154 African American Registry, "George Middleton, Patriot Born," last accessed January 16, 2025, https://aaregistry.org/story/george-middleton-patriot-born/.

155 Friends Journal, "Rethinking William Penn," last accessed January 16, 2025, https://www.friendsjournal.org/rethinking-william-penn/.

156 BBC, "Benjamin Lay: The Quaker Dwarf Who Fought Slavery," last accessed January 16, 2025, https://www.bbc.com/news/uk-england-essex-42640782.

157 Smithsonian Institution, "Benjamin Lay," last accessed January 16, 2025, https://www.si.edu/object/benjamin-lay%3Anpg_NPG.79.171.

158 Battlefields.org, "Sarah Bradlee Fulton, Mother of the Boston Tea Party," last accessed January 16, 2025, https://www.battlefields.org/learn/biographies/sarah-bradlee-fulton.

159 Mount Vernon, "Mercy Otis Warren," last accessed January 16, 2025, https://www.mountvernon.org/library/digitalhistory/digital-encyclopedia/article/mercy-otis-warren-1728-1814.

160 National Women's History Museum, "Mercy Otis Warren," last accessed January 20, 2025, https://www.womenshistory.org/education-resources/biographies/mercy-otis-warren.

161 "Mercy Otis Warren's Revolutionary Impact," last accessed January 20, 2025, https://www.usconstitution.net/mercy-otis-warrens-revolutionary-impact/.

162 Mercy Otis Warren, *History of the Rise, Progress and Termination of the American Revolution* (ISBN: 9781015707108).

163 Library of Congress, "Benjamin Banneker: Surveyor, City Planner, Astronomer?" *In Custodia Legis: Law Librarians of Congress* (blog), February 2, 2024, https://blogs.loc.gov/law/2024/02/benjamin-banneker-surveyor-city-planner-astronomer.

164 History.com, "Abraham Lincoln and Black Resettlement in Haiti," last accessed January 16, 2025, https://www.history.com/news/abraham-lincoln-black-resettlement-haiti.

165 William L. Stone, *Life of Joseph Brant—Thayendanegea*, Vol. 1 (New York: George Dearborn & Co., 1838), 281–283; see also Charles S. Hall, *The Oneida Indians and the Coming of the Revolution* (Boston: Grafton Press, 1905), 198–201.

166 "Report on Lafayette's Reconnaissance Expedition," *Papers of George Washington: Revolutionary War Series*, ed. Philander D. Chase, Vol. 14 (Charlottesville: University of Virginia Press, 2004), 120–123; Robert S. Allen, *His Majesty's Indian Allies: British Indian Policy in the Defence of Canada, 1774–1815* (Toronto: Dundurn Press, 1992), 46.

167 Relief Web, "Modern Slavery by Country," last accessed January 16, 2025,

168 U.S. Department of Labor, "Child Labor Report," last accessed January 16, 2025, https://www.dol.gov/agencies/ilab/reports/child-labor/list-of-goods-print.

www.ingramcontent.com/pod-product-compliance
Lightning Source LLC
Chambersburg PA
CBHW061354010526
44107CB00011B/931